THE NATIONAL INSTITUTE OF
ECONOMIC AND SOCIAL RESEARCH

STRENGTH IN NUMBERS
LEARNING MATHS IN JAPAN AND ENGLAND

by

Julia Whitburn

Published by
The National Institute of Economic
and Social Research
2 Dean Trench Street, Smith Square, London SW1P 3HE

© The National Institute of Economic
and Social Research 2000

First published 2000

Printed in Great Britain by
Whitstable Litho Printers Ltd,
Whitstable, Kent

Cover design by Ed Walker

ISBN 0 952 6213 6 3

Contents

List of tables and illustrations

Illustrations

Acknowledgements

It is good to have the opportunity to express my thanks to the many people who have given help and advice in the preparation of this book.

First, grateful thanks go to Joy Hendry and Morag MacLean, both of Oxford Brookes University, who supervised the doctoral thesis on which this book is based. Funding contributed by the Japan Foundation Endowment Committee in 1995 and 1996 enabled the fieldwork to take place and their generous support is warmly acknowledged.

At the National Institute of Economic and Social Research, I have been fortunate to benefit from the wisdom and experience of Professor Sig Prais, who, throughout the last four years, has been a constant source of encouragement. Also at the National Instutite, Fiona Thirlwell has been an unfailingly helpful colleague and Fran Robinson has helped enormously in turning the thesis into a book.

Particular thanks go to all the teachers and the pupils at the schools visited, both in England and Japan, for welcoming me so warmly and for answering all my questions. In Japan I have also been grateful for continuing help from Dr. Eizo Nagasaki of the National Institute for Educational Research and for his willingness to answer endless queries on the finer points of the Japanese educational system. In England, I appreciate the valuable comments of Professor Geoffrey Howson who has been generous with his time and in making suggestions.

I should like to thank many friends for their willingness to debate particular issues and my family for their tolerance and support over a number of years. Finally, I am perhaps most of all indebted to my good friend Hisako Shiina for her insistence nine years ago that I should visit Japan and for arranging my initial experience of Japanese schools.

Julia Whitburn
London
November 1999

Preface

by S.J. Prais FBA

Japan's 'economic miracle' in the past half-century has become a commonplace of our everyday life; from being a low-wage country producing cheap-quality copies of manufactures of the Western world it has risen in only a few decades to become a leading producer – often *the* leading producer – of precision cameras, reliable cars, television sets, calculators, computers, electronic equipment, ... A workforce has been created there capable of working to the highest standards of precision and highest reliability; there is a capability within their economy of planning production on a large scale to be sold at prices attractive to a world market, of rapid product-improvement and innovation. That such a workforce is based on high educational standards, particularly high in mathematics, has been repeatedly confirmed by international tests of schooling attainments based on representative samples of pupils, carried out more or less every decade since 1964 (mainly by the IEA – the International Educational Association). But we have been short of adequately clear accounts of the practicalities of how those high schooling attainments have been achieved there.

To produce an account of Japanese schooling with the hope of being helpful to teachers and educational policy makers in England (as perhaps equally in many other Western countries), an observer has to know the Japanese language, to have experience of teaching in an English school, to be expert mathematically, to have an understanding of statistical survey work, to have the time and resources to carry out a sufficient number of visits to Japanese schools and, finally, to be able to present the findings in a way that others can benefit. The author of the present book, my colleague at the National Institute, has that rare combination; having recognised the importance – from the point of view of schooling and of our economic system – of understanding how the Japanese educational system works, she took part-time leave from her researches on European education at the Institute to undertake an observationally-based doctoral dissertation on Japanese schooling. The present publication is a slightly edited version of her dissertation.

The manifold results presented here demonstrate the value of direct classroom observation of teaching methods, going much beyond what can be gathered from international written tests of pupils' attainments such as those carried out by the IEA. The same observer needs to be actually present in the classroom of both countries that are being compared. Even classroom videos (carried out as part of the 1995 IEA mathematics survey) do not provide the same quantity and quality of *relevant* observations as gathered by an experienced teacher whose eyes move rapidly to that right spot in the classroom where pupils are actively responding, writing or, perhaps, not attending. For example, we learn from the present study that in a Japanese primary school mathematics lesson, pupils are 'on task' for an average of 88 per cent of their time, compared with an average of only 62 per cent for English pupils of the same ages (see p. 182); that is, Japanese lessons are relatively about 40 per cent more efficient – an obviously important contribution to faster learning. While the pace of the early-years syllabus in Japan is more moderate and less ambitious than under the English National Curriculum, it pays much greater attention to consolidating foundations: for example, numbers over a hundred are expected to be introduced to English pupils in our Year 1, while in Japan they are not introduced until the child is two years older (in Grade 2, corresponding to our Year 3, see p. 239). Before that age Japanese pupils are engaged on procedures associated with number bonds with smaller numbers, with which they are taught to be thoroughly familiar – virtually to a reflex (automated) response; unless that earlier stage is fully mastered, and mastered by the *whole* class (not just the majority, as so often in English schools), it is thought that further progress cannot ensue in an efficient way. In that respect the Japanese approach is close to that of Switzerland – a successful European educational system that has much occupied our research energies in recent years at the Institute, and has formed the basis of successful schooling reforms in mathematics in the London Borough of Barking and Dagenham (based on a systematic series of visits to Swiss classrooms, for direct observation of teaching practice by Engliah teachers: an initiative undertaken jointly by Institute researchers and senior school inspectors and teachers from that borough).

Indeed, many features of the successful teaching of mathematics in Japanese schools will be recognised in the ensuing pages as being similar to those of schools in European countries with high mathematical attainments, such as Switzerland, and still differing from England even after the most recent reforms in mathematics teaching here, though less than previously. I might perhaps be permitted to mention two features that struck me. First, the understanding in Japan that the earliest years in a child's education, in what we call Nursery and Reception Years, need to be spent – *not* in anticipating schooling work by the early teaching of numbers and letters, and of addition and the reading of simple words – but on general learning skills: in training the child's memory, extending the child's attention span, learning how to be co-operative in a classroom setting. Julia Whitburn presents Japanese views and thinking on such foundation learning clearly in the following pages. The second feature is the emphasis on whole-class teaching, in contrast to the individualised ('child centred') teaching characteristic of much of English schooling of the past generation. Even under the latest Literacy and Numeracy teaching reforms in England, it is still recommended that the class be divided into about three attainment groups for a significant part of each lesson. Thirdly, the much greater variety of difficulties faced by pupils in an English mathematics class, and the greater variety of learning activities in which English teacher has to be engaged (see table 6.1, p.153).

Fundamentally at issue is the degree of uniformity of pupils' attainments within a class that is required for the teacher successfully to teach the whole class together. The Swiss – as most Continental schooling systems (as also the United States) – find it necessary to engage in Procrustean procedures: one or two slow-maturing children move from Swiss kindergarten to primary school a year later, and thereafter in Swiss primary schools an occasional child repeats a class (about one child per class every other year). In Japan, no such flexibility seems to be required; in England class-repetition has been regarded as demeaning and demotivating, and is virtually unknown today. The question that springs to mind is whether Japanese children, by the time they reach schooling-age, are less variable in their 'educational potential' – whether because of social norms in upbringing, diet or genetic inheritance – than English school-children.

A major difficulty in approaching such a question is that IQ tests are inevitably culturally-linked, making it difficult to draw convincing conclusions on international comparisons of averages of measures of mental capabilities, and probably even more so of the variability. The author of this book kindly drew my attention to some comparative statistics on the physical heights of children which can be no more than suggestive for our purposes, and are clearly not irrelevant to rates of general maturation and its variability. The summary figures are as follows:

Heights of children (cm.) in UK and Japan by age

Age-	Boys				Girls			
range	Average		Dispersion*		Average		Dispersion*	
	UK	Japan	UK	Japan	UK	Japan	UK	Japan
6–10	128	128	6.0	5.5	128	128	6.3	5.8
11–14	153	156	8.1	7.4	154	154	7.4	5.9
15–17	172	170	7.2	5.8	162	158	6.1	5.3

Sources: UK: Department of Education and Science, *Body Dimensions of the School Population* (HMSO, 1985, p. 6). Japan: Tokyo Metropolitan Education Committee, *Physical Strength and Sporting Activity of School Children* (Tokyo, 1995).
Note: *Standard deviation (cm.)

The figures, based on school inspections, suggest a greater disparity of heights in England – by about a tenth at ages of primary schooling, rising to a fifth at ages of early secondary schooling for English girls, and to a quarter at ages of upper schooling for English boys. Interestingly, the 1995 IEA tests of pupils' attainments in mathematics at ages 8–9 showed English pupils with a 14 per cent greater standard deviation than Japanese pupils (p. 21 below): clearly of much the same order of magnitude. In both countries the disparities in heights are greatest at 11–14, the ages of puberty. These figures on heights seem consistent with greater pressures (a) to divide an age-cohort into sub-groups when it reaches puberty; and (b) for those pressures to be greater in England.

To appreciate the intuitive significance of such differences in the size of the standard deviation, the following hypothetical calculation may help: removing the bottom and top pupils from a hypothetically normally-distributed class of 25 children (the bottom pupil being presumed to start school a year later, and the top pupil a year earlier) reduces the standard deviation by about 16 per cent, which is broadly of the same magnitude as the average gap between the dispersion of UK and Japanese heights shown in the above table. Such a classroom promotion procedure broadly corresponds with Continental schooling practice. It would clearly be of interest to compare similar distributions for other countries; but this is not the place to speculate further – that must remain as a task for another research project.

1

Introduction

Background

The success of any country depends on the capability of its people. This is particularly true for Japan and England, which share the characteristics of an over-abundant population combined with a relative dearth of natural resources (Ishida, 1993). Traditionally, the strength of the educational system in England has been in its ability to produce a highly educated elite, often drawn from privileged backgrounds, to hold positions of influence at home and abroad (Kanako, 1988). The capability of the ordinary workforce – which can be improved through raising educational standards in the general population – is recognised as a major factor in the economic success of a country. In England it was only relatively recently that the focus of education changed from producing an academic elite through the independent and selective state schools to a wider concern with the education of the whole cohort of school-children of all abilities by means of the comprehensive school system.

Japan, however, under the influence of American policymakers, adopted a single-track approach to education at the time of the reconstruction of the educational system at the end of World War II. Central to its educational philosophy is equality of opportunity for all pupils, and the state system claims to provide a relatively uniform educational experience which is independent of social, economic or geographical factors. Thus the structure of the Japanese educational system has been able to provide comparable educational opportunities for children of all abilities for a longer period than in England.

During the last generation, both countries have recognised the need for higher levels of education and vocational training (Robbins, 1963; Cummings et al., 1979; Passin, 1982; Dearing, 1994). In the case of

1

England, while its past contribution to the industrial revolution and international trading is unquestioned, it is doubtful whether the systems currently in place for education and training are either sufficient or appropriate to meet the needs of technological development (Prais, 1993). Questions have also been asked regarding the capability of school-leavers for rigorous vocational training, and, in particular, whether the average levels of mathematical competence are adequate to meet the increasingly technological demands of such training. Reliable evidence over time with regard to the standards achieved in England and performance of school-leavers is sparse, but there is little to suggest that the mathematical standards attained by either the elite or the ordinary population of school-leavers has improved during the last generation. Indeed, the most recent comparative evidence from international studies indicates that, relative to international norms, the performance of English pupils has deteriorated during the last three decades. This is a critical time for the future direction of mathematics education in England, and we need to understand why standards of mathematics achievement have failed either to keep pace with those in other countries or to show any improvement in real terms.

The changes that have focused society's attention on the importance of education – the changing mix of jobs in highly industrialised societies from manufacturing towards services; the need for flexibility and adaptability in attitudes towards learning; above all the need for literate, numerate and trainable workers – have forced governments to be more outward-looking with regard to their educational provision, and to reconsider their ways of doing things from the perspective of other nations, and especially those who appear in many ways to be achieving the highly desirable aim of mass education to enviable standards. With increased intensity of global economic rivalry, there is corresponding pressure on governments to compare the effectiveness of different educational systems and their achievements. This is a further reason why there is a need for comparative studies that provide valid and reliable evidence with regard to the organisation, methods and effectiveness of different educational systems.

Reflecting this concern to improve our understanding of learning mathematics within a comparative context, this research examines the acquisition of children's understanding and competence in mathematics in the early years of schooling within the educational systems of England and Japan and considers the reasons for the different levels of attainment.

Evidence on standards in mathematics from comparative studies

Increased global awareness combined with technological advances in computing have facilitated the growth of international comparisons in the field of education – these began over thirty years ago with the establishment of the International Association for the Evaluation of Educational Achievement (IEA) as an international co-ordinating research centre in 1959. From the first large-scale international study in which twelve countries participated, the comparative studies have grown – in terms of scope, level of participation by different countries, in terms of the sophistication of the methodology used, and in the speed of the analysis of the results (Husén, 1967; Goldstein, 1993; Keys *et al.*, 1996). For several valid reasons these international studies have tended naturally to focus on education in mathematics and science: the discipline of mathematics, for example, has unique qualities in that it possesses an agreed body of knowledge which is reflected in the school curriculum; the problems of language are perhaps less acute than in many other subject areas; and standards are to a large extent conducive to objective measurement (Reynolds and Farrell, 1996). While the area of science possesses some of these qualities – albeit to a lesser degree – there is also considerable transnational variability in the extent, nature and content of science teaching in schools which creates fundamental difficulties for making valid comparisons. The discipline of mathematics is also widely recognised as one in which adequate levels of average attainment among school-leavers as a whole, and not just for an intellectual elite, are crucial for developing the key skills needed in a modern industrial society in which technology plays an increasing part. It could also be argued that mathematics is one area of the curriculum where the effects of home background on progress of pupils are less than the effects of the educational system, which enables a more realistic appraisal of the effectiveness of the educational systems of the participating countries (Coleman, 1979; Fogelman *et al.*, 1978; Mortimore *et al.*, 1988). Finally, on a more practical level, the participation by England in international educational studies has been more consistent in the area of mathematics than in other subject areas.

From the first major study by the IEA (Husén, 1967), which included only pupils in the lower years of secondary schooling, to the most recently available data from the Third International Mathematics and Science Study (Harris *et al.*, 1996; Keys *et al.*, 1996; Beaton *et al.*, 1996; Mullis *et al.*, 1997), a consistent finding has been the relatively low achievement

of English pupils in comparison to their counterparts in Japan. The validity and reliability of the evidence for this finding are discussed in some
detail in Chapter 2, together with information provided by the most recent survey concerning structural and organisational factors affecting
pupils' performance.

The existing comparative studies of English and Japanese education
and mathematical attainment (the large-scale international studies
previously mentioned) raise many questions which are left largely unan-
swered. For example, the studies point to the superior performance of
Japanese pupils with regard to mathematical attainment at the ages of
18 and 13, and the most recent study provides evidence of similar differences being apparent among pupils who are only 8–9 years old, but
they do not tell us at what age the differences *begin* to appear. The purpose of this study is to identify at what stage of schooling differences in
mathematical attainment between English and Japanese pupils first become apparent and then to examine the major contributing factors. It is
recognised that the process of learning is affected by many factors that
are external to the classroom – for example, by the value placed on education by society, and cultural attitudes towards learning. Within the
classroom the acquisition of mathematical understanding is a further
complex process, involving teaching, learning and cognitive development
(Light and Butterworth, 1992; Nunes and Bryant, 1996).

Social and cultural influences on learning

Children's attitudes to learning reflect the values of society absorbed during their early childhood years, either from their parents or close family
in the home environment. The influence of social values on children's
learning has been well documented in relation to Japan (Cummings,
1980; Stevenson *et al.*, 1986; Hendry, 1986b; White, 1987; Shields, 1990;
Boocock, 1991; Stevenson and Stigler, 1992) and to England
(Blackstone, 1971; Davie *et al.*, 1972; Mortimore *et al.*, 1988). The value
placed on education by society – not just for the financial rewards that
accompany better career opportunities, but for the intrinsic personal
benefits of learning and desire for self-improvement – is reflected in the
opportunities provided by the educational system. The aspirations and
expectations of parents for their children are also a reflection of society's
attitudes towards education – these in turn affect the home–school relationship and the support given by parents to children's learning outside

school. Children's attitudes towards schooling – for example, their commitment, motivation and willingness to persevere – are also influenced by the values of society and these attitudes will start to be formed during their early socialisation in the home and by their family. This study will examine the way in which these attitudes affect their learning of mathematics.

The socialisation process begun at home is continued by pre-school education where the cultural and behavioural values of society are transmitted to children. Earlier research studies have documented the ways in which cultural values and traditions absorbed during pre-schooling are reflected in attitudes towards learning (Tobin, 1992; Lewis, 1995). During pre-schooling, children may begin to learn about their responsibilities as individuals to themselves, to one another and to the wider community. The content and methods of the pre-school curriculum has implications for later formal learning and the extent to which behaviour learned during pre-school education helps or hinders later learning at school will be examined.

Influences from the educational system on learning in the classroom

In addition to the cultural influences from the family and from pre-schooling that affect children's attitudes and capacity for learning, children's learning within the classroom is also affected by the structure of the educational system as a whole and the organisation of the school. The educational systems of Japan and England have been discussed by a number of authors who have identified the underlying educational philosophy. For example, the way in which the single-track, co-educational state system prevailing throughout Japan may be perceived as a reflection of the aim of equalising educational opportunity and the provision of a relatively uniform educational experience has been discussed by Cummings (1980) and may be contrasted with the diversity of educational provision that exists within the state sector in England. Throughout the years of compulsory schooling, the use made of the private sector schools in Japan is relatively small, both in comparison to the percentage of pupils in private institutions in the pre- and post-school years and to the percentage of pupils in private sector schools in England. Further, the attitude that achievement is a reflection of effort rather than innate ability leads logically to the expectation that all children are capable of achieving the standard set for their age group and of moving forward together in developing understanding. This is in marked contrast to the educational philosophy of 'differentiation' that characterises English schooling, in which it is assumed that the individual nature of children's development is such that highly differentiated rates of progress are only to be expected – and even encouraged. It has been suggested that this philosophy contributes to the 'long tail of underachievement' which has been identified in the distribution of mathematical attainment in recent years (Prais, 1987). The influence of the philosophy of 'moving forward together' in Japan is also apparent in organisation at the school level, with mixed ability classes dominating throughout the years of compulsory schooling in Japan. This type of organisation contrasts with current practice within English primary schools, where there has been a tendency to 'group pupils by ability' for the teaching of mathematics from the beginning of Key Stage 1 (and sometimes even earlier) in order to reduce variation in attainment within pupils in the group to a level which makes teaching a more manageable task. The policy in England, however, ignores the evidence of the widening effect that grouping has on attainment levels (Slavin, 1987) as well as possibly detrimental effects on behaviour, unity and co-operation of the class group that may well result from the construction of different teaching groups. The effects of these differences in educational organisation on the learning of mathematics will be examined.

A major difference between the two educational systems that has a far-reaching effect on classroom practice is the greater centralisation of decision-making educational powers in Japan. Two important areas in which the power of the Ministry of Education in Japan (*Monbushō*) has an immediate influence on children's learning are those of deciding the curricula for each subject and controlling the publishing of approved textbooks; the effect of centralised control of these two areas will be examined in detail.

Approaches to cognitive development

Different approaches to cognitive development may be seen affecting the teaching and learning of mathematics within the classroom. In recent decades, and especially in the West, ideas of cognitive development have been greatly influenced by the work of Piaget, who has probably been one of the most powerful influences on educational thought on infant development (Piaget, 1941; 1965; 1969). In essence, his view was that children's psychological development should have reached a certain level of maturity before any teaching process begins, and that children learn principally through interacting with the environment. After conducting detailed observational studies of individual children, he proposed that cognitive development depended on the processes of assimilation and accommodation: that children would attempt to use existing mental structures to assimilate new ideas, but, if these were found to be inadequate, then they would be adapted as appropriate (Meadow, 1993). As children moved from a state of disequilibrium created by their inability to assimilate the new ideas to a state of restored equilibrium when the necessary accommodation is made, cognitive development was thought to occur. Changes in equilibration (he postulated) were likely to occur throughout life as children attempted to assimilate new concepts; this led to his view that children's thinking is qualitatively different from that of adults. The second idea that was central to Piaget's thinking was that the child is an active participant in his/her own learning and not a passive organism. This principle that children learn 'by doing' and that activity and experience aid development can be found in the earlier thoughts of Pestalozzi, Froebel, Rousseau and Dewey. The influence of these ideas may also be seen in the report of the Plowden Committee (Plowden, 1967) which to a large extent determined the direction of primary education in England in the following thirty years.

Piaget's ideas, however, reflect his concern with the *nature* of knowledge and not with problems of *instruction* (Hughes, 1996). Indeed, his views imply that children will acquire logical forms of thought independently of any instruction at school, and the Piagetian approach led to a theory of teaching concerned more with child development than pedagogy (Alexander, 1995). Critics of Piaget point out that his theory makes no practical suggestions to teachers regarding effective ways of promoting intellectual development and is inadequate as a pedagogic model (Dearden, 1976). Vygotsky, who in the final years of his life was largely concerned with the relationship between teaching and cognitive development, criticised Piaget for concentrating on the content of children's thinking and neglecting the operational aspect, and developed his own theories of cognitive development which involved effective instruction. The development of understanding of mathematical concepts may be seen as differing from that of many other disciplines since, whatever the level of concept being introduced, relatively complex thought is required. Vygotsky argued that in order for pupils to move forward from understanding one concept to the next, help from a teacher – or 'scaffolding' – is needed (Wertsch, 1985).

Critics of Piaget's work included Bruner (1966), who had greater concern for the *processes* that enabled cognitive development in children to take place and was less concerned than Piaget with the *nature* of knowledge. He developed a theory of instruction which interacted with his theory of development, arguing that the child is constantly striving to understand the complexities of the world and to make sense of it.

The relationship between the theories of teaching, learning and cognitive development are central to this study. Their interpretation and implementation within the Japanese and English educational systems have a crucial effect on the development of mathematical understanding.

Influences on teachers and their teaching

Society's view of education will affect the status of teachers; tangibly, in terms of pay and conditions but also intangibly in the social position of teachers. The status accorded to teachers by society – as well as pay and conditions of service – determine the desirability or otherwise of teaching as a career. Recruitment and selection of potential teachers for teacher training is enhanced by higher social status of teachers, attracting better students both in terms of academic qualifications and the many personal qualities such as communication and organisational skills which are a prerequisite for a successful teacher. In the earlier years of this century in England, the occupation of teaching offered a route to upward social mobility for children of academic talent from modest backgrounds – today this is arguably more appropriate in terms of Japanese children. Attitudes regarding the value of education are also demonstrated by the quantity and quality of early years' or pre-school education, and the commitment by the state to adequate levels of provision of such education.

At the level of the educational system, decisions are taken, often by the appropriate official department at national or local level, regarding, for example, curricula, teacher training, examination systems, school inspection systems, and desirable pedagogy, although in each of these areas the effect of societal attitudes may also be identified. At the institutional level, while the organisational/structural nature of a school will be predetermined to a large extent by the views formed at the societal or systemic levels, other decisions regarding the day-to-day administration will be taken by the head or school principal: the extent of the influence exerted at the official level over school organisation, however, differs greatly between Japan and England, with many of the roles and responsibilities of the school head in England being pre-empted by officials. This reflects the greater extent to which aspects of the educational system are prescribed by *Monbushō* (Ministry for Education, Sport and Culture) compared with the Department for Education and Employment (DfEE) in England. In addition to prescribing school curricula, and approving textbooks, *Monbushō* also has responsibility for deciding on the length of the school year and school week, the subject allocation of time, the level of financial contribution from parents, and for the system of appointing teachers. However, whether responsibility for the decisions made in respect of these areas lies at the systemic or institutional level, the effect on the class teacher is the same – namely, that these areas are decided outside the classroom. The range of choices and possibilities open to the class teacher with regard to teaching methods and materials and classroom practice is, in reality, severely limited by factors and decisions taken above the level of the classroom. The way in which the limiting of these choices affects children's learning of mathematics will be examined.

Within the classroom

Factors affecting the teaching of mathematics within the classroom which will be addressed here may be classified into five broad areas:

- management and climate of the classroom;
- teachers' attitudes towards cognitive and social development;
- teaching approaches to instruction, including strategies for calculation;
- nature and use of teaching materials;
- expectations in relation to minimum standards for all children.

The *management and climate* of a classroom provide the setting within which teaching and learning can take place: the atmosphere is, to a great extent, teacher-determined and controlled and depends on organisation, physical arrangements of desks and other classroom furniture, seating arrangements for pupils, standards of discipline and codes of behaviour. Teachers may choose whether the atmosphere of the classroom is largely one of co-operation or of competition. Pupils also contribute to the climate of the classroom; for example, by their standards of behaviour and their ability in listening and in answering questions.

Teachers' attitudes towards children's development, pedagogy and learning affect the nature of instruction. Attitudes may reflect a broadly 'transmission' approach to learning, or a broadly 'constructivist' approach, or some adaptation of these.

Teaching approaches and methods of mathematics instruction affect children's learning experience: the differences between English and Japanese teaching approaches will be of considerable interest (Galton *et al.*, 1980; Mortimore *et al.*, 1986; Croll and Moses, 1988). It may be that the distinctively cumulative nature or 'linear' character of mathematical development requires that instruction in mathematics should build upon those concepts and skills which children possess, and should explicitly take children through the next stages of those concepts and skills, in a logical and step-by-step manner (Case, 1983).

The nature of textbooks and other teaching materials and the way in which these are used affect the learning process. In particular, the use made in Japan of the detailed teachers' manuals – which is inter-related to the use of a whole-class teaching method – will be examined. In England, the use of a wide range of teaching materials drawn from a variety of publications is intended to enable teachers to provide a highly differentiated range of activities commensurate with pupils' individual levels of attainment.

Lastly, the attitudes of pupils, teachers and parents to *standards expected* of pupils will affect teaching and children's learning. The concept of a minimum standard for all pupils may affect teaching approaches, monitoring of progress and the use of strategies for 'catching up' slower or weaker pupils.

Research hypotheses and questions

The purpose of this study is to consider, first, at what stage of schooling differences in mathematical attainment between English and Japanese pupils first become apparent and, secondly, to examine the major contributing factors for this.

Specifically, it is hypothesised that:

(i) At the age of six when children begin formal schooling in Japan, their average mathematical competence does not exceed that of children of the same age in England;

(ii) Between the ages of six and seven, children in Japan make faster progress in mathematical development and understanding, so that after one year of formal schooling their average mathematical competence is significantly ahead of that of children of the same age in England.

Other major research questions relate to the reasons for the differences in the development of mathematical understanding. These include:

Influences from outside the classroom:

From society

(i) In what ways are the educational systems of Japan and England a reflection of their different cultures? Are there fundamental differences in educational philosophy that affect children's learning?

(ii) To what extent do children's attitudes to learning reflect the values of society they have absorbed during their early childhood years?

From pre-schooling

(iii) Are there differences in children's experiences of pre-school education which affect their subsequent learning in formal schooling? What are the aims of the Japanese and English models of pre-school education? To what extent does pre-school education continue the socialisation process begun by parents, family or the home?

At the systemic level

(iv) Are there differences in the degree of centralised control of the two educational systems? Are there particular aspects of children's educational experience that are significantly affected by these differences?

(v) Are there differences in the way in which the curriculum is specified by the government?

(vi) How do the teaching and other lesson materials used in the classroom compare, and how do they affect the development of mathematical understanding? What is the role and function of teachers' manuals?

Models of children's development and attitudes to pedagogy

(vii) In what ways is the nature of the instruction provided affected by the attitudes of teachers towards cognitive and social development?

(viii) How is the teachers' theoretical knowledge translated into a practical teaching model in the classroom? What are the levels of pedagogical and subject knowledge?

Influences from inside the classroom:

Teachers

(ix) Are the qualifications, educational backgrounds and age profiles of teachers comparable? Does the financial status of teachers differ, affecting recruitment of potential teachers?

The teaching of mathematics

(x)   Are there differences in the management and climate of the class-room that affect learning? Are there differences in the responsibility of an individual towards the larger community that affect the class-room atmosphere?

(xi) Are there differences in teachers' attitudes to the importance of de-veloping conceptual competence and/or procedural competence?

(xii) Are there differences in classroom practice that affect mathemati-cal development? For example, what importance is attached to oral work, and to interaction between teachers and pupils? To what ex-tent do lessons follow a particular structure or format which is familiar to children? Does this help development?

(xiii) Are there differences in levels of pupil motivation and/or partici-pation?

(xiv) What are teachers' and parents' expectations in relation to stand-ards expected of children? Is there an expectation regarding the achievement of a *minimum* standard? Are strategies used for the 'catching up' of pupils who fall behind or below the average stand-ard? Is variation in attainment acceptable, and to what extent is this expected?

Research methods to be used

In order to understand fully the particular nature of the teaching and learning of mathematics in Japan and England, we shall need to exam-ine carefully, *inter alia*, the following:

(i)   the content of the mathematics curriculum, as prescribed by the government;

(ii) examples of the delivered curriculum and the precise way in which it is delivered;

(iii) the sequencing of topics within the curriculum, and the way in which a particular exemplified topic is introduced and developed;

(iv) the use made of explanation and discussion;

(v) the nature of the interaction between teachers and pupils; the nature and levels of questioning used;

(vi) and the use made of contextualised word problems and practical demonstrations.

The nature of mathematical learning is highly complex, and the danger of simplification with regard to observations of educational approaches and culture is readily acknowledged. Questions of understanding teaching and learning can only be addressed through the nature of culture, social structure and socialisation, and the way these become institutionalised in education and the school in terms of pedagogy, curricula and classroom practice. We need to examine how children succeed in the classroom in the context of school experience being tied to, and resonating with, their social and cultural background and continuing experience.

While understanding of the *learning framework* for the child can be gained by examination of the written curriculum, the pupils' textbooks, the teachers' manuals, examining other available documentation, and by talking to teachers and other professional educationalists, examination of the *learning environment* of the child, as indicated by the classroom experience, can only be attempted through intense first-hand detailed observation.

Research methods used in this research, therefore, include:

• Detailed classroom observation of samples of 6- and 7-year-old children in Japan and England matched by age;

• Objective assessment by means of a short written test of the levels of mathematical attainment of these children;

• Analysis of text book and other lesson materials used in the teaching of mathematics to these children, including analysis of teachers' manuals;

• Analysis of curricular requirements; comparison of government specification of curricula, and the content of mathematics curricula for this stage of schooling;

• Discussions with class teachers and educationists regarding mathematical pedagogy;

- Informal observational visits to Japanese kindergarten and English nursery classes;
- Informal discussions with children in the classes selected for field-work regarding mathematical strategies and understanding of number structure.

Summary

This chapter has outlined the research questions to be addressed in the remaining chapters. Chapter 2 examines in more detail the existing evidence relating to comparisons of mathematical attainment of Japanese and English pupils and identifies the need for a small-scale observational comparative study to improve our understanding of the reasons for the differences in mathematical attainment. The methodology of the present study is described in Chapter 3, which identifies some of the particular methodological problems of educational and comparative research. Chapters 4 and 5 respectively are concerned with the different levels of influence on teaching and learning – namely, from society and from the educational systems. Chapter 6 examines different models of children's development and attitudes towards pedagogical knowledge. Central to this study are the examples included in Chapter 6 that illustrate the differences between lessons and children's activities in learning mathematics (Tables 6.1 and 6.2). The causes for these differences and their effects on the subsequent mathematical development of children are examined in the following chapters. Chapter 7 considers the backgrounds of teachers, their teaching methods and classroom practice, and identifies instructional variables involved in achieving greater progress in understanding mathematics and higher levels of competence. Case studies of the teaching of two topics are analysed in detail in Chapter 8, together with an outline of the associated implications for teaching and learning. The concluding Chapter 9 makes recommendations for changes in educational policy and practice and considers to what extent the recent changes made by the government are likely to solve the problems identified.

2

International comparisons of mathematical attainment

Introduction

International differences in mathematical attainment among secondary school age pupils are well documented and indicate that the performance of pupils in England lags behind that of many other countries. In particular, evidence shows that the average attainment of 13-year-old pupils in Japan is significantly higher than that of the corresponding co-hort of pupils in England (Husén, 1967; Comber and Keeves, 1973; Travers and Westbury, 1989; Beaton *et al.*, 1996; Mullis, *et al.*, 1997). Attainment at 13 years is the result of several years of formal schooling, and indications of earlier relatively poor performance by English pupils may be identified among 8- and 9-year-old pupils, reflecting both the rela-tive 'linearity' of development of mathematical understanding and the cumulative effect of failure (Bynner and Steedman, 1995; Harris *et al.*, 1996). Other evidence suggests that those pupils who fail in mathemat-ics at an early age are unlikely to be successful thereafter. We need to begin by considering how valid the evidence is regarding the differences in attainment between England and Japan. Are the apparent differences between the average levels attained by Japanese and English pupils at the ages of 9 and 13 years attributable, for example, to differences in the relationships between their curricula and the test questions? Are the different emphases in the contents of the mathematics curricula respon-sible? Are there significant differences between the response rates in the different countries which may account for the differences in results? To what extent is the educational system responsible for the between country differences in attainment, or for the variation in attainment? The problems of comparability, methodology and language associated with large-scale cross-national quantitative studies are immense – some detail is provided in the following section – and any consideration of results from international surveys should be set in this context.

The major studies of mathematical attainment have been conducted during the last thirty years by the International Association for the Evaluation of Educational Achievement (IEA) and by the International Association for International Planning (IAEP); Japan did not however participate in the study by the latter organisation. The IEA was established as an international co-ordinating research centre in 1959, shortly before the beginning of its first study. With the publication of the reports relating to the Third International Mathematics & Science Study (TIMSS) (Harris, *op.cit.*; Keys, *op. cit.*; Mullis, *op. cit.*) an immense quantity of statistical data on the mathematical attainments of school children in 46 countries – including Japan and England – has become available. For the purposes of this study, the results relating to the achievements of 8- and 9-year-old children in primary education are most relevant, and the majority of comments made here relate, therefore, to the findings in respect of primary and not secondary age children.

Large–scale comparative studies of mathematical attainment

Background

In many areas of the social sciences, quantitative studies may be regarded as performing the function of a skeleton, since by providing fundamental information on social structures they give shape and form to the field of study and assist the progress and advance of ideas. This applies as much to the field of comparative education as to any branch of the social sciences: accurate, systematic information relating to different educational systems and their societies is required as a basis for testing hypotheses in the search for explanations of educational phenomena. There are, however, particular difficulties associated with comparative educational data which need to be examined in some detail.

The early comparative educationists of the nineteenth century made cross-national comparisons by means of juxtaposing data from different countries and attempted quantitative measurement of simple variables relating to the structures of educational systems, such as the numbers of pupils attending different types of different schools at different ages.

Their approach to the measurement of variables, however, was simplistic and problems of language, interpretation, comparability and accuracy of information were largely ignored. Jullien (1817) was particularly ambitious in his plans for systematic and comprehensive inquiry (Fraser, 1964) and other educationists such as Matthew Arnold and Victor Cousin were inspired by his ideas. The ideas of Michael Sadler at the turn of the century placed a new emphasis on dynamic analysis and explanation, including an appreciation of the importance of the concept of causation (Sadler, 1902).

The first major comparative study of mathematics education began in the years leading up to World War I, organised by the body that is now known as ICMI (International Commission on Mathematical Instruction). Both Japan and the UK participated in this study, whose main achievement was to prepare a summary of teaching practice in 33 countries (Howson, 1984). Work on this was interrupted by World War I, and although the Commission was re-established in 1928, major work was not resumed until 1952, by which time UNESCO, OECD and the World Bank were also contributing to the collection of educational data although there were difficulties with poor data sources, inferior means of collection and limited analysis of results. By the 1960s, the beginning of the development of computing technology made it possible to undertake previously unthinkable levels of analysis of large-scale data. The first attempt at large-scale collection and analysis of comparative educational data was undertaken in 1963 by Husén in conjunction with the International Association for the Evaluation of Educational Achievement (IEA): the First International Mathematics Study (FIMS) concentrated on attainment in mathematics of secondary age pupils in twelve industrialised countries (Husén, 1967). It sought to explain mathematical variation in a way that would be relevant and useful for educational policy, especially at a time of considerable controversy over the desirability of comprehensive or selective education; single or multi-tracking; and single sex or co-educational schools. It was methodologically relatively sophisticated for its time, paying particular attention to question design and the effects of school, home and societal variables on education. The results were quickly and widely used by educationists to draw attention to the hierarchical ranking of countries by mathematical achievement, but it is possible that the wider publicity that these rankings received helped to give the study greater status and to ensure its continuity.

During the 1970s there was the beginning of an acceptance that large-scale transnational studies represented the only way in which data could be collected in a systematic, controlled way. Alternatives, such as the use of small-scale studies or government statistics, were accepted as being very limited either in sample size, and thus open to methodological criticisms, or in depth. There was a growing awareness of the need to apply the techniques of the social sciences to the field of comparative education using a more empirical and quantitative approach followed by detailed analysis (Anderson, 1977). By the early 1980s, the development of the micro-chip had transformed computing technology, improving dramatically the possibilities of large-scale multivariate analysis. The Second International Mathematics Study (SIMS) conducted by the IEA in 1982 benefited from this, being more ambitious in its coverage than the first study and including 19 countries (Robitaille and Garden, 1989). The Third International Mathematics and Science Survey (TIMSS) was extended even further and is discussed in more detail below.

Methodological problems

Despite improvements in methodological techniques, coupled with vastly improved technology permitting sophisticated methods of statistical analysis, in the early 1990s serious problems remained in relation to the validity and reliability of the data obtained from these global surveys. Detailed criticisms were discussed in the context of SIMS notably by Goldstein (1993), Bracey (1992) and Huelskamp (1993). Although some of the problems were successfully addressed inTIMSS, conducted during 1995 and involving pupils in 41 countries, it is important to be aware of the main areas of methodological difficulty which remain in the conduct of large-scale comparative studies. The problems outlined by Professor Goldstein may be classified broadly into five categories.

First, problems arising from language. English has been the main language used for the construction of materials such as questionnaires in the IEA studies. These have then been translated into other languages as necessary, and 'back-translated' to English for comparison with the original text. Yet this does not ensure that the meaning is translated correctly. There may not be a specific 'one-to-one' translation of a particular word: the relationship may be 'one-to-many' yet if the word has a 'many-to-one' translation back to English, it appears as though the translation is straightforward and non-problematic. Some words may not have an equivalent meaning: for example, 'family' is a word existing in most languages, yet the definition and concept of family varies with culture and social structure. In attempting to define simple concepts such as 'full-time schooling', differences in assumptions and attitudes may be revealed. Words may be ambiguous: Goldstein refers, for example, to the ambiguity of the word 'expect' in the English language, which according to its contextual use, can refer to a wish, an intention, and obligation or a prediction. Research to assess the comparability and equivalence of back-translated questions used in the 1981 IEA study was carried out by Hanna (1993) who found that, out of the 174 test items examined, 70 differed significantly in their language meaning. There may also be bias arising from using English as the original language for the test material, but little research has been done in this area. However, it seems that even with more research into the effects of bias, the problems of meaning and equivalence in language are likely to remain to some extent: for example, it is not possible to ensure that the meaning of a question in two different cultures is precisely the same, because there is a lack of external criteria against which comparisons can be made. Thus in the presentation of results deriving from global surveys it is crucial that awareness of language problems is appreciated and that the difficulties which language presents for the validity and reliability of cross–national data is not underestimated.

Secondly, sampling procedures and response rates are likely to give rise to serious methodological problems. In the 1981 IEA study the stratified sampling procedure used the school as the basic sampling unit, stratified by type, size and region. It was not possible, however, to standardise completely this sampling procedure across all countries. In addition, the use of the school as the basic unit of sampling makes inter–school comparisons difficult due to the small number of schools with a given characteristic (Reynolds and Farrell, 1996). In relation to response rates, although some countries (such as Taiwan, Japan and Korea) achieve consistently high rates, others which struggle to reach 50 per cent may be subject to bias. Where the nature and extent of the bias is unknown, these potential biases are a matter of considerable concern (Reynolds and Farrell, *op cit*.). Other methodological problems relate to difficulties of categorising pupils by age or grade. In some countries such as France, successful completion of examinations is a prerequisite for progression to the next grade and thus repeating a year is common. Are those pupils repeating grades to be excluded from the survey for reasons of age? And, if so, what bias will this introduce into the results?

Thirdly, there are problems of analysis of results. So far, there has been a tendency for results to be aggregated by country in order to facilitate transnational comparisons, but this tends to obscure the within-country differences. The IEA studies have collected valuable information relating to curriculum, school organisation, teacher experience, attitudes of parents, as well as characteristics of pupils and schools; multivariate analysis of this information within countries could shed light on the effects of different educational policies and could contribute to the construction of explanations of observed educational relationships.

Fourthly, the IEA studies have been criticised for concentrating too much on measurement at a single point in time and for collecting cross-sectional rather than longitudinal data over more than one year, which are necessary if progress of pupils over time is to be assessed.

Fifthly, an important problem arises with the difficulty of interpreting change. If there is, for example, a difference in the pattern of questions correctly answered on a test of mathematical attainment, is this to be interpreted as evidence of a real change, or of a discrepancy in translation? Is change in mathematical achievement a reflection of mathematical change or other structural change? This problem, like the difficulties arising from language equivalence, cannot be solved adequately because of the absence of external criteria against which to measure change. This difficulty relates to responses to questions classed as 'anchor items' in the IEA studies and which were repeated between SIMS and TIMSS in order that changes in performance might be identified. A further difficulty with interpreting the change in the pattern of responses to these questions arose from the fact that while it is clearly essential for such questions to be presented to successive cohorts of students in exactly the same format, this was not always the case in SIMS and TIMSS.

The design of TIMSS was aimed to eliminate as many of these criticisms as possible, and to a large extent was successful in this aim. The samples of pupils selected for testing were examined carefully in order to avoid bias, and the sampling of schools permitted replacement schools which could be used if necessary. Testing sessions were monitored, and all data were carefully checked for within–country consistency before analysis. Despite these efforts, some of the problems associated with language and comparability of meaning remain; it is doubtful whether they can ever be completely eradicated from even the most sophisticated survey.

Results from the Third International Mathematics and Science Study

Primary-school pupils included for testing were 8- and 9-year-olds; in most countries (including Japan) such pupils were in the third and fourth

Table 2.1 *Maths scores of primary pupils: Japan and England*[a]

	Pupils aged 8		Pupils aged 9	
	Mean	Standard deviation	Mean	Standard deviation
Japan	538	75	597	81
England	456	87	513	91

Source: Mullis *et. al.*, 1997, Tables C3 and C4.

[a]These scores were standardised by TIMSS to an international mean of 500 for all participating countries.

grades of compulsory formal schooling. In England children begin schooling at an earlier age than almost every other country, and so pupils tested in English schools were in Years 4 and 5. The fact that English pupils in the survey had experienced, on average, at least one additional year of schooling should not be overlooked when making comparisons of attainment levels. Efforts were made to ensure that the content of the test items was appropriate for pupils in the different countries and reflected their current curriculum. The test covered six content areas: whole numbers (25 per cent of test items); fractions and proportionality (21 per cent); measurement, estimation and number sense (20 per cent); data representation, analysis and probability (12 per cent); geometry (14 per cent); and patterns, relations and functions (10 per cent). About one quarter were 'free response' or 'open-ended', with the remainder being multiple choice (one answer out of four). The broad results achieved by pupils in Japan and England are shown in table 2.1 above.

Without the benefit of more sophisticated analysis, these results indicate that:

- by the age of 8, Japanese pupils were already achieving higher mean scores than pupils in England;
- this difference was maintained (and slightly increased) during the next year of schooling;
- the variation in scores of English pupils (as measured by the standard deviation) was higher in both age groups;
- assuming a steady rate of progress, the average pupil in Japan was nearly eighteen months ahead of the average English pupil (at both ages);
- there was some slight increase in standard deviation between age

groups for both countries. If coefficient of variation[1] is taken as a measure of variation, however, this showed a slight decrease between age groups.

A number of questions follow from these results, the first of which concerns their validity in the context of differences in, for example, sampling procedures, response rates and exclusion rates. On examination, it would appear that where differences in methodology do exist, they operate to enhance the English results. For example, in England a higher number of replacement schools was used in the final participating sample, which may bias the sample in favour of higher attaining schools. Also, in England 12 per cent of pupils were excluded from completing the test compared with 3 per cent of pupils in Japan and it may be assumed that many of these pupils were from the weakest level of achievement (Mullis, 1997, *op. cit.* Table A.2). In addition, the percentages of pupils failing to complete the tests for reasons of absence were about 5 and 3 per cent for England and Japan respectively (*Ibid.* Table A.5). Taking these factors together would suggest that about 10 per cent fewer of the pupils in England participated compared with the participation rate in Japan: since many of these would have been lower–attaining pupils, this supports the view that the figures for England have benefited artificially from this and that the true comparable scores for English pupils were lower.

The results from previous international comparisons had generated concern that the relatively poor performance of pupils in England arose largely from content areas or topics involving number, indicating a weakness in basic arithmetic; it had been suggested that this was counterbalanced by the fact that pupils in England scored above the international means in the topic *Data representation, analysis and probability*. Yet if the broad results for England and Japan from TIMSS are broken down into the different topic areas, it is clear that the poor performance of English pupils was far from restricted to the topic of 'number' (see table 2.2). It was only on questions involving the topic of *Geometry* that pupils in England obtained (marginally) higher average scores than pupils in Japan; this is perhaps due to the greater amount of attention given to the topic of *Geometry* in primary schooling in England than in Japan.

In addition to considering figures for average attainment for all pupils, it is also instructive to examine the achievements of the top attaining

---

[1] Coefficient of variation is calculated as $\dfrac{\text{standard deviation}}{\text{mean}}$

Table 2.2 *Mean scores[a] by content area: Japan and England*

	Pupils aged 8			Pupils aged 9		
	Japan	England	Difference	Japan	England	Difference
Number	72	46	+26	82	58	+24
Fractions and proportion	52	34	+18	65	45	+20
Measurement	60	42	+18	72	52	+20
Data handling	69	50	+19	79	64	+15
Geometry	62	63	−1	72	74	−2
Patterns	64	43	+21	76	55	+21
Average	63	45	+18	74	57	+17

Source: Mullis, *op. cit.*, Tables 2.1 and 2.2.
[a]These mean scores are mean percentages of questions correctly answered in each topic area.

pupils, and the achievements of the lowest attaining pupils: results from earlier international studies suggested that pupils at the top of the attainment range in England performed as well or better than the best pupils in other countries including Japan. However, using the score obtained by the top decile of pupils internationally as a measure, we can see that in England only 6 per cent of 8-year-old pupils performed at this level, compared with 24 per cent of pupils in Japan. The figures for 9-year-old pupils are scarcely more encouraging: the percentages for pupils who reached the top decile level of achievement internationally were 7 per cent and 23 per cent for England and Japan respectively. It seems possible that the levels of achievement in England of the best pupils may have deteriorated only recently since in the 1991 survey by the IAEP (in which Japan, however, did not participate), the best pupils in England obtained high scores when compared internationally (Lapointe *et al.*, 1989).

Another way of comparing the results of the highest attaining pupils is to compare the actual mean scores (standardised to an international mean for all countries of 500) of the top 5 per cent of pupils in the two grades (table 2.3). These figures suggest that even the best pupils in England are now performing at a level which is almost one year behind their counterparts in Japan. These figures have serious implications for the future, since they relate to the nation's future capabilities with regard to research and technology (Psacharopoulos, 1972; Prais, 1995).

Turning to the other end of the achievement scale, it can be seen that the mean scores obtained by the weakest 5 per cent of pupils in England

Table 2.3 *Mean scores in mathematics of the top and bottom 5 per cent of pupils: Japan and England*

	Pupils aged 8		Pupils aged 9		Change	
	Top 5%	Bottom 5%	Top 5%	Bottom 5%	Top 5%	Bottom 5%
Japan	659	410	726	458	+67	+48
England	603	318	672	366	+69	+48
Difference						
Japan/England	+56	+92	+54	+92		

Source: Mullis *et. al.*, 1997, *op. cit.*, Tables C1 & C2.

were further behind Japanese pupils. This suggests that the lowest attaining English pupils have a lag of almost two years behind such pupils in Japan; if it is further accepted that many of the weakest pupils in the English sample would not have participated in the assessment exercise (as discussed earlier in this section), this provides even greater cause for concern.

In relation to performance on individual questions, detailed results from TIMSS have so far been made available in respect of only a small number of questions – it is to be hoped that more of these will gradually become available, because it is from the answers to the specific questions that most can be learned. On the topic of 'Whole Numbers', the percentages of correct responses are available in respect of five specific questions, three of which were multiple choice and two were open–ended. The results show a dramatic gap between the percentage of correct responses among Japanese and English pupils. Indeed, *in all the five questions*, the performance of 9–year–old English pupils is way behind the performance of 8-year-old Japanese pupils, and at the estimated rate of improvement of English pupils as indicated by the difference between the scores of the 8- and 9-year-old pupils, the performance of the English pupils shows a 'lag' of between two and five years behind that of the Japanese pupils. The results are shown in table 2.4. If the usual adjustment is given for a 'multiple choice question', the differences become even greater.[2]

---

[2] For example, in a multiple choice with four possible answers (as used in TIMSS), a percentage of correct answers of 60 per cent suggests that approximately 47 per cent of pupils knew the correct answer, and the remainder guessed. It is therefore clear that 8-year-old pupils in England (of whom only 23 per cent obtained the correct answer) would have been expected to have done better by guessing.

Table 2.4 *Percentages of correct responses to questions involving whole numbers: Japan and England*

| | Pupils aged 8 | | Pupils aged 9 | |
Questions	Japan	England	Japan	England
Which of these is the largest number? A. 2735 B. 2537 C. 2573 D. 2753	91	69	94	83
4+4+4+4+4=20 *Write this addition fact as a* *multiplication fact.*	86	39	92	53
2000+?+310+9=2739 *What number goes where the ? is* *to make this sentence true?*	73	28	86	49
25x18 is more than 24x18. *How much more?* A. 1 B. 18 C. 24. D. 25	48	27	59	37
Subtract: 6000 –2369 A. 4369 B. 3742 C. 3631 D. 3531	73	23	89	36

Source: Mullis *op. cit.*, Tables 3.1, 3.2, 3.3, 3.4, 3.5.

Table 2.5 *Percentages of correct responses to a subtraction question by primary and secondary pupils: Japan and England*

	Pupils aged 8	Pupils aged 9	Pupils aged 13	Pupils aged 14
Japan	73	89	89	93
England	23	36	59	65

Source: Mullis *op. cit.*, Table 3.3.

The algorithmic question involving vertical subtraction is particularly interesting, because this was one of the 'linked' questions which were also administered to the 13- and 14-year-old pupils at secondary school and it is thus possible to compare achievement in the primary years and lower secondary years. The results are summarised in table 2.5.

While this question may be criticised as mundane, it is a reasonable test of competence in numerical skills: it was not a test of mental arithmetic, since it was set out in vertical form, and primary school pupils in

England would be expected to have been taught the algorithmic approach to subtraction by or during Year 5. Yet it is clear that even by the time they are 14 and have completed nearly *nine years* of compulsory schooling, the percentage of English pupils able to select the correct answer from a choice of four (65 per cent) was less than the percentage of Japanese pupils aged 8 in their *third year* of schooling (73 per cent). It has been suggested that on the basis of these figures we should expect a third of English school-leavers to be unable to carry out such a basic sum (Prais, 1997, p. 57).

Despite all the documented problems of making valid and reliable comparisons in international studies, it seems, therefore, established beyond reasonable doubt that in almost all aspects of mathematics, the average performance of English pupils is significantly inferior to that of Japanese pupils of a similar age but with one year less schooling. There is thus a considerable body of indisputable evidence relating to the current weaker performance of English primary school pupils when compared to attainment in Japan, *throughout all levels of ability*. Some leading British educationists have attempted to argue that such findings are either invalid or irrelevant to the deeper understanding of mathematics, and suggest that the approach to learning mathematics experienced by children in England encourages skill in problem-solving that is of greater value in the application of mathematical ideas in the 'real world'. As yet, however, there is little in the way of evidence to support this view.

While the results from the large-scale international studies – especially the methodologically-improved TIMSS – provide a valuable comparison of levels of mathematical attainment, they are restricted in their *diagnostic value* since they are unable to provide any information on the nature of the errors made by pupils which would improve understanding of the difficulties pupils experienced in developing mathematical/numerical competency.

The next question to consider is: 'Are these large-scale international comparative studies able to identify the *reasons* for the differences in attainment levels, or to suggest any causal factors?' Apart from the results of mathematics scores of pupils, the latest TIMSS survey included a great many questions relating to background factors affecting performance – for example, on pupils' attitudes towards learning mathematics, teachers' experience and their teaching methods, the importance attached to homework and the use of calculators. Much of the data relating to background of Japanese pupils, however, were not made available – and for English pupils the data on 'time spent in homework' were not available.

Table 2.6 *Comparisons of perceived and actual achievement of pupils aged 9: Japan and England*

Pupils' perceptions about usually doing well in mathematics	Japan	England
	Mean scores	
Agree/strongly agree	617	518
Disagree/strongly disagree	539	477
Difference between mean scores	78	41

Source: Mullis *op.cit.*, Table 4.12.

The range of comparisons that can be made between Japan and England is, therefore, limited to those areas where information is available concerning both countries. For example, pupils in England spent more time than Japanese pupils on each of the categories identified for 'leisure' activities (although the patterns of time spent watching television are difficult to interpret) (Mullis, *op.cit.*, Table 4.11). Another aspect concerned pupils' perceptions of mathematics; 90 per cent of English pupils agreed that they 'usually do well in mathematics' compared with 74 per cent of Japanese pupils. These perceptions of their performance in mathematics are consistent with their attitudes to liking/disliking mathematics – 84 per cent of English pupils in year 5 said that they liked mathematics compared with 71 per cent of Japanese pupils in the fourth grade.

The relationship between perceived and actual performance was more evident among Japanese than English pupils – the average score difference between those who agreed that they usually did well in mathematics and those who disagreed with that statement was only 41 points for English pupils, compared with 78 for Japanese pupils (Table 2.6). Whether this suggests that teachers are misleading their pupils with regard to the actual level of their achievements, or whether the work demanded of pupils is set at too low a level is not clear. The results of other data included in TIMSS, for example, relating to teachers' backgrounds and contact time, are discussed in the appropriate later chapters together with their implications for understanding mathematical development.

From the results of the recent TIMSS study of primary school pupils, the following points can be made in relation to comparisons of the performance of Japanese and English pupils:

- On average, English pupils aged 8–9 years old are about eighteen months behind Japanese pupils of a similar age (who have had at

least one year less in terms of experience of formal schooling);
- this perceived 'lag' is particularly marked among the low attaining English pupils who are about two years behind their Japanese equivalents;
- for the first time in a major international comparative study, high attaining pupils in England appear to have been overtaken by their Japanese equivalents;
- a major deficiency occurs in arithmetical competence;
- variation in levels of attainment is greater among pupils from both age groups in England;
- results of English pupils may have been enhanced by the exclusion of a larger proportion of weaker pupils, and the true position might show Japanese pupils with an even greater advantage.

While it is easy to dismiss the need for arithmetical competence and to argue that it is more important for pupils to develop an understanding of broader mathematical issues – as presented in the National Curriculum, for example – yet a sound foundation in numeracy is a prerequisite for later mathematical progress and scientific understanding. One of the aspects of the TIMSS data which causes concern relates to the performance of the 'best' pupils: whereas hitherto the levels of attainment of the top English pupils were as good as, if not better than, those attained by the top pupils in Japan, this is clearly no longer the case, and, moreover, the shift appears to have taken place in the last few years.

The TIMSS study provides a wealth of valuable information, and represents a major contribution to the body of knowledge regarding educational systems, structures and standards: the importance of the IEA studies is widely acknowledged by comparative educationists of international standing (Psacharopoulos, 1990; King, 1986). Yet the TIMSS study does not provide the necessary insight into the factors associated with, or underlying, the different attainment levels. Such insight, it is argued, can only be provided by smaller-scale, more narrowly focused studies which involve carefully structured detailed classroom observation and discussions with practising teachers regarding pedagogical factors. In order to understand the difficulties experienced by children in developing conceptual understanding in mathematics, we first must carefully analyse the nature of the errors made in answering questions on focused questions involving specific concepts. Only then can we hope to advance children in their cognitive development and understanding of the structure of number.

Smaller-scale studies

Since 1980 there have been a number of comparative studies of mathematical attainment involving Japan that have been less ambitious in terms of their coverage than those conducted by the IEA. These studies mostly involve comparisons between two, or at the most three, countries. Most of them involve comparisons between the US and Japan; none is concerned with comparing mathematical learning development in *England* and Japan.

Studies of Japanese and American performance in mathematics achievement include those by Harnisch (1986) and by Azuma *et al.* (1981; 1986). The former showed the mathematical achievements of the high school students in Japan to be significantly higher (by more than two standard deviations) than the achievements of the students in Illinois. The studies by Azuma *et al.* were more concerned with the influence of family background factors on achievement and school readiness.

Other studies of mathematical achievement relating to pupils in Japan were conducted by the University of Michigan: these are summarised by Stigler and Baranes (1988). The first of these studies compared samples of children in Japan, Taiwan and America, and was concerned to identify the stage at which differences in performance first began to appear.[3] This first study found that Japanese and Taiwanese children were ahead of American children even in the first grade and this difference became more pronounced by the fifth grade. The second Michigan study examined performance on a wider range of mathematical skills, in order to test the hypothesis that the achievement of Japanese children lay primarily in the field of computational proficiency and not in the field of creative problem–solving mathematics. The study concluded, however, that the performance of Japanese children was superior to that of American children in all areas of mathematical competence in both the first and fifth grades. The main differences in classroom practice found by these studies may be summarised as:

---

[3] A study by Song and Ginsburg (1987) lies outside the main focus of this present study, since it compares standards of Korean and American children, yet it has important findings that are relevant to the issues being investigated here. It established that whereas between the ages of 4 and 6 years old Korean children did not do as well as their American counterparts in informal mathematics, and that there was no significant difference at this stage in knowledge of number facts, calculation skills nor understanding of number structure, yet by the age of 7 or 8 years old Korean children were ahead of American children on both informal mathematics and number knowledge.

- greater amount of time spent teaching mathematics in Japan and Taiwan;
- greater use of whole-class teaching in Japan and Taiwan;
- greater use of discussion and reflection in Japan and Taiwan;
- greater teacher–pupil interaction in Japan and Taiwan;
- different ways of using concrete materials (or 'manipulatives' such as cubes and blocks).

A further study of mathematical development of elementary school children in Japan and the USA by Stevenson and Stigler (1992) attributed the relatively poor standards of mathematical achievement of pupils in America to low levels of individual effort rather than innate lack of ability. The authors identified five major factors within the elementary school system in Japan which, they argued, were instrumental in producing the high attainment standards:

- the Japanese educational system recognised the need for order and structure by children at an early age and provided techniques for group functioning;
- children in Japan shared responsibilities for classroom discipline and also for practical activities such as cleaning and the serving of food;
- development of a group identity in Japan was increased by activities (during break and lunch time, before and after school), and by class trips;
- there was greater continuity in Japan between home life and school life;
- the emphasis given to the importance of whole-class activities rather than individual activities was apparent in the use of ritual and the development of social skills.

The authors emphasised the importance of socialisation with respect to achievement, commenting on the effect of Confucian philosophy on effort and the school environment. Relatively little attention, however, was paid to variables associated with teaching.

A small-scale comparative study by Stigler (1988b) was more tightly focused on a single aspect of teaching mathematics, namely, the nature of verbal explanation in the teaching of mathematics in Japanese and American classrooms. This demonstrated that verbal explanation in Japan was likely to be more frequent, more complicated and more abstract in nature, and that lessons in Japan were generally at a more relaxed pace.

Stigler also pointed out that young children are capable of understanding and responding to complex verbal explanations, and that concrete experiences and verbal explanations may be demonstrated simultaneously (Chapter 7): however, the extent to which Stigler's comments may be validly applied to teaching mathematics in England is again limited. Finally, two further small-scale comparative studies should be mentioned. These relate, first, to pupils' abilities with problem-solving tasks (Stigler *et al.*, 1982) and, secondly, to classroom observation of pupils in grades I to IV, in which large cross–cultural differences found in classroom structure and management paralleled differences in achievement in the three countries examined (Stigler *et al.*, 1987).

Although these studies of Japanese elementary school children provide valuable insight into possible reasons for high mathematical attainment, none included Britain in their comparisons with Japan, reflecting the general tendency for comparative research with Japan to be conducted by American researchers and, therefore, to focus their concerns on the US. The extent to which their findings are relevant in relation to the English educational system thus is limited, and the need for a small-scale tightly focused study of the differences between the Japanese and English approaches to the development of mathematical understanding and acquisition of mathematical skills is further underlined.

Summary

The large-scale international comparative studies of mathematical attainment have contributed a great deal to the awareness of achievement on a global scale. Many of the methodological problems associated with the early surveys have been successfully addressed, and with an increasing number of countries participating in the IEA studies, data on both attainment and classroom practice are greater than ever before. Yet these large-scale studies raise as many questions as they answer, and there is a need for smaller-scale in-depth comparative studies of the practice in two countries if we are to understand the differences in the learning experiences of young children in the two cultures. There is an acute lack of comparative studies of Japan and England, primarily because the majority of research undertaken is US-financed and thus has a US perspective. This study addresses this lack and aims to provide a detailed analysis and understanding of the mathematical learning process of young children in schools in Japan and England.

3

The research method within a
comparative education framework

Introduction

Questions of research method and design are never easy to answer, and
often solutions consist of reconciling what is theoretically desirable with
what is practically possible. Problems of understanding different cultures
and societies provide further complicating factors in designing research
studies within the field of comparative education. Some of the problems
arising in comparative educational research are outlined here, together
with a summary of approaches to research developed during the establishment of comparative education as an accepted academic discipline
and in recent years. An assessment of the current thinking with regard
to methods appropriate for use in comparative research provides the
context within which the methodological problems of the present study
are considered. Resolution of such problems led to the design of the
present study which is outlined at the conclusion of this chapter: details
are also provided regarding the selection of schools and classes to be sampled, the nature of the fieldwork, methods of recording and subsequent
analysis.

Methods of comparative education: background and development

Before the 1960s, contributions to the development of the comparative
method in education had been made notably by Hans (1949) and Kandel
(1933; 1955; 1959). Hans had stressed the importance of identifying factors affecting education and tradition within a country. He argued that

32

in order to maintain unity of national culture there were five factors where homogeneity needed to be maintained – namely, race, religion, language, compactness of territory and political sovereignty.

Kandel, on the other hand, was more concerned with the identification and analysis of the causes shaping educational systems and, while recognising the dangers of simplistic stereotyping of national character, argued that a main influence on education was the cultural environment of the nation. Both Hans and Kandel were concerned to develop a more scientific approach to comparative education, which was continued in the work of Noah and Eckstein (1969). In their work *Toward a Science of Comparative Education*, they identify weaknesses of existing quantitative knowledge and argue for the construction of a complex transnational data base which could help to explain educational relationships, and understanding thus acquired could be used to predict the changes likely in society as a result of educational changes. In a sense, the large-scale international comparative studies of the IEA, such as the recent TIMSS in mathematics and science, are beginning to provide information on the global scale proposed by Noah and Eckstein *(ibid)*.

Thus by the 1960s, comparative educationists were beginning to demand a systematic, rigorous, and, above all, scientific, approach to the field of study, with consequent implications for appropriate methodology. Bereday (1964) notably argued for thorough awareness of the cultural, social and historic backgrounds of the countries to be compared, in addition to systematic data collection and comparison.

Bereday, with his ambitious plans for the comparison of area studies, provided a bridge between the historico-philosophical approach of comparative educationists before the 1960s and the later methodological awareness and applications of concepts derived from the social sciences, which characterised the work of later comparative educationists such as that by Holmes (1965, 1985), Altbach and Kelly (1978, 1986) and Schriewer and Holmes (1988).

Holmes was largely concerned with attempting to provide solutions to the practical problems in education. His method began with the identification of a particular problem within a school and moved out into the wider national context and then to cross-national comparisons – although he was doubtful of the likelihood of being able to develop a precise predictive approach to comparative education.

While Holmes was concerned with the identification of national characteristics which affected education and the distinction between these and national factors, other comparative educationists such as Anderson

(1977) did not agree with the attempts to identify the field of study by the methods used, arguing that since the field of comparative education was basically a combination of a number of disciplines with a common interest in analysing the relationship between school and society, it could more properly be defined by its content. Anderson, concerned with the theoretical development of complex ideas relating school and society, proposed that any of the methods available from the social sciences might be used – and that a single method by itself would be insufficient to meet all of the complex needs presented by a piece of comparative research. In concentrating more on the relationships within a national context and less on comparative studies, and attempting to relate specific aspects of education to social and economic factors, he accurately identified the development of comparative education in the later 1960s and 1970s, away from cross-national comparisons and the quest for a single methodology, towards an analysis of the relationship between school and society.

Comparative education within the framework of social sciences

Throughout the development in the field of comparative education, it is important to be aware of the contemporary and often parallel development in other fields within the social sciences. At the time of the early 1970s there was considerable interest in the techniques of the different methodologies available: for a while, large-scale studies were fashionable and were seen as the only means of providing data to test hypotheses. This approach has already been observed in the context of the large-scale international comparative studies such as the IEA in the field of mathematical attainment. Later, the small-scale in-depth approach of the ethnomethodologists and anthropologists replaced the statistical or analytical approach previously advocated – and, since the early 1970s, the concerns of comparative education have moved away from methodological debate and have been more concerned with defining the content of the field of study. By the end of the 1970s, the two major strands in the development of comparative education that could be identified related to the macro- and micro-approaches. While some comparative educationists were increasingly concerned with world systems analysis and the identification of characteristics and factors which would affect all educational systems, others concentrated on analysing the variation in classroom practice at the local level. At the micro-level, studies were often small-scale and frequently were ethnographic, phenomenological or interpretative in approach, reflecting the many views of sociologists and anthropologists in the field regarding the understanding of reality. The findings of the IEA studies regarding the extent of the differences in educational practices within as well as between nation states have given support to this view, and the two broad strands of comparative educational method clearly identifiable today – namely, an appreciation of the value of the small-scale qualitative study in parallel with the large-scale quantitative study – may be combined in order to link research effectively with the development of educational policy.

Whereas the methodological developments of the 1960s elevated the status of the discipline of comparative education, its viability as a discipline is seen here as dependent on the three factors identified by Kazamias (1972):

- its relevance to educational problems;
- the extent to which it illuminates contemporary issues
- the extent to which it informs proposals for change

The present study

This study, which is concerned with differences in mathematical attainment between pupils in Japan and England, satisfies each of the above criteria. The problem of poor mathematical performance of English pupils relative to pupils of a similar age in almost all other industrialised countries is widely recognised as being currently one of the most urgent educational problems: this also carries with it serious implications for the quality of the future work-force. Without adequate levels of mathematical competence among school leavers, it is doubtful whether the rigorous standards of vocational and educational training now recognised as necessary can be achieved on a suitably wide scale, and this question directly affects future levels of economic productivity. At the upper end of achievement in mathematics, concern has been expressed in recent years by professors and others in university departments of mathematics regarding the perceived falling quality of undergraduates and their poor grounding in mathematical knowledge and understanding (Royal Society, 1988; Howson, 1991). A number of different and wide-ranging initiatives have been introduced in order to improve mathematics standards, but so far there is little evidence to suggest that they will effect a significant improvement in average standards. In fact, it is slightly surprising that, given the considerable diversity of institutional and classroom practice, it has not been possible to identify a model of educational practice for the teaching of mathematics that would facilitate the improving of standards.

It becomes increasingly urgent, therefore, to address the problem from a different perspective – namely, by examining the educational model provided by a country more successful in the teaching and learning of mathematics. From such a perspective, it becomes possible to understand the nature of the problem more clearly: however, it is also necessary to understand fully the extent and the precise nature of the *context* within which the comparative educational model is set. This underlines, yet again, the need for identification and detailed analysis of the factors affecting the educational model at the different levels (societal, systemic and classroom). Only when the nature and effect of these factors is fully understood will it be possible to make proposals for change in the educational system in England which will facilitate an improvement in standards. Moreover, since it is now clear that differences in the performance of average pupils in the two countries emerge at an early age, a comparative study that informs proposals regarding a model for the effective teaching of mathematics should be concerned with educational practice at the beginning of formal schooling (Harris *et al.*, 1996; Keys *et al.*, 1996).

From the evidence presented in relation to existing international comparative studies of mathematical attainment, and particularly in relation to the large-scale international studies, it becomes clear that in order to answer some of the detailed questions regarding reasons for differences in mathematical attainment in Japan and England, a smaller scale 'in-depth' study is needed. While an appreciation of the effect of factors at the societal and systemic levels is essential, and any analysis should be conducted within this framework, we need to consider carefully what happens at the classroom level and the effect of this on pupils' learning. There are many questions relating to teaching methods, the nature of teacher–pupil interaction, the development of strategies for understanding mathematical processes, the nature and use of lesson materials, and so on, which can only be answered by direct first-hand classroom observation. The employment of an observational method of research, however, especially in the context of comparative education, is far from straightforward and some of the more obvious associated problems should be outlined.

While the technique of observation has long been used in studies of early childhood in order to enhance understanding of social and cognitive development in young children, until relatively recently within the context of educational research it has been treated as less important than other methods such as those involving questionnaires or structured interviews (Simon and Boyer, 1970). This is partly due to the difficulty of achieving the appropriate level of systematisation required in the observing and recording of phenomena if 'observation' is to be used as a research method (Genishi, 1982). Traditionally, a distinction has been drawn between quantitative studies which depend on numerical or statistical data and their analysis, and qualitative or non-statistical studies. A major distinction between these two types of study, however, relates to the attitudes of researchers regarding hypotheses or assumptions to be tested. Within quantitative studies, the researcher is likely to have previously constructed specific hypotheses for testing, to have identified analytical methods to be used in relation to the data, and to have constructed categories for the analysis: in contrast, within a qualitatively based study, the researcher is likely to retain a more open mind to aspects of interest and emerging patterns and to avoid predetermining categories for subsequent analysis. Qualitative studies tend to lead to an understanding of events and are thus interpretative or constructive in outcome, rather than predictive as is often the aim of quantitative studies.

Frequently in research with an educational focus, the two distinct approaches become merged; a dominant qualitative approach utilising an observational approach becomes supported by quantitative data obtained through objective testing or through structured interview. This is the nature of the research described here: the observational approach predominates, but is supported by some quantitative testing of children's mathematical attainment in order to provide an opportunity for some structural error analysis.

Different types of observation that exist include approaches that may be broadly anthropological, sociological, ethnographical or use participant observation. Ethnography (which literally refers to a written account of a cultural group of people) is often used in connection with cultural anthropological studies; however, this commonly involves extended periods of participant observation which, for a variety of reasons – many of them practical – are difficult to achieve at the institutional level in education. Instead, the term 'microethnographical methods' has been coined to describe observation at the classroom level (Genishi, op.cit.). Educational researchers using this approach include Mehar, who, influenced by the sociological perspective on ethnomethodology, emphasised the importance of the retrievability of data through, for example, the use of video recording methods, and of the need for comprehensive analysis and treatment of data, including the use of examples to provide evidence and to support conclusions (Mehar, 1979).

Problematic issues resulting from using an observational method for research include, firstly, that of reliability of observations and the conclusions drawn from them (Hollenbeck, 1978). Reliability of observational data depends essentially on the judgement of the researcher, and his/her skill in recording what activity is actually taking place, and interpreting this correctly. In a research context involving only one observer, it is important that the observer should be as experienced as possible in terms of background knowledge of the dynamics of the situation under observation. It is also helpful if a single observer has had some previous experience in comparable situations involving more than one observer, where some check on the extent to which agreement is reached on recording and interpretation of events has been possible.

Secondly, it is important to appreciate the issues of validity of observational methods – whether what has been measured or recorded is what we say has been measured or recorded. A high level of validity is perhaps easier to achieve in a quantitative approach, where the researcher intrudes as little as possible: this is harder to achieve in a qualitative study where an observer inevitably intrudes to some extent on the situation being observed. It is clearly helpful for the researcher to be as unobtrusive as possible – in a classroom situation the extent to which this is possible depends partly on the physical arrangement and organisation of the classroom, and partly on the nature of the teaching method used. While it is often argued that the use of a video camera makes valid observation an achievable reality, because by replaying the tape a series of 'microanalyses' becomes possible, yet a camera cannot record everything that takes place in a situation (and the use of two cameras, while improving the sight lines, increases disruption and intrusion). In the present study, some limited use was made of a video camera – its use was deliberately restricted, since it is not possible for a single researcher simultaneously to observe and to record. While using a video camera, it is possible for a researcher to miss the impact of important interaction taking place which in the normal course of events would have been observed and noted. The use made of a video camera, therefore, was largely as a visual record of classroom organisation, together with some sample or demonstration lessons of teaching methods in developing concepts and strategies. The subsequent analysis made of video film has proved invaluable as an *aide mémoire*, but is no substitute for the detailed written lesson observation made contemporaneously.

A third problem arising from small-scale studies relates to the extent to which the results are generalisable or applicable beyond the population studied. Whereas in-depth qualitative studies of a small number of classroom situations may have high internal validity, their findings are less capable of generalisation than those from a large-scale quantitative study. While this problem can to some extent be reduced by the careful selection of the small number of classrooms to be observed – this point was given particular consideration in the present study – it is generally accepted that there is some 'trade off' in benefit between the two types of study. Educational researchers acknowledge that large-scale studies alone cannot provide the detail of classroom processes: rather, direct classroom observation is necessary for this. Discovering exactly what occurs in a particular classroom setting, without manipulation or experimentation, is the goal of all educational research studies in which a technique of classroom observation is used – which is also reflected in the goal of this study.

The method adopted here reflects the lessons learnt by the earlier comparative educationists and the development of their methodology – it also reflects the need for a largely qualitative study supported by objective quantitative data. As a foundation, the ideas of Bereday (*op.cit.*) regarding the value of understanding the cultural, historical and social influence of society on its education system have been heeded, together with his advice to be proficient linguistically in the languages of the appropriate countries (although the researcher's competency in Japanese language was limited to the level of six- and seven-year-old pupils in elementary school). Existing relevant comparative data have been used as a starting point, as recommended by Holmes (*op.cit.*), which have assisted both the design and extent to which it has been possible to focus the study.

Particular methodological problems arising from the present study

In attempting to make comparisons of the experience of pupils within the Japanese and English educational systems, some specific methodological issues arise due largely to structural differences between the two systems. These include:

(i) *Age of statutory schooling*
Children in Japan, in common with children in most other countries, are required to begin formal schooling later than children in England. Japanese children begin elementary school (*shōgakkō*) at the start of the school year following their sixth birthday (*Monbushō*, 1995b): in England, on the other hand, the legal requirement is for all children to be in full-time education by the term following their fifth birthday (Ofsted, 1996a). (The provisions made in Japan and England for pre-school education are discussed in Chapter 4.)

(ii) *Actual age of beginning formal schooling*
Whereas in Japan all children start formal schooling together – at the beginning of the school year following their sixth birthday – in England the majority of children begin formal schooling in advance of the statutory requirement. Admissions policies vary between and within local educational authorities, but it is not uncommon for an education authority to have a policy of admitting all children to full-time schooling in the September following their fourth birthday – such children would then have two years of schooling *before* Japanese children began formal schooling. Available statistics suggest that at least half of all children in England begin school at this age (National Foundation for Educational Research, 1995). Educational authorities may, however, decide to have a policy of admitting children twice a year, or each term, or let schools decide on their own admission policy.

(iii) *Beginning of school year*
In Japan the school year starts in April: England (in common with many European countries) has a school year which begins in September.

The effect of these three structural differences between the two educational systems presents methodological problems for comparing the nature and levels of mathematical understanding of children within the schooling systems. After considering various alternative strategies, it was decided that this study should include samples of children *matched by age* rather than by schooling experience. The difference in the time at which the school years in Japan and England begin then became a distinct advantage, as this enabled fieldwork to be carried out at comparable points in each school year.

Components of the study

This study of the development of mathematical understanding included a number of separate strands:

- *Fieldwork* with samples of classes of six- and seven-year-old children in Japan and England. The fieldwork included:

(a) extensive classroom/lesson observation in order to obtain as complete an understanding as possible of children's mathematical development. This was supported by discussion on an individual basis with a small number of children in each class regarding, for example, their strategies for mental calculation;

(b) use of an objective written test of numeracy/mathematical competence administered to all children in the study, which would permit both cross-national comparison and also some measurement of progress between the two age groups of children in the study;

(c) discussion with classroom teachers regarding teaching methods and classroom practice.

- Analysis of available *documentation*, including;

(a) national curricula for mathematics;
(b) textbooks and associated lesson materials;
(c) content and function of teachers' manuals.

- *Discussion* of pedagogical approaches with other educationists, academics and researchers also informed a number of aspects of the study. Issues discussed included sequencing of topics within the mathematics curriculum; the teaching of strategies for mental calculation; and how best to help slower learning children within the classroom.

Fieldwork

Selection of sample

The samples were designed to include classes of children who were six years old at the beginning of the school year who were first-graders (*ichinensei*) in Japan but in England, given the earlier age of starting school, had reached Year 2 of primary schooling.

Since the study was concerned to examine the development of mathematical understanding in the early years, it was appropriate to observe children as soon after their entry to formal schooling as was practicably possible. Fieldwork began about six weeks after the beginning of the school year which was thought to be the earliest point in the school year at which an observer in the classroom would be welcomed. Due to the difference in the timing of school year, the fieldwork took place in May/ June in Japan, and in October/ November in England.

Decisions relating to the optimum size and selection of the sample were not easy. First, with regard to selection of schools, the decision was taken to sample from within the state or public sector elementary schools in order to increase the representativeness of the sample, and thus to improve the generalisability of the findings. Pupils attending elementary schools in the independent or private sector constitute a small minority of pupils in the two countries (about 5 per cent in England, DfEE, 1998d, and 3 per cent in Japan, *Monbushō*, 1997) and tend to be unrepresentative of the population of similarly aged pupils, being privileged either in terms of financial/social background or by ability.

Secondly, although using a large sample of schools would have tended to improve the representativeness of the subsequent findings, this needed to be balanced against the greater depth of understanding possible if fieldwork resources were more concentrated. It was finally decided to select a small number of schools in each country for the purposes of study – three or four – which would improve the generalisability of the findings without significantly affecting the quality of the insight gained.

Thirdly, the question of the geographical locations of the schools selected was decided by reference to practical considerations – due to the smallness of the study and the limited nature of the budget for travel, it was sensible to concentrate efforts on schools in or near the capital city of each country.

Fourthly, it was decided that no help either in choosing the schools for study or in obtaining their co-operation would be sought from the respective governmental departments of the two countries. From earlier experience of observing, arranging and participating in exchange visits to other countries for the purposes of improving mutual understanding of educational systems, it is clear that it is difficult for a 'host' country to resist the very natural inclination to select only the 'best' schools for foreign visitors to see. Thus, in this study, having identified a small number of schools suitable on the grounds of size, geographical location and with the benefit of as much background knowledge of the schools as possible, the head teacher or principal of each school was approached directly for the purposes of establishing co-operation. Permission to visit and observe classes for an extended period was sought directly from the head teachers and official channels were not used. Head teachers were happy to co-operate; it seemed that the fact that the researcher had spent many years as a mathematics teacher encouraged head teachers to give their permission. It also seemed that informal visits by an ex-teacher were less likely to be seen as 'threatening' and gave less cause for concern than visits arranged through official channels. Moreover, whereas official school visitors arriving from a government department tend to be given special treatment and shown only the 'best' classes, an unaccompanied ex-teacher is more likely to be accepted into all classrooms and to be able to observe unobtrusively. This is not to suggest that the classrooms visited were not to some extent affected by the observation, but that this was minimised as far as is possible. From the children's point of view, it appeared that the 'novelty' value of the visit wore off after about a day and a half.

Schools

The final sample of schools included three elementary schools (*shōgakkō*) in different parts of Tokyo and four primary schools in or close to London. The inclusion of an additional school in England was deliberate in order to balance the numbers of children observed in the two countries. Visits were also made to a number of other elementary schools in Tokyo and primary schools in and around London to check the validity and representativeness of the schools selected for inclusion in the study; these visits to additional schools also included periods of classroom observation. In England, it was possible to obtain additional information regarding background characteristics of the school selected – information relating to, for example, the percentage of children having free school meals, attendance rates, and performance in the tests forming part of the SATs assessment of children at the end of Key Stages 1 & 2. This information was also used as a check on the extent to which the schools were representative.[1]

---

[1] Using the standard indicator of school attainment in mathematics, namely the percentage of children gaining Level 4 or better at Key Stage 2, the schools in the sample

Within each school one class of six-year-olds and one class of seven-year-olds were studied in depth.[2] Selecting a class *(kumi)* of pupils in each of the three elementary schools in Japan provided a sample of just over 100 pupils for each age group (the average class size for elementary schools in Japan was then about 34 pupils, it has since fallen and is now closer to the English level: *Monbushō,* 1995a). In England, a class in each of the four primary schools included provided a similarly sized sample of just over 100 pupils (average class sizes in England, although increasing in size, remain slightly smaller than those in Japan, with a median figure of about 28 pupils per class, Ofsted, 1996b).

Timing of fieldwork

There were two main periods of fieldwork in each country.[3] The first focused mainly on observation of six-year-old children within the classroom context; during the second period, observation focused mainly on pupils a year older, thus enabling the nature and extent of their progress in mathematical understanding between the two periods to be assessed.

The first period of observation took place in Japan in May/June 1995 and in England in October/November 1995. This involved detailed classroom observation of lessons in the first grade/Year 2 classrooms selected, together with supporting observations from other schools. In Japan, in order to meet the conflicting aims of, on the one hand, spending the complete week with the particular *kumi* of the *ichinensei*, but, on the other hand, observing as many mathematics lessons (more correctly or prop-

---

Footnote 1 *(continued)* were exactly in line with their boroughs and with England as a whole. In 1997, the SATs results showed a percentage of 62 per cent children in the four sample schools gaining this standard; this showed a remarkable degree of consistency with standards achieved at both the borough level (for the boroughs in which the schools were located) and the national level; in both cases the figure for children at KS2 attaining Level 4 or better was 62 per cent (DfEE, 1998c). In terms of KS2 results, therefore, the schools sampled may be regarded as representative of English schools nationally.
[2] In England, the shorthand 'six-year-olds' refers to Year 2 pupils who had become six years old before September; a few had in fact turned seven by the time of the fieldwork. In Japan, the first-grade pupils had become six years old before 1 April and so a comparable proportion had turned seven by the time of the fieldwork. A similar situation existed in relation to pupils in the 'seven-year-old' classes.
[3]Since the beginning of the study there have been several government initiatives in England relating to the provision of mathematics education, including the National Numeracy Strategy and its more detailed framework; the likely effects of these initiatives are discussed in the concluding Chapter 9.

erly described as *sansū* or arithmetic lessons), a compromise was adopted whereby attachment to a particular class was established, but some mathematics lessons with other first-grade classes were observed whenever the timetable permitted it. In addition, some observations of other grades occurred in response to the wishes of individual teachers, who invited me to observe their teaching of mathematics (for example, to second-grade children) and on one occasion to assist with a lesson on 'international understanding'. A similar approach was adopted as appropriate during the fieldwork in English schools.

The second period of fieldwork took place in Japan and England exactly twelve months after the first period of fieldwork, namely during May/June 1996 in Japan and in October/November 1996 in England. This second period had been designed to follow the progress of pupils who had been observed the previous year, within the same class grouping; however, it was found that in one of the schools in Japan, due to falling numbers, the class no longer existed – its pupils had been divided up and distributed among the remaining two parallel classes. The replacement second grade (*ninensei*) parallel class selected for observation thus included some, but not all, of the pupils observed the previous year.

As in the first period of fieldwork, the attachment to the particular class dictated which lessons were observed, with the proviso that advantage would be taken of any opportunity to observe the teaching of mathematics to parallel classes of similarly aged pupils. Teachers in Japan appeared relaxed and content to welcome a visitor to their classroom: it was evident that it is common for teachers to visit each others' classes for observation and subsequent pedagogical discussion in order to improve teaching effectiveness. Although the presence of a visitor had some novelty value for the children, in general, following the example of the teacher, this was accepted without fuss or undue attention. Due to the intensive nature of elementary school teaching – which includes teacher responsibility for lunch supervision of first- and second-grade children – there were restricted opportunities for pedagogical discussion with the teachers within the school day, and arrangements were made whenever possible for discussion after school. During the second period of fieldwork in Japan more opportunities for discussion with the class teachers arose or were created, which included, for example, their views on pedagogical approaches and other aspects of classroom practice, such as treatment of 'slow learners' or children with behavioural problems.

The pattern of visits to primary classes in and around London was similar: a relationship with a particular class was established but mathematics teaching to other parallel classes was observed when the opportunity arose. More time was available for discussion with the relevant class teachers in England than in Japan – this took place mainly at lunch time over sandwiches, when English teachers are comparatively free of responsibilities for pupils.[4] As in Japan, there was a warm welcome by teachers and pupils, although English teachers appeared less accustomed than the Japanese teachers to having their lessons observed – on those occasions when lessons are observed by outsiders in England this tends to be for reasons of inspection, and it appears that it is relatively uncommon for teachers to observe each others' classes.

Recording of data: classroom observation

Structured observation forms were used to record details of aspects of classroom practice including:

- background information about the class and the pupils;
- the teaching objective(s) of the lesson, as explained by the teacher and supported by the text-book, and the extent to which the lesson was successful in achieving the stated objective(s);
- teaching methods used, and the distribution of lesson time between them;
- teaching materials used – textbooks, worksheets, board materials, concrete materials;
- teacher behaviour – with respect to discipline, atmosphere, management of classroom;
- the nature of questioning of children by the teacher – the level of questioning, the extent and detail expected in the answer, the precise questions asked both by teachers and pupils, the treatment of errors and misconceptions of pupils, introduction of new mathematical concepts by a step-by-step approach or an open-ended investigative approach;
- learning behaviour of children – enthusiasm, time 'on task', participation of individuals in answering questions, demonstrating to others, level of involvement;

---

[4] In contrast, elementary school teachers in Japan were observed to be responsible for lunch arrangements for the pupils in their *kumi* or class. The ritual of lunch in the classroom has been described by Lewis (1995); the relevance here is that in Japan teachers had free time only after their pupils had finished lunch, cleared away, swept up; pupils were in the playground for a period of perhaps twenty minutes before the beginning of afternoon school.

- social behaviour of children – evidence of co-operation and help-ing other children, listening to others, showing consideration to others (especially to slower learners), examples of unsocial behav-iour;
- the extent and nature of interaction – teacher-pupil and pupil-pupil, treatment of slower learning children within the classroom;
- arrangements or additional help provided;
- interruptions to lessons – both from within and outside the class-room.

In addition, classroom practice was recorded in photographic and video form; however, as explained previously, the extent to which a video cam-era was used as a method of recording was deliberately restricted.

The experience of lesson/classroom observation has been drawn on extensively in Chapters 7 and 8, and has been used as illustrative of much of the evidence relating to the instructional variables associated with the observed differences in the development of mathematical under-standing.

The mathematics test

A short objective test was administered to some of the pupils in the classes observed during the first period of fieldwork; however, partly because it was not practically possible to administer this test to all the pupils in the sample on this first occasion, and also because it became clear that certain questions included in the test required modification, this was re-garded as a 'pilot study' test and subsequently altered in the light of experience for use with all the pupils observed during the second period of fieldwork in order to make meaningful comparisons of children's achievements in mathematics.[5] All the questions in the objective writ-ten test were constructed to test the skills and concepts within the learning experience of children; contextualised word problems were care-fully tested for language and context transferability. The content of

---

[5] Thanks go to Professor Stigler for his permission to include a number of the questions from the test of numeracy he administered to first grade children in Japan, Taiwan and the US (Stigler *et al.*, 1982). The questions used in his test had been carefully constructed to test the skills and concepts to which children had been exposed, and the language used had also been carefully tested for comparability of meaning and relevance in the different languages.

textbooks in popular use with six-year-old children in Japan and England was analysed in order to identify what topics and concepts would be expected to be within the experience of six and seven-year old children and accessible to them (*Atarashii Sansū*, 1995; *Sansū*, 1996; Ginn Mathematics, 1993; Cambridge Series of Mathematics, 1995). The content of the final test reflected the content of the mathematics curriculum prescribed for children in the first and the early part of second grade of schooling in Japan that was also common to the mathematics curriculum normally covered by children during the early part of Key Stage 1 in England. This test included 26 questions, of which 12 included language and were, therefore, read to the children by the class teacher administering the test, in order that levels of mathematical skill should not be confounded with children's levels of literacy skill. The questions involving language were translated by a native speaker of Japanese, and were then back-translated in order to check on consistency of translation and meaning. Verbal and written instructions for the completion of the test were carefully constructed in each language by native speakers. The test papers were, except on one occasion (one school later posted the test papers), collected in by the researcher, who marked the papers, analysed the scores, and conducted some error analysis in order to gain further insight into the level and nature of children's understanding and also the nature of their misconceptions in these early years.

In Japan, due to the timing of the fieldwork, the teaching of two topics within the mathematics curriculum received particular attention. These were, for first- and second- grade children respectively, an introduction to the concept of subtraction, and the development of an understanding of place value in the context of larger numbers. Concepts involved in the teaching of these two topics and differences in the teaching approaches observed in Japan and England are discussed in detail in Chapter 8, which also draws on the results of the relevant test questions.

Discussions with teachers and other education specialists

In addition to pedagogical discussion with Japanese classroom teachers during the school day, or after school, other opportunities for discussion were arranged with other practising teachers and educationists in Japan, and especially at Tsukuba *Daigaku* (University) *Shōgakkō*, which has a particularly high reputation for teaching mathematics. This school is known for its success in organising national conferences for practising teachers, for publishing mathematics journals and for the contribution of its teachers to the widely used text books. It was also possible, through contact established on previous visits to Japan, to have extensive discussions on the teaching of mathematics in Japan with internationally-known researchers at the National Institute for Educational Research; the help and encouragement received from such sources was invaluable.[6]

Purely by chance, one of the schools selected for study in Japan had a particular interest in the teaching of mathematics and had sought to be designated as the 'maths research school' for the area. This interest led to the systematic observation of mathematics teaching to each of the classes in turn, by all the teachers plus the principal, once a term on a regular basis. This represented a significant commitment in terms of time and effort – not only for the time of teachers observing the lesson, but for the preparation of immensely detailed information regarding the achievement and progress of individual pupils in the class concerned, and for extended discussion subsequently of the success of the lesson in achieving its stated aims, and the possible ways for improvement. The opportunity to observe these demonstration lessons, and to examine the carefully prepared background information, provided invaluable insight into teachers' views of mathematical pedagogy. A further opportunity for observing demonstration mathematics lessons occurred at the main teacher training university in Japan: two lessons on the topic of 'division of fractions' were demonstrated by specialist mathematics teachers of acknowledged exceptional capability and experience. These two lessons, observed by approximately 100 academics, teachers and specialists in mathematical pedagogy, were followed by intense discussion for a further three hours, during which the precise mathematical processes involved in the topic were unpicked and related to the appropriate teaching strategies.

Document analysis

Careful analysis was made of all available documentation, including nationally prescribed mathematics curricula: particular attention was given to content analysis of the textbooks most widely used in the two coun-

---

[6] In particular, thanks are due to Dr. Eizo Nagasaki and Ms Senuma, both of the National Institute for Educational Research in Tokyo, for their continuing patience in answering questions.

tries, together with the supporting teachers' manuals, and other materials used in the course of lessons, such as published or teacher-produced work sheets, written tests and diagrams. Consideration was given to ways in which a new mathematical concept was introduced and how this related to the approach suggested in the teachers' manual or pupils' textbook: the detailed nature of teachers' manuals in Japan in providing a step-by-step approach and indicating the precise questions and issues to be covered was thought to be especially helpful in providing a framework for instruction. This analysis has been drawn on extensively and used to inform much of Chapter 5, which concerns the effect of centralised decision-making in regard to, for example, prescription of curricula and control of text-book approval, on classroom practice.

Results of the objective written test

Results of the test of numeracy/mathematical competence administered to all children in this study give clear support to the two initial hypotheses associated with this research; firstly, that when Japanese children begin schooling at the age of six, their mathematical competence is not greater than English pupils of a similar age, and secondly, that by the time they are one year older and have had the benefit of one year of formal schooling, their levels of average attainment in mathematics are higher than those of their English counterparts. Table 3.1 gives summary results for this test and provides evidence to support these two hypotheses.

These results are in line with the findings of the TIMSS survey (discussed in Chapter 2) relating to mathematical performance of children aged 8 and 9 years old. For example;

- while the performance of six-year old English pupils shows the advantage of an earlier start to formal schooling, one year later this early advantage has disappeared, and English pupils aged 7 have been overtaken by Japanese children of a similar age;
- the progress made by Japanese children between the two ages at which the test was administered was much greater than the progress made by English pupils;
- at both ages the variation in performance is twice as great among English pupils.

Although the summary results of this test provide evidence to support the hypotheses outlined in Chapter 1, by examining the detailed results

Table 3.1 *Results of mathematics test: Japan and England (percentage of correct answers)*

	Pupils aged 6			Pupils aged 7		
	Mean	Standard deviation	No. of pupils	Mean	Standard deviation	No. of pupils
Japan	37	10	94	92	9	106
England	67	20	107	82	13	108

we can see the nature of the errors made by English children, and what this tells us about their fundamental insecurity with number structure and its inherently logical character, and their weakness with arithmetical operations. The results show, for example, that in all the questions which involved an application of subtraction procedures, Japanese children (at the age of seven) achieved significantly higher levels of correct responses than English children of a similar age. The full question-by-question analysis of the results is given in Appendix B; in addition an analysis of the errors made in two of the questions involving subtraction procedures is included in Chapter 8.

Summary

While recognising the value of the large-scale international comparative studies of mathematical attainment, there is a need for a small-scale comparative study which provides greater understanding of the various factors and their levels of influence on teaching and learning within the classroom. To achieve such understanding, detailed classroom observation is a prerequisite for any study, but this needs to be informed by the inclusion of background and other related information which is available from the study of available documentation. Discussion with practising teachers and other education specialists helps to highlight particular classroom issues that might not be readily apparent to an observer. In addition, some form of objective testing enables some comparison to be made with the findings of the large international studies, whose methodology is now generally accepted to be achieving a high level of validity and reliability.

The two-stage nature of the fieldwork was found to be particularly helpful, since it permitted reflection on the experience and insight gained as a result of the first period, and the opportunity for building on this understanding during the second period. By the second period of fieldwork, observation was more focused on areas of particular interest, such as the introduction of concepts in particular mathematical processes and progress of 'slow learners' within the classroom.

The results of the mathematics test provide support for the two hypotheses outlined in Chapter 1. The results show that the attainment levels of Japanese children in mathematics on beginning schooling were not higher than those of six-year-old children in England but that during their first year of schooling Japanese children made faster progress in acquiring mathematical knowledge than children in England so that, one year later, they had achieved significantly higher attainment levels. This demonstrates the difference in progress in mathematical understanding and competence made by the two groups of similarly-aged children in the two countries. The central question of this study relates to the reasons for these differences.

4

Influences on teaching and learning

Introduction

It is all too easy to regard what happens in a classroom as being within the control of the teacher who determines the lesson structure, format and content, and who decides on the teaching materials and the pedagogical approach to be used, and all aspects of classroom organisation and management. Teachers may themselves feel that classroom practice and their pupils' educational experience is within their control, and express the view that "Within the kingdom of my classroom, I am king". Yet any classroom is firmly located within a particular school organisation, which is part of an educational system, in turn constructed by a particular society with specific values and attitudes towards education and learning. Thus teaching and learning within any classroom are subject to influences from outside. The nature of these influences and the level of their effect will vary between countries and curricular subjects but it is not possible to place any classroom in a vacuum and seal it off from society. The purpose of this chapter is to locate this study of children's mathematical learning in the classroom within the context of society and its influences.

The relationship between education and society is complex and the influences are two-way; in this study, however, we are concerned more with the way in which education is influenced by the values and attitudes obtaining in the wider society than the reverse process. This chapter outlines the development of the educational systems of Japan and England, their present structure and the way these reflect the values and attitudes of the wider societies. It may be that the interdependent relationship between education and society is particularly strong in Japan, with resulting implications for schooling. For example, specific values of the educational system in Japan that contribute to its success can be identified as emanating from society and culture – such as a positive attitude towards learning, emphasis on the role of effort in achievement, and individual responsibility for achievement (Stevenson *et al.*, 1986; Azuma, 1986; Shields, 1991).

We also need to consider the way that current educational models adopted in the two countries both reflect social values and affect classroom teaching. We need to understand how specific cultural values towards learning can be used to increase the effectiveness of classroom teaching, together with attitudes regarding what types of knowledge are important and the ways in which these are best transmitted. Differences in attitudes to education as development of human resources also affect the educational models produced.

Finally, we need to examine the way that children's attitudes to learning in the classroom are shaped. The roles of the two main agencies of socialisation and transmission of cultural values before the stage of formal schooling – namely, the family and pre-school education – in the two countries are contrasted. In relation to Japan, the importance of the mother in the socialisation process has been relatively well-documented (Befu, 1986; Hendry, 1986a; Stevenson *et al.*, 1986); of parallel importance, however, is the continuation of the socialisation process by the pre-school educational experience of a child at kindergarten or nursery schooling (Hendry, 1985; 1986b; White, 1987; Lewis, 1995). This experience is also instrumental in determining the skills that children take with them to formal schooling and providing them with a positive attitude towards learning.

Values of society and social attitudes

Understanding the contrasting natures of the two societies is a complex problem, compounded by the social change that is a feature of the late twentieth century. Moreover, the values of Japanese society reflect a complex network of tradition, beliefs and historical background. Several authors have provided rational and convincing analyses of Japanese society (Befu, 1971; Beauchamp, 1978; Hendry, 1993). It is possible here only to identify those differences in values held and transmitted that affect children's learning, while trying to avoid the pitfall of making 'dichotomous broad-brush contrasts commonly drawn between British and Japanese cultures' (Dore, 1987, p.7). Additionally, the effects of western influences on the physical appearance and behaviour of Japanese teenagers have, in recent years, become more apparent. While such effects are not yet visible in the same way among children as they begin schooling, it is important to be aware that young people are beginning to challenge traditional values and attitudes.

It should also be stressed that in Japan, perhaps more than in some other countries, appearances are deceptive and that an understanding of the concept of *tatemae* and *honne* is central. Azuma distinguishes between them in the following way: "*Tatemae* is how things should be according to the officially recommended ideology; *honne* is that state of affairs that, although it contradicts the *tatemae*, represents what people actually want" (Stevenson *et al.*, 1986, p. 6).

Azuma cites the example of the impact of outside influence on Japan, especially at the end of World War II, when ideology introduced from abroad became the *tatemae*; this, however, did not replace previous attitudes but accompanied the *honne* of existing traditions. Other notable explanations of the difference between *tatemae* and *honne* have been provided by Hendry (1986a, p.176) who described them respectively as 'the face shown to the world' and 'own thoughts and feelings' and White (1993, pp.39 and 188) who defined them as 'the accepted norm or rule' or 'official form and reality'. Within the context of social behaviour, the self-control practised by individuals enables the 'expected' behaviour to be maintained on the surface (*tatemae*) while innermost feelings may still be held (*honne*). An ability to understand and appreciate what is appropriate behaviour in a particular situation (*kejime*) and to distinguish this from feelings is regarded as essential for maintaining social standards.

It is proposed that there are two major areas of difference in the values and ideas prevailing in the two societies that have most influenced the development of their educational systems. The first of these relates to different perceptions of ways in which success may be achieved. Western societies, including England, view innate ability (that is, intelligence, IQ or talent) – obtained either genetically or environmentally – as a major contributing fact in achievement. In contrast, Japanese society places a greater emphasis on the importance of perseverance, hard work and diligence in the achievement of success, which may be summarised in the term *gambaru* (to persevere). This has been discussed by a number of authors, including Singleton (1990, p.8), Blinco (1991; 1993) and Befu (in Stevenson *et al.*, *op.cit.*, p.24). Dore points out that the value of emphasising the role of effort in relation to achievement lies in the fact that it is under the control of the individual and his/her will, rather than attributing it to genetics or environment. Befu (*ibid.*) suggests that developing the desirable quality of self-discipline involves persistence, hard work, effort and endurance. From the days of infancy, mothers encourage children to persevere in the face of difficult mental and physical demands and that through hard work, diligence and, above all, persistence (*gaman*) comes achievement. Hess in his study (Stevenson *et al.*, 1986, Ch.11) found that low achievement in mathematics was more likely in Japan to be attributed to lack of effort rather than to other factors, which he contrasted with the position in the United States where lack of ability, effort and poor training were thought to be of equal importance. The view that educational success is based on effort rather than innate ability reflects the influence of Confucian philosophy that is drawn upon to provide an incentive for educational achievement among Japanese society as a whole. This in turn increases the importance attached to education within society; if it is believed that achievement and success are accessible to all, then parental motivation (as well as pupil motivation) is improved.

Attitudes of Japanese teachers towards children's progress echo these ideas: teachers' behaviour is consistent with the belief that all children can be motivated to learn, and that with hard work and persistence all can achieve. In contrast, variation in potential for attainment is readily accepted in England. Evidence for this view is provided by a number of sources; a few are mentioned here. For example, in his report *Mathematics Counts*, Cockroft (1982, p.100) commented on the range of mathematical attainment at age 11.[1] Further attention was drawn to this by the APU Mathematics Monitoring Unit (Foxman *et al.*, 1991) and more recently was the subject of a government statement (DfEE, 1997c). Official educational policy assumes that a significant minority of children will have identifiable 'special educational needs': a recent document quoted an expected figure of 18 per cent (DfEE, 1997b, p.12). A greater degree of variability at the pupil and school level in England found in mathematical attainment in the most recent international study provides further support for this view (Mullis, 1997, Tables C3 and C4).

---

[1] Cockroft (para.342) states: "It therefore seems to me that there is a 'seven year difference' in achieving an understanding of place value which is sufficient to write down the number which is 1 more than 6399. By this I mean that, whereas an 'average' child can perform this task at age 11 but not at age 10, there are some 14 year olds who cannot do it and some 7 years olds who can."

The effects of these different values on the educational systems are clear. If it is accepted that educational success is achievable by all, and depends primarily on effort rather than ability, then it is a logical step to provide a common educational system for all. It also follows that it is logical to have a single-track, co-educational system and a common curriculum throughout the compulsory years of schooling, and to have standards of attainment which all are expected to achieve. These are principles of the Japanese educational system today which espouses a philosophy of providing equal educational opportunities for all through an apparently uniform, standardised system (Shields, 1991). Primary education in Japan was significantly altered after World War II to incorporate the democratic principles of American education (Schoppa, 1991); during the elementary school years children are taught in mixed-ability groups for all subjects.[2] There is a professed expectation that all children in a class will progress together and that the same curriculum will be mastered to the same level during each school year, although the extent to which this is achieved is unclear. It may, more cynically, be regarded as an example of the *tatemae* of the official policy, publicly transmitted by teachers and supported by parents, while in reality teachers recognise that achievement by pupils is likely to vary and are also aware of individual differences in ability. The veneer of homogeneity between schools may also conceal diversity at the local level (Sato, 1996, p.120) and the role of *juku* in containing diversity of pupil achievement should also be acknowledged. Certainly, as pupils progress through their schooling, the system becomes increasingly meritocratic and there is a fierce contest for places at the 'top' high schools (Rohlen, 1983). However, all may enter the competition (Cummings, 1980), and the belief that performance can be improved through increased effort is undoubtedly a motivating force and helps to explain why parents are willing to dedicate so much time and effort to supporting children's academic work (Stevenson *et al.*, 1990, p.67).

In contrast, the educational system in England is known to provide a diversity of educational opportunity and experience both between and within schools, which is related to the perceived needs and abilities of

---

[2] Mixed-ability teaching also prevails throughout compulsory secondary schooling. At the end of the compulsory schooling (the end of lower secondary), however, pupils compete for places in upper secondary schools. This creates a degree of streaming between (rather than within) schools, but effectively groups pupils of similar attainment levels together.

children. Schools within the educational system in England are diverse in organisation, structure, management and output (Gipps, 1992; Alexander, 1995; Marks, 1998). Within schools in England, the greater value attached to individual needs and perceived potential leads to a variety of treatment and teaching (Ofsted, 1995a). Teaching approaches recommended for use in primary classrooms have emphasised the need for learning to be child-centred and to reflect the wide range both of attainment and likely future progress. This has resulted in highly differentiated teaching in primary classrooms, which until very recently was organised on an individual or small group basis.

The second major difference in the values of the two societies that affects their educational systems and learning within the classroom relates to the emphasis given to being a member of a group or behaving as an individual. In Japan, importance is attached to the advantages of belonging to a group and a consequent loyalty to that group, whether the group is a class, a community or a nation. Western culture, however, emphasises the concept of the individual and the goal of developing personal potential. The values placed in Japan on group membership and responsibility were reinforced by the neo-Confucian philosophy from the nineteenth century (McLean, 1995) which placed less emphasis on the individual and his/her achievements, and greater emphasis on living as a member of a family and a community. Individual obligations and achievements are acknowledged, but as part of the wider notions of social responsibility. Individual loyalty to a group may be identified as a major cultural characteristic of Japanese behaviour (Blinco, 1991, p.130), and is linked to the value placed on the qualities of perseverance and self-discipline which has already been identified. By persevering to make their individual contribution to their group's achievement, members of the group can gain self-recognition and reward. Children learn that through group loyalty, effort and persistence, achievement and happiness can be attained. These Japanese values of individual responsibility for group achievement, accomplished through self-discipline and a belief in the ability of all to succeed, could scarcely be more different from the values in English society which emphasise the rights of the individual and the importance of personal achievement, in which effort is perceived to play only a small contributory part.

The effects of these different emphases were noticeable at the class level. In the lessons observed in Japan, whole-class teaching was observed to predominate, and all children participated in the questioning and answering sessions. In contrast, the classroom practice observed in England included virtually no examples of whole-class teaching.[3] In Japan, group tasks were set in such a way as to encourage co-operation rather than competition with other children whereas individual tasks set in English classrooms were intended to encourage self-discovery. In Japan, displays of children's work included examples from the whole class (Hendry, 1985, p.5) in contrast to displays in English classrooms that contained selected examples, usually only the best. In sports events in Japanese elementary schools, all children were observed to take part, often in team or group events, in contrast to school sports events in England in which typically only the best compete on an individual basis, in spite of the perceived traditional importance attached to team sports in England.

The ways in which the differences in these two major areas affect children's learning are discussed further in the following sections. At this point, however, a brief outline of the development of the educational systems of England and Japan is provided and the current educational models are broadly identified.

The educational system in Japan

Although the system of universal compulsory education in Japan followed the Meiji Restoration of 1868, during the Tokugawa period from 1603 a significant educational system was already in place (Dore, 1997; Marshall, 1994). The contribution of Matsudaira Sadanobu in achieving this is widely recognised: Matsudaira Sadanobu, who as chief minister initiated a return to neo-Confucian orthodoxy and rejected the increasing heterodoxy of the time (1790), encouraged a commitment to education as a means of advancement. Tests of literary skills and knowledge of Confucian studies became a standard requirement for the advancement of administrators. Some 'domain' schools had already been established;[4] these flourished and increased in number, together with private

---

[3] Since then, the introduction of the National Numeracy Framework into all primary schools in England has required that children be taught together for the beginning part of a lesson, following which they may work as a whole class, in groups, in pairs or as individuals.

[4] Altogether there were some 250 fiefs or domains ('*han*'), although the number was never constant. The first of the domain schools was established during the seventeenth century; more were established during the eighteenth and nineteenth centuries when the rate of expansion increased and by 1867 there were schools in over 200 of the domains (Dore, 1965; Jansen, 1989; Simmons, 1990).

academies (*shijuku*) and parish schools for commoners (*teragoya*). By 1830 there were about 260 private academies and over 1500 parish schools. By the middle of the eighteenth century, schools were available for the children of the *samurai* warrior class, for children of the urban merchant class, and, to a lesser extent, for children of farmers. By 1850 it was estimated that one quarter of the total population was literate; a figure which bears comparison with literacy rates in Europe at that time. Dore estimated that by the 1860s between 40 and 45 per cent of boys were receiving some formal schooling outside their home, together with 15 per cent of girls (Dore, 1965, p.100).

The most influential schools at this time were those for the children of *samurai* in which the emphasis was on Confucian studies. The Confucian analogy of the family with society, with the virtues of loyalty and obedience to superiors being of paramount importance, assisted the ideological support of order and authority. Book learning combined with martial arts was seen as contributing to spiritual growth; the attributes of hard work, challenge and discipline were also seen as central for development. The example and guidance of a teacher was crucial; the comparatively high status of teachers in Japan today may well derive from the considerable influence of teachers at this earlier time. The private academies and parish schools were modelled on the domain schools, and emphasised the value of persistence and effort.

Since the overthrow of the feudal system of Japan in 1868, however, there have been three major periods of educational reform; each period of reform may be seen as a response to outside influences and at times of great social, political and economic upheaval. The first period of educational reform resulted from the realisation of the need to respond to the challenge of Western technology and industrialisation. This followed the dramatic arrival of American warships in Edo Bay in 1853, and the beginning of an appreciation of the significance and need for education as a tool for modernisation. Thus the first period of educational reform in the modern era took place in the 1880s when, under the Meiji Restoration and following considerable observation of educational systems in Europe and the United States, a national system of education was created. It was established under the central authority of the *Monbushō* which today remains the centre of educational control. The then Minister for Education, Mori Arinori, played a central role in determining the new educational policy, emphasising that "education is not for the sake of the student but for the sake of the state" – thus indicating that the relationship between the success of a country and the quality of its people had already been understood. With the introduction of government subsidy for compulsory education in the late 1880s the stated goal of universal attendance at primary school became a realistic possibility. This laid the foundation for equality of educational opportunity and the examination system contributed to a meritocratic order which was open to all regardless of family background.

The second period of educational reform took place at the end of the Second World War, following Japan's surrender. During the postwar period of military occupation, the aim of American policymakers was to democratise the Japanese education system, which was perceived as being nationalistic and militaristic. The United States Education Mission made recommendations for changes on American lines which were incorporated into the framework for postwar education provided by the Fundamental Law of Education and the School Education Law of 1947. The educational system introduced during this period of reform featured structural similarities with the American system of education, being based on a 6-3-3-4 system of 'single-track' public education, and including nine years of compulsory education (from 6–15 years). This aimed to create not only a more democratic system of education, but one which incorporated a comprehensive, co-educational approach providing equality of educational opportunity for all pupils. Competition between pupils naturally exists to some extent, but this is played down in early schooling which emphasises co-operative work and interpersonal skills, and aims to develop a sense of pride in group effort (Lewis, 1995, p.115). Although the competitive spirit contributes to the meritocratic nature of the education system, the important principle established was that all pupils might take part in the competition. At the same time less emphasis was placed on the theme of nationalism which had been promoted during the years leading up to the Second World War (Tsuchimochi, 1991).

The system created during this second period of educational reform was, by the 1970s and early 1980s, widely admired throughout the world for the high standards of pupil performance it achieved. By 1988, 95 per cent of the age cohort stayed on at school beyond the compulsory age of schooling of 15, and over 90 per cent graduated from high school at age 18 (NIER, 1991). Average attainment was high, especially in mathematics and science; teaching was generally of a good quality; pupils displayed a high degree of social sensitivity and discipline was not a major problem (Cummings, *op. cit.*; Lynn, 1988). To many, and especially to those outside Japan, the educational system represented an ideal to be aimed for which, moreover, was achieved with approximately the same proportion of GNP as was expended on education in Britain (Rohlen, 1983; Howarth, 1993).

The extent to which this second period of educational reform was successful in creating a system with a remarkable degree of uniformity of educational opportunity has been well-documented. Cummings (*op.cit.*), for example, identifies five reasons for this success:

- promulgation of egalitarian educational values;
- provision of equal facilities;
- equal treatment of pupils by teachers;
- less pressure during primary schooling;
- support for egalitarian values by teachers' unions.

Yet there were criticisms of the system on a number of grounds and from a number of directions: some of the pressure came from Japanese economists and industrialists who were concerned about Japan's ability to meet the demands of the 21st century (Ohta, 1986; Schoppa, 1991). In particular, they argued that the educational system needed to be more outward looking with a greater spirit of internationalism. Thus the period of the third major educational reform was provoked by a desire to meet the challenge of the outside world: western educational systems were perceived by many within Japan as providing a diversity of educational opportunity and experience that is essential for future economic success.

The National Council for Educational Reform (referred to as the 'Reform Council') was thus established in 1984 to consider and define the educational problems facing Japan and to make recommendations relating to what the educational system should provide as preparation for life in the 21st century. Yet the nature of the reforms requested by Nakasone, the Prime Minister at the time, may be seen as inherently paradoxical and self-contradictory: for example, the diversification that was seen as desirable would have undermined the strength of the homogeneity of the system and its broadly egalitarian aims. The relative equality of educational opportunity provided by the system is a major factor controlling the variability in academic attainment, especially at the elementary school level (Stevenson and Stigler, 1992; Lewis, 1995). This was seen as restricting development of the most able pupils and discouraging the growth of individuality; however, while Japan clearly envied the degree of individualism and independence of mind exhibited by foreign students, any changes that might have jeopardised the existing high attainment standards were viewed with mistrust (Horio, 1990; Schoppa, 1991; Lincicome, 1993).

The contradictory nature of the desired reforms, combined with the lack of agreement as to the desired direction of the reforms and the inner conflict within the Reform Council, led to a Final Report (1987) which was relatively anodyne in content; this was subsequently reflected in the implementation of the recommendations and the impact of the reforms on the schools. The reforms that were finally introduced into schools were relatively slight in comparison to Nakasone's original ideas. A little flexibility was introduced into the curriculum, some ideas were expressed about creativity and some small moves were made towards adopting a more international approach to education. The changes effected may be perceived as a further example of *tatemae* and *honne*; the *tatemae* of educational reform in response to outside criticisms apparently being promulgated and put into practice may be contrasted with the *honne* in which internal pressure resulted in the system continuing largely as before. On the whole, it is not unfair to conclude that the third period of educational reform in Japanese history is the least significant of the three and that the educational system that exists today remains largely unchanged since its introduction fifty years ago and still reflects 19th century values drawn from Confucian ideals. Three important principles of the Japanese education system may be identified which directly affect children's learning experience:

- the aims of equality of educational opportunity for all;
- the emphasis on the contribution of effort to achievement;
- the importance attached to individual responsibility for group behaviour, and training for behaving as a member of a group.

The educational system in England

A system of universal elementary education was introduced in England in 1870; prior to that education had been reserved for those privileged by social class or wealth. Public schools – formed as a group from the nine leading grammar schools in the 18th century – have had a significant influence on the values and aims of English education. They provided the impetus for a liberal education, in which the training of moral character was fostered in order to develop personality. The content of English education prior to 1870 was largely in the 'humanist' tradition. This, it has been suggested, can be explained by the need

produced by the 'imperialist mission' for young men with a clear understanding of moral duty and ability to make decisions (McLean, 1995).
The influence of the liberal humanist ideals of the 18th and 19th century can be identified in the content of 20th century state secondary
education (Holmes, 1985).

The report of the Hadow Committee (1933) began a new era in English education by attempting to provide a 'non-academic' post-elementary
education to run in parallel to the existing academic schools. This was
largely frustrated and it was not until the Education Act of 1944 (which
implemented many of the recommendations of the report by R.A.Butler
and also the Spens Report of 1938) that a new system of secondary education for all was introduced. This established a tripartite system of
secondary education for all pupils from the age of eleven which provided
academic education in the grammar schools, technical education in the
technical schools, and a more practical education to be provided in the
'modern' schools. In reality, a largely bipartite system existed, with about
30 per cent of children attending grammar schools; places at technical
school being created for a mere 3 per cent, and with the remaining children – the majority – attending secondary modern schools. The failure
to create a significant number of technical school places at that time may
be seen as a major factor in the relatively low level of vocational qualifications among the work-force of today and also indirectly related to the
underachievement of current school-leavers.

This allegedly three-track system of education continued into the
1960s, when moves towards a 'comprehensive' single-track system of secondary education were encouraged – notably by the DES Circular 10/
65 which asked all local authorities to submit plans for comprehensive
reorganisation. The intention behind this new policy was to reduce the
inequality in opportunity that existed in the previous tripartite system.
By the end of the 1970s, over 80 per cent of children attended a comprehensive school, seen as a major step from the 'sponsorship' form of
education in which an 'elite' was identified at the age of eleven, to a more
'open contest' form in which all could compete on equal terms (Turner,
1971; McLean, 1995). Some local education authorities (for example,
South Devon, Kingston upon Thames) chose to retain the earlier tripartite system including selective grammar schools. Currently, the state
sector of secondary education in England includes local authority maintained comprehensive schools, city technology colleges, grant maintained
schools, maintained grammar schools, middle schools, 11–16 schools,
11–18 schools, sixth form colleges and tertiary colleges.

Within the state primary sector a similar diversity exists and currently includes: infant only schools (Years 1 and 2); junior only (Years 3–6); all through schools (Years 1–6); lower primary (Years 1–4); middle schools (Years 5–8), and a few for pupils aged 5–9 (Years 1–5). Differences in educational practices in primary schools include, for example, structure (mixed age classes, family groupings): organisation (setting, mixed ability teaching); use of specialist/generalist teachers; and treatment of children with 'special needs' (specialist helpers inside the classroom or children withdrawn for help).[5]

The exceptional diversity of provision and practice within the education system of England limits the extent to which comments or findings have general applicability; it also increases the difficulty of making valid comparisons with the learning experience of children in other educational systems.[6]

Current models of education: Japan and England

The differences between the educational systems of Japan and England may be seen as reflecting, to a large extent, the differences in values held by the two societies. The stated aim of education within Japan is to provide equality of educational opportunity and in many ways Japan can be regarded as successful in achieving this aim; the egalitarian nature of elementary school instruction has been documented by Shin-Ying Lee *et al.* (Rohlen and Letendre, 1996, pp. 167–8). Although a few well-off parents send their children to 'elite' private elementary schools and it is common to use the *'juku'* system or private tutors to increase chances of success in the competitive entrance examinations to upper secondary school, Rohlen concludes that in spite of these exceptions: "the fact is that up until the tenth grade, the Japanese population is neither tracked nor sorted in any manner" (Rohlen, 1983, p. 119).

---

[5] The diversity of types of schools and their organisation is matched by the variability in standards of attainment. At the primary level, this has been examined *inter alia* by Marks (1996b); Sammons *et al.* (1995).

[6] This difficulty must be borne in mind throughout this study, together with the dangers of assuming that what was noted during the periods of detailed classroom observation was typical of the practice in schools throughout the country. It is hoped that this limiting factor was minimised as far as possible by the selection of schools that did not appear in any identifiable way to be exceptional, but it is not possible to eliminate it completely. Reference has already been made in Chapter 3 to the representativeness of the sample of schools in terms of KS2 results.

He makes the point that during the compulsory years of schooling an essentially equal education is offered: "Nor is there any tracking within these schools: quite the reverse, in fact. In the schools I visited, teachers sought to mix and balance abilities in each classroom. They wanted to create a spirit of comradeship and egalitarian sharing." (*ibid.*, p.120). The degree of diversity in many aspects of Japanese society is acknowledged, yet Japanese education appears more homogeneous with respect to ideology and values than England and many other societies (Cummings, *op. cit.*). There is little evidence of conflict between values of teachers and parents and their goals for a child.

The high degree of central control exercised by the *Monbushō* over the education system in Japan is undoubtedly a contributory factor in achieving its relative uniformity by controlling the curriculum for each school grade, the allocation of contact time for each subject, and requiring all published textbooks to have *Monbushō* approval. On the other hand, while the degree of state control within the Japanese education system may be perceived as controlling resources and improving accountability it may also be perceived as restricting initiatives by individuals or institutions (Kaneko, 1988; Stephens, 1991). Equally, it may be that the perception of reduced scope for initiative is an example of '*tatemae*'; for example, Sato (1996, pp. 120-1) suggests that although the system appears rigid and restricting, the reality is that Japanese teachers have considerable professional latitude. She also refers to examples of individual expression, creativity and initiative at the elementary school level which were given official endorsement by the recommendations of the Reform Council (1987).

The Japanese model of education may be viewed as a prototype of the Asian model of education which, according to Cummings (1995), has four main characteristics:

- a high degree of state control;
- an acceptance of individual responsibility for achievement and for attaining the minimum standard;
- priority is given to primary education over secondary or tertiary education;
- consideration given to the need for human resources in manpower planning.

This Asian model, it is argued by Cummings, results from a realisation that for a country with few natural resources, the key to economic success lies in the development of the potential of the human resource – and that this has since been recognised by the Pacific Rim countries such as Singapore, Korea and Taiwan, which have successfully adopted similar educational models in order to facilitate their economic and financial growth. In order to develop potential, it is vital that a strong and successful primary sector is developed.

The English system of education may be seen as an example of the Western model, which tends to have a lesser degree of central control and attaches greater importance to individual development, rights and freedoms. In contrast with the Japanese system, the English education system can be seen as having:

- a lower degree of state control;
- emphasis on individual achievement through the development of innate ability;
- a higher level of spending on secondary/tertiary education than primary;
- no element of manpower planning.

While the policy of comprehensivisation of secondary schooling in England may be perceived as demonstrating a broadly egalitarian desire for social change, the success of a single-track system was sabotaged, effectively if unintentionally, by changes made contemporaneously to the primary stage of education. These changes resulted from the report of the Plowden Committee which emphasised that greater attention should be given in the classroom to the needs of the individual child and suggested that a range of teaching methods should be used to accommodate these individual needs. The translation of this aim into practice led to the widescale use of individualised schemes of work, and to the almost total abolition of any whole-class teaching within the primary years. Evidence suggests that a policy of encouraging children to work at their own pace and differentiated teaching within the classroom increases the range of attainment (Mortimore *et al.*, 1988). A 'single-track' secondary system sits uneasily on a primary system in which a wide variation in standards of attainment is encouraged. It is also possible that the discontinuity between primary and secondary educational philosophy adds to the difficulty, for some pupils, of transferring from Key Stage 2 to Key Stage 3; it is known that problems relating to poor school attendance and alienation increase at the beginning of secondary schooling.

At the institutional level, the major organisational differences between the countries relate principally to the lack of any 'setting' by ability of pupils of a similar age in Japan. Setting by ability is a relatively common educational practice in the teaching of mathematics at primary level in England; recent Ofsted reports suggest that about one third of upper primary classes were set by ability for the teaching of mathematics. There remains considerable support for this principle which – without any clear evidence – is seen as facilitating progress in mathematical understanding for all pupils, and preventing pupils who are perceived to possess greater mathematical ability from being 'held back' by their less able peers. This reflects society's concern to maximise the progress and level of attainment of individual pupils, regardless of any resulting effect on the cohesiveness of a class. In Japan, 'setting', streaming' or 'tracking' does not officially take place within the state system until the beginning of high school, when streaming between schools results from the competition for places. The reason given for the mixed ability approach is often ethical – that to do otherwise could be interpreted as discriminatory. Yet there are sound pedagogical reasons why, in the early years, children benefit from being taught mathematics in a mixed ability class. For example, in order for a secure understanding of a new mathematical concept to be grasped by all children, it is necessary for the full range of misconceptions and errors to arise and to be discussed, and this is only likely to occur if the children in the class reflect the full range of ability. It is also widely recognised that less able pupils derive considerable educational benefit from the opportunity of observing how their more able peers approach mathematical problems – how they 'think' mathematically. Equally, it is regarded as important that children who are quicker at grasping new mathematical concepts should learn to appreciate and be considerate of those in their class who are slower. The Japanese system also recognises that these considerations are relevant not only for learning within the classroom but also for living and contributing to society as a responsible adult citizen.

The diversity of the English educational system is paralleled by the diversity of cultural values, moral values and social behaviour apparent within English society. While teachers are expected notionally to assist with the transmission of moral values by discussing issues in context (Ofsted, 1995b), this has no specific place on the time-table. Given the diversity of both educational opportunity and cultural values in English society, it is scarcely surprising that there is little literature which addresses the area of cultural relationships between school and society: studies have rather tended to concentrate on an individual school or schools within a particular societal context (Alexander, 1992; Croll & Moses, 1988). (Notable exceptions to this are the more statistically orientated surveys of school and social class; Davie *et al.*, 1972; Bynner and Steedman, 1995.)

The view that the educational system in England contributes to the perpetuation and even growth of class division, providing little or no motivation for achieving academic success, is expressed by Howarth (*op.cit.*), who contrasts this with Japanese education in which, he argues, there is a high level of motivating incentives. Further, the 'low common cultural capital' in England, evidenced by the conflict between individual goals and those of society, contributes to the lack of educational urgency evident among many school children in England and is symptomatic of the illogicality of the situation in which children are required to attend school until 16 but are not required to learn anything. The educational system in England requires children to attend school for a minimum of eleven years – two years more than the period of compulsory schooling in Japan – but children may progress from Year 1 through to Year 11 without being required to attain any minimum standard in any subject. The further illogicality inherent in the system, whereby children are expected to have widely differing abilities and rates of development yet are uniformly tested at the ages of 7, 11, 14 and 16 without any flexibility in terms of age, is almost beyond belief. That a significant minority of children in England continue to leave school at the age of 16 without any qualifications is a matter for the utmost concern (Woodhead, 1996): there is an urgent need to break the cycle of underachievement, to halt the devaluing of education and to prevent the adoption by those in the later years of compulsory schooling of an 'anti-learning culture'.

Children's behaviour and attitudes towards learning

At the classroom level, differences between the values of the two societies directly affect the nature of teaching and learning. In particular, the attitudes of children towards learning and the behaviour of children towards others in the classroom reflect the social values that have been acquired before they begin formal schooling. Even young children in their first term of formal schooling in Japan were observed to take responsibility for their satisfactory progress in learning, which was apparent in their willingness to persevere until they achieved success. (A frequently heard encouragement to young children in Japan was '*Gambatte kudasai!* Please persevere!)

It is argued here that Japanese children at the beginning of schooling display levels of independent behaviour that are considerably in advance of those observed among children of a similar age in England. Some examples from the fieldwork observation of this study are described here in detail in order to demonstrate the precise nature of the independence or self-sufficiency of young Japanese children, in contrast to those of a similar age in England.

For example, in Japan children from the age when they begin formal schooling are expected to travel to school independently of parents. In Tokyo children attending their local neighbourhood state school are likely to walk to school although children attending a private sector school may have a journey by subway or bus. Benjamin (1997, p.15) describes how, at the meeting for parents of 'beginning children', each child was assigned to a 'walking group' of children living close to each other, with one child being designated as the group leader and a mother in charge of gathering the group together each morning at the appointed place. She suggests that neighbouring children are expected to walk together; older neighbouring children may be relied upon at first to help younger children (p.32). Different arrangements may be made for children in rural communities facing longer or more difficult journeys. Children from the age of six upwards were observed walking to school along routes prescribed by the school in order to maximise safety[7] (this was particularly important in relation to one of the schools visited in Tokyo which was situated within a criss-cross of level crossings for railway lines), wearing distinctive school hats, carrying possessions in their *randoseru* (rucksacks – designed not only to improve posture but also to leave hands free), and crossing the road at points supervised by a rota of mothers who came on duty at 8 a.m. every morning (wearing distinctive yellow uniform, carrying the yellow 'children crossing' flag, and putting out road blocks for the twenty minutes or so when children were travelling to school). Children mostly walked in pairs or groups and only occasionally was a child seen on his/her own. Children are encouraged to be self-sufficient in this respect from their first day of elementary schooling, and it is seen as part of the maturing process and as part of their individual responsibility (Benjamin, *op.cit.*).

In contrast, it is extremely rare for children of primary school age in England to be responsible for their own arrangements for going to and from school. In poorer areas crowds of parents – often, but not

---

[7] School routes are described in more detail in White (1993) pp. 225–6.

exclusively, mothers – may be seen at school gates or inside the school playground (depending to a large extent on the attitude of the school head), and in more affluent areas, children may be dropped at the school gates by parents in cars – often on their way to work but sometimes on a 'car run' rota.[8] Observation of primary school children arriving in the morning at a number of different schools and at different times of year have failed to provide more than a handful of examples of children bringing themselves to school (Joshi *et al.*, 1997).

A further example of the greater independence or self-reliance of young Japanese children in comparison to English children was demonstrated by the ritual-like routine behaviour of children on arrival at school. In England, children were generally observed to stay outside school in the playground – some playing, some talking to their friends, some remaining with their parent or carer – until a bell signalled the beginning of schooling. At this point, observed behaviour was for children to 'line up' in classes under the supervision of their class teacher, who then escorted them into their classroom. In contrast, children arriving at elementary school in Japan were free to choose whether they remained outside in the playground until the school day officially began or entered the school building. From observation, it appeared that virtually all children on arrival at school chose the latter. On entering the school building, all children performed the routines they had learnt at kindergarten (Hendry, 1986b). Entering by the appointed door (not the one used by visitors), the first routine was that of changing outdoor shoes for indoor ones – usually plimsolls of the 'pull-on' type for young children – and storing their outdoor shoes in their space on the labelled rack (one rack for each *kumi* or class). Umbrellas, when brought to school in the rainy season would also be stored in an appropriate rack. Coats were hung on personally labelled pegs outside the classroom, and possessions unpacked from rucksacks onto the appropriate shelf space, or into drawers beneath individually labelled desks. Only after completion of this organisational routine – a further example of children's independence at this age – did children choose their activity for this 'free time'. Some sat at their desks and drew – using exercise books and crayons provided for that purpose; such drawings, while apparently influenced by the 'cartoon' culture prevalent in Japan (evidenced by the '*manga*' or cartoon books widely read by all ages), were highly detailed and elaborate in their depiction

---

[8] There has been concern expressed recently that much of the 'rush hour' traffic congestion in inner cities is attributable to children being taken to school by car.

of people or familiar situations. Other children found enjoyment in using the *origami* paper that was a standard item in the children's individual
storage boxes – demonstrating considerable levels of fine motor skills and
memory (visual and spatial) in their ability to fold paper precisely. A few
children would be engaged on 'cutting out' activities using scissors from
their individual boxes, together with glue if necessary, and showing similar levels of dexterity in their use of scissors. Other 'desk' activities in the
before-school period of the day included colouring in, reading, and
writing. These activities within the classroom might be conducted at an
individual level, in pairs or in groups, according to personal preference:
whatever the nature of the grouping or the classroom activity, children
appeared contented to choose their own activity, demonstrating levels
of intense concentration. From time to time, children took the initiative
to talk to me, to show curiosity in what I was writing down – some
choosing to copy some '*rōmaji*' script – and at other times advantage of
this 'free time' was taken for informal discussion with individual children
regarding their mathematical capabilities, understanding and strategies
used in mental calculation. Not all children, however, were engaged
at this time in constructive activities within the classroom – many ran
around the corridors and played games accompanied by a great deal of
noise.

The common strand, however, running through all the activities in this
'free time' in all the schools observed was the complete lack of adult supervision. No teachers or parents were present to oversee the arrival of
children into the playground, nor in taking off their outdoor shoes and
coats, nor during the activity period. Yet no difficult situations were observed arising between children during this period of unsupervised time
– there were apparently no arguments, scuffles, pushing about and no
incidents of bullying. The atmosphere was happy and relaxed – children
appeared perfectly contented in choosing their own activity. That a relatively large number of children (up to forty children in a class) were
capable of organising themselves peacefully without adult supervision or
intervention was surprising in the context of the expectations and norms
of the English educational system. In the Japanese system, however, it
is standard practice and illustrates the behavioural expectations of teachers and parents for their children (Benjamin, *op. cit.*, p.40-1). Sato (*op.cit.*,
p.138) comments that: "students are always supervised, whether or not
adults are around, because peer-supervision and self-supervision form an
integral part of authority and control mechanisms at work in Japanese
schools".

The emphasis given to the development of self-reliance (*jibun no koto o jibun de suru*) is also discussed by Lewis in the context of organising oneself for lessons (Rohlen and Letendre, 1996, p.93). The willingness of the children to be responsible for their actions, for choosing their activities, and to behave as a responsible member of a clearly defined community indicated the extent to which they were able to act independently. It also reflects the consistent standards of social behaviour successfully developed among the children during experience prior to beginning school; the way in which this is achieved is examined in the following section.

A formal beginning to lessons in Japan served to focus the attention of the class. This was observed to be an important routine, in which all members of the class took turns on a rota basis in calling the class to order, treating this as a serious responsibility. The *tōban* system, in which classroom leader duties are rotated so that each pupil has a turn, has an important role in developing children's capability to be responsible (Sato, *op.cit.*, p.137). Benjamin (*op.cit.*, pp. 58–9) suggests that experiencing the difficulties of leadership is a good way to learn how to be a follower. The need for acceptance of, and compliance with, standards of behaviour may best be learned through experiencing the difficulty of achieving this as a leader. The *tōban* pupils may be responsible for the time between lessons and for maintaining class discipline as well as for organising the formal beginning and end of lessons. A formal beginning of lessons also gives a clear demarcation of lesson time, separating it distinctly from break time when exuberant, noisy behaviour is perfectly acceptable, and thus helps to minimise wasted lesson time. Children were observed either to have laid out the books needed on their desk in advance of the lesson, or to have ready access to the necessary books on the shelf under their desk.

It has been argued here that Japanese children aged six years old displayed greater independence of learning than English children of the same age and that their knowledge and understanding of social and behavioural skills enabled them to observe the correct school routines. This raises the question as to what enables Japanese children beginning school to have such skills, knowledge and understanding that make whole-class instruction a possible teaching style from the beginning of schooling. The first-grade children observed had been in the formal school environment for as little as six weeks, and thus it is reasonable to assume that their patterns of social behaviour had been established by their earlier experience; this is examined in the following sections.

The socialisation process begun by the family

Japanese society has been described as patriarchal, with the position of head of the family being awarded to the eldest male, and a wife, typically although not invariably, taking the name of her husband's family (Azuma, *et al.*, *op.cit.*, pp.6–8). Yet in Japanese society today the wife or mother is the dominant figure in a household, and the husband or father has a role which is respected but of lesser significance (Stevenson *et al.*, 1986, p.6). The husband/father is likely to be the main bread-winner, and the household depends on his financial contribution, but the wife/mother is responsible for the household management, financial budgeting and all decisions relating to child-rearing. Azuma regards this as an example of the concept of *tatemae* and *honne* in which the public perception of the father as head of the household may be contrasted with the reality in which the mother is the main influence in the household. Although an increasing proportion of mothers in Japan are in paid employment, their principal responsibility is still perceived as being for their children, family and home. With this continued responsibility, the mother is the main transmitter of cultural and social values to children within the family, and so it is the values of the mother which are important (Befu, 1986, p.25).

One of the most fundamental aspects of influence in the home is on character formation and moral development. Befu (*op.cit.*, p.23) argues that Japan differs from Western practice in its aims for child-rearing: whereas in the West parents aim to make their children as 'independent' as possible at an early age, Japanese parents want to maintain interdependence with the child. In this way, with the closeness of the mother-child relationship, the child will receive and be influenced by the parents' values and ambitions. Yet it is not clear precisely what is understood by Befu when he refers to the 'independence' of a child: the examples he gives are in the context of children taking decisions for themselves, or making choices, and he ignores the 'capability' or 'self-sufficiency' aspect of children's independence. Similarly, his definition of the state of dependency of children on their mother – often termed *amae* – is unclear. A more correct understanding of the term 'dependency' in this context may be obtained by appreciating that a mother's role in Japan is to prepare her children for life, and to socialise them to the values of society whilst recognising their strengths and weaknesses. Through close attention to a child, the mother promotes social values, the need for effort and self-discipline and individual responsibility for achievement. First-grade children displayed levels of self-discipline when, rather than demanding the teacher's attention for themsleves, they contented themselves in discussing problems with friends until the teacher reached them to check on individual progress.

Looking more closely at the particular ways in which Japanese mothers effect the development of desired qualities in their children, it would be easy to conclude that the intense level of attention given to the needs of individual small children could amount to over-indulgence on the part of the mother. In the Western view, this could be seen as encouraging selfishness, lack of consideration for others, and inability to participate as a member of a group, yet in Japan the need to keep a child happy and contented is crucial for developing a co-operative attitude in the child. White (1987, p.96) describes the mother as avoiding open confrontation with the child and protecting her relationship with the child at all times. White and Levine (1986, p.56) identify two groups of qualities that they believe Japanese mothers seek to develop in their children; the first group relates to those benefiting children's growth into an '*ii ko*' (good child) and includes, for example, the quality of compliance or guilelessness ('*sunao*'). Hendry (1986a, pp. 87–8) draws our attention to the range of meanings for the quality of '*sunao*' which also includes honesty, frankness and straightness. The Japanese view is that if a child is given enough love and attention by the parents, a feeling of reliance and trust will develop and, as a result, children will be willing to comply.

The second group of qualities relates to those that are perceived as beneficial for development – such as the ability to persevere ('*gambaru*'), to strive ('*doryoku*') and to reflect on one's own weaknesses ('*hansei*'). Studies of the patterns of Japanese child-rearing, and the ways in which these differ from Western patterns suggest that Japanese children may develop a greater feeling of security which enables them to be self-confident, to have self esteem and thus to be able to act independently at school (Hendry, 1986b; Stevenson *et. al.*, 1986).

It is also possible that there is some implicit and unarticulated understanding between the apparent over-indulgence of the Japanese mother and the subsequent socialising of the child's behaviour.It is almost as though there is an unstated agreement between the mother and child that the child may behave badly towards the mother as long as s/he behaves appropriately towards the outside world, because sucess in motherhood is judged by the public standards displayed by the child.

When the child makes the transition from the home, firstly, to kindergarten and then to elementary schooling, the mother bridges the gap between self-fulfilment and social integration. The emotional security provided for the child by the unswerving devotion of the mother is also an important factor in this transition. The possessions that a child takes with him/her are a constant reminder of that devotion – from the carefully sewn hand-made shoe bag, lunch mat, cushion cover, the beautifully presented *bento* (packed lunch box), to the individual naming of every single item within the child's personal *sansū setto* (mathematics set) – each is a statement to the child of the mother's love and care.

In contrast, the qualities perceived in England as being desirable and meriting further development in young children include the qualities of curiosity, showing initiative, originality and creativity (Joshi and MacLean, 1997). It is these qualities and values which parents are urged to encourage among their young children. This encouragement continues during pre-school education, although this does not fit easily with the aim of social development. The role of the family in the socialisation process in England is, however, thought to be declining in importance: with the growth of both the single-parent family and the high percentage of mothers of young children who work full-time outside the home, the greater influence in the socialisation process is arguably provided by those responsible for child-care – and in England this is more likely to be found outside the network of family relationships.

The socialisation process continued by pre-schooling

Background

The importance of early years' or pre-school education for a child's social, emotional and intellectual development is widely acknowledged today. This understanding has developed during the last two hundred years from the ideas of Rousseau (1762) who was the first of the child-centred educationists to stress the child's point of view, developed by Pestalozzi into his notion of *Anschauung* or 'observation of the senses' as the basis of knowledge, to Froebel, who was the first to postulate a comprehensive theory of pre-school education and to propose a detailed method. However, although in England in the late 19th century one strand of nursery schooling developed based on Froebel's ideas, another strand of nursery education developed in parallel to "rescue the working-class child from degrading conditions and exploitation" (Katz and Mohanty, 1985) from which came the early but persistent confusion in

England over the purpose of nursery or pre-school education – namely, whether it is primarily for educational or child-care reasons.

Although the report by the governmental commission in 1908[9] advocated the public provision of early education and training for all children whose background was inadequate – thus reflecting a perception of nursery education as a 'leveller' – this was never implemented and, in fact, perversely led to a reduction of opportunity for 'under fives' who became prohibited from entering primary school as they had done previously. Nursery education in England has always lagged far behind all other types of educational provision – both in terms of quantity of places provided and in quality of provision – to the extent that it has often been perceived as the Cinderella of the education sector, even though as early as 1924 it was recognised that "There is no doubt that many of the failures in adult life … are due to faulty training or a lack of opportunity for self-expression and self-development in the early years of childhood" (Pickett and Boren, 1924). Provision of places for young children increased during the Second World War in order to meet the child-care needs of the additional numbers of working women (yet a further example of the confusion in England regarding the purpose of nursery education) – but fell back after the war. In spite of reports consistently pointing to the need to increase provision – for example in the Plowden Report (1967) and the HMI report (1989a) and supported by research in both the United States and in Britain which demonstrated the relationship between pre-school experience and later success in school (Berrueta *et al.*, 1984; Osborn and Millbank, 1987), nevertheless provision of nursery places remained patchy and piecemeal. By the early 1990s, children were able to obtain pre-schooling in a variety of ways; mainly through attending a nursery school (state or private), nursery class or nursery unit attached to a primary school, or a privately-run play group. Provision of separate nursery schools by the state was unusual; in 1992 only 4 per cent of three- and four-year- olds attended local authority nursery schools (Ball, 1994, p.33).

In Japan, public pre-school services began in the late 19th century with the establishment of the first kindergarten by Tokyo Women's Normal School in 1876 (OMEP, 1992). Although this was intended for the children of privileged families, it served as a model and the idea spread throughout Japan; free kindergartens were provided in 1900, which later became day nurseries and served a different purpose. These early kindergartens were based on the ideas of Froebel, and incorporated, for

---

[9] Report of the Consultative Committee of the Board of Education.

example, his use of 'gifts'. The precise origins of the pre-schooling philosophy in Japan today are unclear: it has been suggested that these have been derived over time from the ideas of Pestalozzi and Froebel and subsequently influenced by Confucian values (Lewis, 1995).[10] Boocock (1991, p. 109) suggests that the influences of Kodai, Montessori and Rousseau can also be found, as well as Buddhist and Christian principles.

After the end of the Second World War, pre-schooling was included in the programme of educational reform; kindergartens ('*yōchien*') with an educational purpose were established under the School Law of 1947, and day nurseries ('*hoikuen*') whose prime function was child care or welfare were established under the Child Welfare Law, also of 1947. In 1965, a Course of Study for Kindergarten was prescribed by the *Monbushō* and remained unchanged until 1989, when the curriculum was classified into five areas of learning: Health, Human Relations, Environment, Language and Expression. Educational objectives were also included in the 'Outline for Day Nursery Upbringing' specified in 1990, emphasising the development of social behaviour and interpersonal relations, language and sensitivity (OMEP, *op.cit.*).

The question of whether pre-school education is provided primarily for educational or child-care reasons does not seem to cause any problems with regard to provision in Japan. The two parallel types of pre-school institutions exist side by side and, for the two years preceding elementary schooling, have similar curriculum classroom routines and learning activities (OMEP, *op. cit.*).

Current provision of pre-schooling

The extent of pre-school provision in Japan has for many years (since the end of the Second World War) been greater than in England: for example, by the early 1980s virtually all children (over 90 per cent) attended pre-school for at least one year prior to formal schooling and the vast majority attended for two years (86 per cent) (*Monbushō*, 1984). By 1991 attendance had risen further; figures are shown in Table 4.1.

---

[10] A further suggestion (although it has not been possible to verify this) is that at a relatively early stage of the development of pre-school education in Japan those concerned with planning issues were able to benefit from a translation of a manual for kindergarten teaching in Hungary – this in turn reflected much of the basic ideas and philosophy of Pestalozzi and Froebel, although subject to interpretation in a different and distinctive style.

Table 4.1 *Percentages of Japanese children in kindergartens and day nurseries*

Age	% of age group In kindergarten (*yōchien*)	In day nurseries (*hoikuen*)	Total
3	20.3	29.3	49.6
4	56.1	33.6	89.7
5	63.8	30.7	94.5
All	47.2	31.2	78.4

Source: *Monbushō*, 1991; Report from the Council for Promotion of Kindergarten Education.

In contrast, although exact figures are difficult to obtain, the proportion of children in England attending pre-school education was much smaller. It is known that in 1994 26 per cent of four-year-olds were in nursery school classes, and 19 per cent were in some form of private or voluntary provision, but the extent to which 'double counting' occurred because some children benefited from more than one type of provision is not known, nor is the nature of the attendance (full- or part-time) known (DFE, 1995).

In making comparisons of pre-schooling, however, it must be remembered that the ages at which children experience pre-schooling differ between England and Japan, since the age at which children begin formal schooling in England is so much in advance of most other countries, including Japan. In Japan, children are likely to benefit from pre-school experience for between one and three years before they begin formal schooling at the age of six. *Yōchien* (or kindergartens), providing classes for children aged three, four and five years old, are generally (although not always) structurally and administratively independent of elementary schools. *Yōchien* are the responsibility of the *Monbushō* (Ministry of Education Science and Culture) whereas *hoikuen* (day care centres), used almost exclusively by working mothers, are the responsibility of the Ministry of Health and Welfare (OMEP, *op. cit.*). There are many similarities between kindergartens and day care centres: they follow the same official curriculum, the classroom daily routines are similar, and, although *hoikuen* hours are longer and allow time for sleep, the activities are broadly the same. The aims of both types of pre-school experience relate to the learning of social, co-operative behaviour and to the developing of skills which will facilitate later learning in a formal environment; learning of a more academic nature is avoided.

Some differences exist between *yōchien* and *hoikuen*, however, in the balance between public and private provision, and also the financial arrangements. Nearly 80 per cent of *yōchien* places are in the private sector compared with about 60 per cent of *hoikuen* places (Boocock, 1991; Monbushō, 1997). The costs of *hoikuen* are evenly divided between parents and government for both public and private places. In *yōchien* the level of subsidy for public places is higher, but many private *yōchien* also receive financial support from the government. There are local variations in the level of this support; for example, private *yōchien* in Tokyo receive more generous governmental support than *yōchien* in many other areas (Boocock, *op.cit.*). The commitment to pre-school education in Japan which is evidenced by society's willingness to share responsibility for the care and education of young children is observed to be unusual in a non-socialist society. It differs from the position in England where, until relatively recently, responsibility for much of the provision of pre-school education in England lay with the parent rather than the state, with many children attending private pre-school play groups or private nursery schools which were unsupported by government funding.

In 1996, however, the then Conservative Government announced its intention to make a nursery school place available to all parents of four-year-old children who would like one for their child, and to effect the necessary expansion of nursery place provision through the implementation of the 'voucher scheme'. After piloting this in four boroughs, the 'voucher' scheme was introduced into all areas in April 1997; this scheme was subsequently abolished following the change of government although the commitment to pre-schooling remained. Early indications relating to the implementation of the voucher scheme suggested that the main effect was to increase the number of four-year-old children in reception classes at primary schools – although this practice of admitting children before the statutory age of schooling has long been criticised by early years' education specialists as encouraging a too early introduction to formal school subjects. An additional hazard faced by schools in England is created by the extent to which the curriculum for children in reception classes is affected by the 'downward thrust' of the National Curriculum, thus creating a climate in which teachers feel pressure to develop formal learning across all the Key Stage 1 National Curriculum subjects and, in particular, to ensure that children develop as early as possible the formal skills of reading, writing and recording of number.

Aims of pre-schooling

If the stated aims of pre-school education of the two educational systems are compared, it does not at first sight appear that there are major differences between the two countries. In 1996, 'Desirable Outcomes for Children's Learning', to be achieved by the end of pre-school education were published (SCAA, 1996a),[11] and an extract showing the areas of learning is given below:

a. personal and social development;
b. language and literacy; which focuses on children's developing competence in talking and listening, and in becoming readers and writers;
c. mathematics; which covers aspects of mathematical understanding and provides the foundation of numeracy;
d. knowledge and understanding of the world;
e. physical development;
f. creative development. (SCAA, 1996a)

The aims for children's learning at *yōchien* or *hoikuen* in Japan are stated as follows:

1. to encourage basic living habits and attitudes for a healthy, safe and happy life, and to nurture the foundations for a healthy mind and body;
2. to encourage love and trust for people and to cultivate an attitude of independence, co-operation and morality;
3. to encourage interests towards one's surrounding nature and society, and to cultivate sensitivity and a capacity for appreciating one's surroundings;
4. to encourage interest toward language in daily life, to develop pleasant attitudes in talking and listening to others and to cultivate language sense;
5. to encourage a rich mind and to enrich creativity through various experiences. (*Monbushō*, 1994)

---

[11] In 1999 these were subject to a review by the Qualifications and Curriculum Authority but the six areas of learning are unchanged (QCA, 1999).

It is unlikely that anyone would seriously argue with the desirability of any of these aims for early education – their general applicability and the broad way in which they are stated make them acceptable as a basic framework. Yet even at this stage a stronger focus on formal learning may be identified in the English framework – namely, that the 'desirable outcomes' refer specifically to mathematics and numeracy and to children becoming 'readers and writers'. This conflicts with the Froebelian principles established in the nineteenth century that "prescribed knowledge in the so-called subjects are not desirable for young children" – he stressed the educational value of play, together with the importance of encouraging a child to do as much as possible for him(her)self. Recent research in the United States has suggested that too-formal early-learning experiences are related to lower achievement later in school (Schweinhart *et al.*, 1986); indeed, the dangers of 'too formal, too soon' have been identified by Zigler (1987) and were echoed by the HMI report in 1989 (*op. cit.*). While the importance of 'learning through play' was recognised in England in the 1970s (Pringle and Naidoo, 1975), this has tended to accentuate 'child-directed' or 'free play', in contrast with teacher-directed play which is more clearly focused on specific learning skills and behaviour. The differences between the Japanese and English approaches to pre-schooling become more apparent when pupils' experiences are contrasted.

Pupil experience of pre-schooling

Two main aims of pre-schooling in Japan may be identified; first, to develop an understanding of the nature of appropriate behaviour for schooling, including behaving as a member of a group, being attuned to the needs of others, how to listen to others, how to respond to questions, and how to participate in group activities, especially those concerned with schooling rituals. Teaching of 'group life' (*shūdan seikatsu*) represents an important transitional stage between that of the home, where the child is the centre of attention and the school environment where the child is one of many taught in a formalised way. Hendry (1993, p.7) says that: "Kindergarten is an opportunity to learn about the concept of peers, people classified in an important way as equal to oneself, certainly equally entitled to the attention of the teacher."

Secondly, Japanese pre-schooling is concerned to put in place those skills that will facilitate formal learning at a later stage, such as memory skills, the ability to concentrate on a particular activity and to persevere with an activity until its completion. The extent of centralised control of the Japanese kindergarten is much greater than in England; very detailed teachers' manuals are published which specify the overall structure for each year of kindergarten, and also examples of specific plans for individual sessions.

The manual of instruction for early years' teachers in Japan reminds teachers of the following basic objectives:

a. While looking after children, one should make an effort to bring out the child's attitude of independence, by encouraging thinking and acting on one's own judgement;
b. understand the development of the child's mind and body and its actual state, and guide the child appropriately according to his/her ability;
c. bring out his/her interest and desire by understanding his/her character;
d. create the right atmosphere for the nursery school by taking into account the area/environment in which the children live;
e. make sure that you know this is different from elementary education and use its special quality to guide children;
f. communicate well and work together with parents in order to achieve a good educational result.

The teachers' instruction manual for the beginning of the school year for children aged five (in their last year of kindergarten) includes the following:

Class:	New friends
Main events:	Opening ceremony
	Entrance ceremony
	Birthday party
	Children's day
	Home visits by the teacher
Aim:	Encourage the children to be nice to their new friends and to be happy about moving up to the new class.
	Encourage them to play and take responsibility for jobs and chores.
Activity:	Take part in the opening ceremony for the new term.
	Listen to the principal's welcome about becoming a member of the 'top' class.
Points to stress:	Be happy about being a member of the top class and encourage them to become more independent.

Health:	Wash your hands after playing with the equipment.
	Use the equipment safely.
Relationships:	Be independent in an activity if you can play with the younger
	children as well.
Environment:	Look after the flowers, plants and pets at kindergarten.
	Make a paper aeroplane and fly it.
Language:	Remember to say 'hello', 'goodbye' and 'thank you'.
	Speak clearly and loudly.
	Be able to say 'yes' and 'no'.
Expression:	Sing a song in tune.
	Make a large flying fish (*koinobori)* for 5 May (boys' festival).
	Make presents for the younger children.

This extract demonstrates the emphasis on the dual and mutually supportive aspects of learning, namely, the development of social behaviour (consideration for younger children, meeting new friends, taking responsibility and being independent) as well as the development of other skills necessary for formal learning. We need, however, to look more closely at the details given in the teachers' manual for a typical session at Japanese *yōchien* or *hoikuen* in order to examine how this is achieved: the following extract is taken from the kindergarten 'teachers' manual' and provides a suggested 'daily plan'. We can see that the session consists of approximately equal periods of time spent in 'free play' and in 'teacher-directed activities'.

Aim: To experience the pleasure of creating and making things and the feeling of satisfaction. Be lively and energetic.

Time	Children's Activity	Teacher's Activity/Notes
9.00	Arrival at kindergarten	Check children's health.
	Free play (indoors)	Give appropriate assistance and encouragement
		(exercise bar, drawing, *nendo, origami,* reading etc.)
9.45	Tidy up, go to lavatory, sit down.	After tidying, play piano while they sit down.
	Greetings, good morning	
	Learn a song	Teach how to sing the song in a lively way.
	Today's promise	Announce today's promise.
9.55	Paper activity – draw a *sumō* wrestler	Ask them to take out their coloured pencils and scissors. Give each child 2 pieces of paper.
	Look at your teacher and listen	Make them sit down quietly and listen to what you have to say. The teacher should speak clearly
	Game of *sumō* wrestling	and plainly with an expressive face.
	Draw a circle on a card	Show your example of the card with a circle

and colour it in	(*dohyō*) so that they understand the size of circle needed. Also show an object the same size as the circle to make it clear.
Tell them to draw 2 lines inside the circle	Make them draw this circle on the card clearly and colour it in. Tell them to draw 2 lines in the middle. Tell them to draw 2 black dots just outside the lines in the circle, which is the place for hitting.
Make a paper *sumō* wrestler. Colour it in Cut it out along the lines Make another one	Make them do this by themselves without help.
10.20 Games with cards Start a match with those sitting at the same table. The rest of the children should cheer them on. A winner should be chosen from one of the 2 finalists.	Children should play the game[12] that they made themselves, and enjoy the feeling of satisfaction. Make them listen to you so that they can understand the rules of the game.
10.50 Outside activity Free play: football, climbing, etc Obstacle race	Make sure that they don't hurt themselves Encourage them to play energetically Make them understand the rules. Encourage them to do their best both for themselves and for their team
11.30 Lunch *Itadakimasu/ Gochisōsama*	Wash hands and get ready quietly Pour some tea Encourage them to eat everything. Brush teeth
12.10 Story on cards (*Yamatano-orochi*)	Encourage them to concentrate on the story and sit quietly. Try to get them to understand the meaning and moral of the story.
12.30 Snack	Wash hands, give them the snack to eat sitting down. Children should tidy up afterwards.
12.40 Outside activity Free play	
13.20 Departing greetings Sing a song	Encourage them to sing in a lively way.
13.30 Going home	Lining up outside the classroom door to say goodbye.

---

[12] The traditional game of '*kami-zumō*' is played by many young Japanese children and the kindergarten manual did not include a detailed description. The game is played by placing two paper sumo-wrestlers, folded in half so that they stand up, on the places marked on the card behind the lines. The two children playing then bang the table until one *sumō* wrestler falls over; the other is then the winner.

The level of detail provided in the teachers' instruction manual (regarding not only the general plan for the beginning of a year but also the detail for a typical session) serves to increase the consistency of children's experience of pre-schooling. While extended observational visits have been made to numerous nursery classes and units attached to primary schools in England, which have provided opportunities for detailed examination of guidelines, frameworks, advice and instruction regarding the nature of the nursery learning and the activities to be provided, nothing has been seen which would suggest that any guidelines with a similar level of detail exist in England.

Visits to nursery classes/units in England have provided opportunities to observe a number of teaching approaches that enable some broad comparisons to be made between practice in England and Japan in three main areas: first, in the use of routine; secondly in the use of 'free play' and, thirdly, in the use of teacher directed activities.

First, pre-schooling in Japan uses routine to a far greater extent; this serves the dual function of providing children with a secure and predictable environment and also with acquainting them with the ritual-like routines to be met in formal schooling (Peak, 1991). For example, children learn how to take off their outdoor coat and to hang it on the correct peg; to change their outdoor shoes and store them correctly; to put on their protective overalls; and to greet the teacher formally. At the formal beginning of the session – when all children have arrived – children sit in a circle when they hear the teacher playing the piano. This is also used to begin the development of responsible behaviour through the use of peer pressure: for example, Hendry (1985, p.7) describes the way that a teacher will continue playing the piano at the beginning of the session until all the children are seated, and will rely on the children to hurry up the stragglers.[13] Once seated in the circle, all children will be greeted individually and will respond clearly: this serves both to acknowledge their importance as an individual of being a member of the group and to introduce them to the ritual of 'taking the register' that they will encounter in primary school. The formalised nature of arrival at a Japanese kindergarten stresses the importance of learning and taking part in routines whereas, in contrast, arrival at a nursery class in England has been observed to be more informal, to lack a formal beginning and to be less

---

[13] Kindergarten teachers are expected to be able to play a piano (or organ) sufficiently well to accompany children.

subject to routine.[14] Other routines that may be observed in Japanese kindergartens include arrangements for the distribution of milk, for 'clearing up' time and for lunch (Hendry, 1986a, p.135). Children in Japan are encouraged to share responsibility for these routines whereas in England the nursery staff are more likely to carry out all routine organisation.

The distinction between 'free play' and teacher-directed activities is clear in Japanese kindergartens, and the two aspects have different learning objectives. In Japanese kindergartens, 'free play' is used to develop children's socialisation (Peak, *op. cit.*, Lewis, 1995; Tobin *et al.*, 1989). Lewis (*op. cit.*) reported that from her observation 'free play accounted for about half the time which was 'unregimented and often even unsupervised'(p. 19).[15] This time enables children to develop socially, and to relate to other children within their peer group relationships. In the normal course of events, no element of teacher intervention or mediation will be involved – children gradually learn to resolve their own difficulties and relationships arising from antisocial behaviour – which helps children gradually to develop an understanding of '*shūdan seikatsu*' or group behaviour. 'Free play' appears to be much 'freer' in Japan than its equivalent in English nursery classes, where teachers/assistants are observed to intercede frequently and quickly in cases of dispute among children. 'Free play' in Japan is perceived as being used as an instrument for learning in order to develop a framework for a feeling of a class spirit, and for children to learn to be a 'responsible, kind member' of that class. It is an essential part of the *preparation* for formal schooling (Hendry, 1986a) and is used to develop the 'child centred discipline' observed in formal schooling (Stevenson and Stigler, 1992). Pre-schooling may also include an introduction to the *tōban* rota system for responsibility used in elementary schooling (discussed above) (Ben-Ari, 1997, p.40). The absence of conflict between the development of interpersonal relationships and rules governing play facilitates the parallel development of self-understanding: the unique combination of individual responsibility and a feeling of group identity underpins later learning in the formal classroom situation. Teachers work hard to develop an awareness among

---

[14] This may not be true of all pre-schooling experience in England. In particular, 'arrival' routine observed in some Montessori schools is closer to the Japanese model.

[15] It should not, however, be assumed that Japanese pre-schooling is entirely uniform in its methods. A survey in 1985 by *Monbushō* of 1500 kindergartens was able to identify eight distinct educational approaches (OMEP, 1992).

children of the needs of group life, and to ease the transition for children who have been accustomed to being the centre of attention at home to being one of many in a class situation. Self-reflection or *hansei* was encouraged during class meetings that were used to reflect on the day's activities and problems that might have arisen during 'free play'. Teachers skilfully questioned children and encouraged them to consider and comment on the behavioural or socialisation problems that they had either observed or experienced.

The element of 'teacher directed' activity in Japan is likely to involve the whole group, and for all children to be engaged simultaneously on the same activity, whether this is *origami*, listening to a story, making a paper aeroplane, or acting out a story. Each activity has a carefully planned learning objective, which, in addition to the general objective of developing social awareness, will be designed to develop memory, co-ordination, language, attention span or powers of observation. Music – particularly 'live' music provided by the teacher – is used successfully to develop rhythm, co-ordination, auditory memory, and counting skills. Children's vocabulary is carefully extended through listening to and discussion of stories – often using traditional 'story cards' ('*kamishibai*'). The opportunity for discussion not only develops children's language skills, it also provides an opportunity for the discussion of moral issues and values. Hendry (1986a, pp.132–3) gives two examples of stories that emphasise the value of 'co-operation' in group activities; this is a further way in which teachers increase children's appreciation of '*shūdan seikatsu*'. Discussion of stories also prepares children to take part in discussion in elementary school classes; they learn how to express themselves to a larger group , and to gain confidence in making an oral contribution. Thus while the teacher-directed activities are carefully constructed to develop specific skills, they are also intended to develop patterns of behaviour appropriate for school, including familiarity with routines to be encountered at school.

In English nursery units, the observed model is likely to lie somewhere between 'free play' and teacher-directed activities. Children are likely to be encouraged to choose their own constructive activity from a teacher-determined range, which prevents the same activity from being selected every day.[16] Having made their choice, a small group of chil-

---

[16] Some nursery classes in England use the High/Scope model involving 'plan, do, review'; however, there is little evidence to suggest that children of such a young age are capable of planning or reviewing, since these skills are associated with later stages of development.

dren (perhaps 3 or 4) will be engaged on the same activity (such as painting, using clay, sand, water, building bricks, jigsaws, sorting, matching). Some will be encouraged in reading and pre-reading activities, including the writing of letters and 'emergent writing', or the recording of numbers. Children are unlikely to receive much formal instruction on these activities, however, due to the number of different activities taking place simultaneously. The observed level of interaction between children in a group is very low; often there may be very little oral communication between children sitting at the same table and engaged on a similar task. This is consistent with the general aims of pre-schooling in England which are more concerned with the development of children at the individual level through the provision of a wide range of learning opportunities and less with the development of those specific skills that will help later learning. Levels of socialisation and interaction among children are relatively low and are, in the main, restricted to activities involving building bricks and playing with train sets. As already mentioned, during such examples of interaction, teachers intervene much more frequently and more quickly than in Japan in order to settle disagreements. In this way, children become accustomed to turn to a higher authority for discipline, rather than, as in Japan, being encouraged to develop their own child-centred discipline.

In English nursery classes, teachers and assistants[17] supervise activities in a general way. Children's attention span was observed to be variable, and little was seen in the way of systematic efforts to extend this. Children may change activities frequently during a session, and, on the whole, teachers do not expect children to persevere with an activity once boredom has set in or they have reached the limit of their capability. Whole-class teacher-directed activity is not often observed; this is understandable given the young age (usually 3–4 years) and number (often 40) of the children in the session. The children may be drawn together at the beginning or end of a session for a song or story, but observation suggests that they are unlikely to have developed sufficient attention span for this activity to be successful.

The limitations of English nursery education are perceived as two-fold; first, the absence of teacher-directed activities in English nursery classes and the consequent greater reliance on children's individual develop-

---

[17] Each nursery unit is required to be under the supervision of a qualified teacher (although s/he need not be physically present). Other staff are nursery assistants with nursery nursing qualifications (NNEB or NVQ).

ment through child-selected constructive activities means that children's learning is highly variable, reflecting existing levels of motivation, attention span and capability. Secondly, children may be introduced to more formal skills, such as the recording of letters and numbers; this may be attempted before an adequate understanding or appreciation of their significance has been established. The pre-school experience of children in England thus lacks the explicit development of the skills and behaviour required for the next stage that is a feature of Japanese kindergartens, and, at the same time, the existing variability in children's earlier development is increased. The kindergarten experience in Japan, therefore, is seen as providing a more adequate *preparation* for learning than that provided in English pre-schooling. Thus although in England the transition from pre-schooling to primary school is more gradual and the interface between the two stages is blurred, many children appear able to cope less well with the demands of formal schooling than Japanese children with their experience of kindergarten.

The transition from pre-schooling to formal schooling

With the development of state nursery provision in England, children are increasingly likely to receive their pre-school education from the state primary school they subsequently attend for their formal schooling (DfEE, 1996b). This provides a degree of continuity between the two stages that facilitates gradual transition. Schools may also have more than one entry point to 'reception' classes thus staggering the entry of children to formal schooling.

In contrast, regulations governing age of statutory schooling in Japan result in all children beginning schooling at the same time in the year, namely, in April following their sixth birthday. The beginning of formal schooling is regarded as an important and major step for a child and the seriousness of the occasion may be marked, for example, by parents purchasing a desk or other equipment for the child at this time (Hendry, 1986a; Peak, 1992; Lewis, 1995). Parents and children alike are aware of the behavioural expectations in formal schooling, and the ways in which these differ from those of kindergarten. Yet the kindergarten experience will have anticipated and gradually introduced children both to the routine and patterns of expected behaviour at elementary school. Parental support and close liaison, mainly from mothers, is vital in establishing understanding of routines and patterns of behaviour. This is helped by the daily exchange of comments between pre-school teachers and mothers, recorded in notebooks which travel to and from kindergarten and home (Boocock, 1991). With their experience and understanding of group life gained in pre-schooling, children adjust more easily to being one of many in a classroom. During pre-schooling, they experience some peer pressure on behaviour and standards that they build on when they participate in the *tōban* system in the classroom and learn to cope with the difficulties of leadership. Thus although schooling is a quite distinct and separate stage, the beginning of it is eased for children by their previously acquired knowledge of how to behave. This is described by Ben-Ari (1997, p.20) who attributes the ease of the transition to formal schooling to the way independence has been fostered in children and the way that they have gradually been accustomed to the needs and expected behaviour of group life. In addition, the care with which the curricular content of kindergarten has been constructed ensures that children will have been helped to develop co-ordination, especially fine motor skills, auditory and visual memory skills, and their ability to concentrate. These skills facilitate later learning and enable children to begin formal schooling with their 'learning tools' already acquired.

Summary

The educational systems of Japan and England may be seen as reflecting their different cultures and social values, both in their structure and their teaching approaches. In spite of the disproportionate influence of a small minority of 'élite' schools, and the role played by *juku* in preparing children for competitive examinations, it has to be accepted that to a large extent the Japanese educational system has been successful in its public claim to provide equal educational opportunities for all. The greater degree of state control in the Japanese educational system is seen as central to the degree of uniformity achieved; this aspect will be examined in further detail in Chapter 5. The English educational system is also perceived as being successful in its desire to provide a diversity of educational provision, in order to meet the widely varying needs of its pupils, and this diversity remains in spite of the comprehensivation of much of the secondary school system.

Japanese children beginning schooling are able to learn effectively and efficiently, and teachers are able to use a whole-class teaching approach. Teaching methods will be examined in greater detail in Chapter 7, but so far it is clear that teachers are only able to use a whole-class approach if all children have appropriate behavioural and learning skills. When children in Japan begin formal schooling, they are well placed to make progress in academic development as efficiently as possible, taking advantage of the effectiveness of the teaching process (Peak, 1991). Children in their first few weeks of schooling were observed, first, to have an awareness of the needs of group behaviour, and an appreciation of the needs of other children, which helped them to resolve any difficulties. Secondly, they were observed to be aware of the routines associated with school and the classroom; they were able to take their turn in the *tōban* rota for bringing the class to order for the beginning of a lesson, and demonstrated awareness of the correct way to respond to questioning and to participate in class discussion. Thirdly, they were observed to have the ability to pay attention throughout a lesson, to organise their belongings, and to be able to carry out instructions. These skills had been developed during pre-school educational experience that had successfully brought all the children to a readiness for schooling and formal learning, but which had not sought to develop the skills of some children to a higher level than that of other children (Hess *et al.*, 1980; Lewis, 1995).

In contrast, the values from English society that stress the importance of meeting the needs of the individual, but without requiring a similar level of individual responsibility, underpin much of the educational system and may be seen affecting the behaviour of pupils within the classroom. Children in pre-schooling in England are observed to develop at very different rates and to display widely differing levels of capability by the time they begin formal schooling. There is little evidence of any 'catching up' of weaker children, or of teachers attempting to ensure that children are 'ready' for schooling. This means that at the beginning of statutory schooling, whole-class teaching is not a realistic possibility, and that the gap between attainment levels of individual children increases. In pre-schooling in England, there is little emphasis given to developing those specific skills that will help later learning, and little emphasis on either the development of social skills or group behaviour. In addition, as required by education policy, children are encouraged to develop the formal skills of reading, writing and recording of number; this is regarded as inappropriate for many children and reduces the time and effort that can be devoted to learning that is more relevant at that stage.

The capability of six-year-old children in England for independent behaviour has been observed to be less than Japanese children of a similar age. Japanese children beginning schooling also appear to be aware of appropriate classroom and learning behaviour and to be able to observe the behavioural standards expected in formal schooling. It is a daunting and difficult task for a teacher to begin to develop standards of appropriate behaviour: that this is achieved at all in English classrooms is a reflection of the skill and dedication of the classroom teachers. Their job would be made far more manageable if children arrived at the beginning of formal schooling with an understanding of appropriate learning and social behaviour. If, as appears likely, this is not likely to be transmitted within the setting of the family, then a greater responsibility is passed to the agencies of pre-school education for developing an awareness of these.

By the time that children in Japan begin compulsory schooling, their counterparts in England will have the benefit of, on average, one year and a half of schooling within the primary school setting. Yet evidence suggests that by the time they are nine, the mathematical attainment of the average child in Japan is eighteen months in advance of his/her English equivalent. It has been argued here that a key factor in enabling children in the Japanese educational system to make such faster progress is their different experience of *pre-school* education. In Japan children beginning schooling are familiar with the routines since they have been introduced to these during pre-schooling, together with patterns of classroom behaviour. They will have learnt how to behave as a member of a group, through the teaching of *shūdan seikatsu* at *yōchien* or *hoikuen*. Teachers will have worked hard to achieve an awareness of this, through the use of 'free play' to develop children's own discipline and the use of *tōban* to accustom children to the different aspects of leadership and responsibility. Finally, teacher directed activities will have been used to develop those specific skills which children need for formal classroom learning.

The preparation for schooling provided by kindergarten, combined with a single date for starting school in Japan, result in children starting from a more equal point at the beginning of schooling. In England, the variable date of starting school, the anticipation of formal learning by some children in their nursery years, and the variable levels of social and behavioural skills mean that among children beginning school there is already a wide range of knowledge. This wide range means that a differentiated approach to teaching and learning is more easily applied than a whole-class approach; one consequence of this differentiated approach is to widen further the range of attainment.

5

Control of the educational systems: effects on the curriculum and learning materials

Introduction

Traditionally, a major difference between the two educational systems of Japan and England related to the degree of centralised control of educational content, teaching and learning. This has already been mentioned in Chapter 4; the task of this chapter is to examine the effect that the difference in central control has on children's learning of mathematics in the classroom.

Cummings' view (1989, 1995) is that a strong degree of state control is a defining characteristic of the prototypical Asian model of education. Hirahala (1995) argued that the Japanese and English educational systems represent two extremes with regard to the degree of centralised state control, with the English system being almost totally free from control. Changes during the last few years have resulted in both countries moving towards each other from their extreme positions. Educational reforms in Japan have relaxed to some extent the *Monbushō*'s tight control over schools (National Council on Education Reform, 1987) and in England a degree of control has been effected through the introduction of the National Curriculum requirements and standardised testing in schools (DES, 1989; SCAA, 1995, QCA, 1999).

Central control and structure of Japanese and English educational systems

As well as reflecting cultural values of society, views relating to a desirable level of centralised control in education involve concern over efficiency in organisation and management (McLean and Lauglo, 1985). This issue was first examined by Kandel (1933), who suggested that a higher degree of centralisation was associated with more equal distribution of educational resources than occurred in a system where control was exercised at a more local level. It is also possible to see other advantages of a centralised system; in relation to the control over textbook approval and publication, economies of scale in producing larger quantities of a smaller range of textbooks operate to the advantage of the consumer. In other areas, however, there may be advantages in localised controls – for example, in allowing head teachers to appoint teachers according to specific local needs. McLean (*op.cit.*) concludes that administrative criteria can often determine the movement towards increased or decreased levels of centralised control. This section contrasts the nature of the control in aspects which directly impinge on the curricula content, teaching and learning at the primary school level.

In Japan, centralised control of the education system is held by the *Monbushō*. At the prefectural level of governing and administering education, each of the 47 prefectures has a five-member board of education, responsible for operating the schools established by the prefecture (primarily upper secondary schools or *kōtōgakkō*), licensing teachers, making appointments and providing advice where necessary to municipal areas (NIER, 1991). At the lower municipal level, each area has a 3- or 5-member board of education (appointed by the equivalent of the local 'mayor'), which is broadly responsible for the operation of public elementary and lower secondary schools, including adopting textbooks for school use (selected from *Monbushō*'s approved list) and making recommendations to the prefectural boards on the appointment and dismissal of teachers. These municipal boards of education, or education committees, have considerable power, yet the process for appointing an individual to the board is not clear. The board members may be retired school principals, or they may be unconnected with education but have considerable standing and respect in the local community, and they may be industrialists (NIER, *op.cit.*). Rarely are teachers represented on these educational boards.

The method of appointing teachers in Japan contrasts with the system in England. An individual wishing to be employed in a state school in Japan must take the teachers' appointment examination set by the relevant prefecture. If successful, s/he will then be allocated to a particular

school by the prefectural board[1] without any choice. Jobs are not, therefore, advertised or subject to application. In contrast, although teachers
in England are required to hold an approved teaching qualification,[2] these
are validated centrally and valid throughout England and Wales. There
is no provision for assigning teachers; teachers apply for jobs advertised
and are subject to selection processes. In Japan, once teachers have obtained employment with a particular prefecture, this is permanent, but
teachers may be moved around between schools by the prefectural
boards. In both countries employment legislation enables women to take
maternity leave and to return to their previous positions[3] although in Japan married women who give up for lengthy periods may be required to
take an examination.

On the financial side, the cost of public sector education in Japan is
shared by national, prefectural and municipal levels. At the national level
Monbushō provides about half the total cost; it finances all the 'national'
institutions, but also allows subsidies to prefectures to assist with the purchase of teaching equipment, construction of schools, and the payment
of salaries. The other half of teachers' salaries is paid by the prefectural
government (Monbushō, 1995b).

Parents of children in public sector schools in Japan are also required
to contribute to the financial costs of education. Parents of first-grade
pupils will typically be expected to purchase equipment to the value of
about £25,[4] and to meet the costs of the daily lunch provided by the
school.[5]

The centralised nature of the educational system in Japan gives rise
to both the strengths and weaknesses of the system. For example, with
rigid control over curriculum content, all pupils during the compulsory

---

[1] Shimahara and Sakai(1995) quote a success rate in 1989 of 1 out of every 4.2 candidates
in Tokyo.
[2] Education (Teachers) Regulations, 1993.
[3] Employment Rights Act, 1996 in England and the Law on Leave for Child-Rearing
(1991, revised in 1993) in Japan.
[4] In 1996, the following equipment for first-grade children was provided by parents: indoor shoes; sports wear (T-shirt and shorts); scissors; *nendo* (modelling clay) and
nendo-board; plain notebook; *origami*; coloured pencils; chalk; glue; castanets; pencil;
board (to go underneath writing paper); report notebook and report case. £25 was the
sterling equivalent of the total cost at that time.
[5] In England, parents may choose to provide their children with a packed lunch, or they
may qualify for 'free school meals'. The proportion of primary school children eating
and paying for a school lunch is comparatively small – less than one third.

years of schooling follow the same broad course of study with no element of specialisation. *Monbushō* has responsibility for the following aspects of education:

- prescribing curricula, standards and requirements;
- approving textbooks;
- providing guidance for the prefectures;
- authorising the establishment of colleges and universities;
- operating national institutions of education;
- generally supervising private higher education institutions;
- regulating establishment of private schools;
- investigating and issuing directives where necessary to local educational boards.

The first two areas of responsibility affect the operation of primary schools to a greater extent than the other areas, and are also the areas of responsibility that give *Monbushō* tremendous power over the nature of the education system. They also give rise to contention; in particular, over the control that *Monbushō* retains over the content and selection of textbooks (Schoppa, 1991).

In England the Education Act of 1944 established the system of organisation and management of education that, in spite of recent changes, remains structurally intact. The central figure of authority is the Secretary of State for Education and the administering body is the Department for Education and Employment (DfEE).[6] This department allocates funds either to Local Education Authorities (LEAs) which have a statutory duty to ensure that children receive a satisfactory education, or, since 1989, direct to schools. While LEAs are accountable to the DfEE and the Secretary of State, the immediate responsibility for ensuring a sufficiency of schools and that children of statutory school age receive education by taking legal action against parents if necessary, lies with the LEA. Since the Education Reform Act (ERA) (1988), the DfEE has had a responsibility for the specification of the National Curriculum that applies to all pupils of compulsory school age; unlike Japan, however, there is no governmental or LEA responsibility with regard to textbook approval.

---

[6] Previously the Department for Education and Science (DES) and the Department for Education (DFE).

Comparison of approaches to prescribing curricula

One characteristic that the Japanese and English educational systems share is the way in which the curriculum for the statutory years of schooling is prescribed by the relevant government department. In Japan, this practice was established as part of the reorganisation of the educational system following the Second World War, whereas in England the defining of a National Curriculum was introduced in 1989 following the Education Reform Act of 1988.

This shared characteristic, however, conceals fundamental differences in governmental philosophy with regard to education. These are revealed in the ways that the curricula are stated. For example, in Japan, the way that the national curriculum specifies both objectives and content for each subject and each year of schooling is consistent with the stated goals of egalitarianism and uniformity of opportunity and experience within the educational system (*Monbushō*, 1989). In England, the National Curriculum is outlined in much broader terms and provides Attainment Targets relating to each of the four Key Stages during the period of statutory schooling (SCAA, 1996c). For clarity, the relationship between Key Stages, ages of pupils and years of schooling is set out below:

Key Stage	Ages of pupils	Years of schooling	
1	5–7	1–2	
2	7–11	3–6	
3	11–14	7–9	
4	14–16	10–11	[SCAA, 1996c]

For each subject (exceptions are art, music and physical education), Attainment Targets are expressed in terms of Attainment Levels 1-8, with 'level descriptions' being provided in order to make summative judgements about a pupil's performance at the end of a key stage' (SCAA, 1996c, p. 7). Levels of attainment, however, are not related to each school year: the 'key stages' cover respectively 2, 4, 3 and 2 years of schooling. The way in which the National Curriculum in England is structured, therefore, reflects an acceptance of the variability of pupil experience within schooling: it does not attempt to establish a standard syllabus for any subject for any year of schooling. Its structure reflects the expectation that pupils of a similar age will vary in their educational progress and rate of cognitive development and consequently children will progress at different rates and in different ways through the levels of attainment.

Table 5.1 *Percentages of lesson time for six-year-old pupils allocated to curricular subjects: England and Japan*

Subjects	England Median % of time[a]	Subjects	Japan % of time
Language (English)	27	Language (Japanese) (*Kokugo*)	36
Mathematics	20	Mathematics (Arithmetic) (*Sansū*)	16
Science	10	Life Sciences (*Seikatsu*)	12
Technology	5		
History	5		
Geography	5		
Art	6	Handwork (*Zukō*)	8
Music	5	Music (*Ongaku*)	8
Physical Education	6	Physical Education (*Taiiku*)	12
Religious Education	4	Moral Education	4
		Special Activities[b]	4

Notes: (a) There is no prescription of teaching time for individual subjects; percentages refer to those observed by Ofsted Inspectors (Ofsted, 1996a). (b) Special activities include classroom activities, student council, club activities and school events such as ceremonies, presentation programs, events related to health/safety/physical education, school excursions, and productive and community service activities (Education in Japan, 1994, p 58, *Monbushô*, 1994).

Some differences between the importance of various curricular subjects for six-year-old children can be identified and are shown in Table 5.1. At the time of writing there is no statutory requirement in England in relation to the proportion of contact time which should be allocated to the different subject areas, although the introduction of the National Numeracy Strategy is likely to reduce the variation between schools in the amount of time devoted to mathematics teaching and learning (see Chapter 7).

Educational philosophy in England not only leads to an expectation of differential rates of progress between individual pupils of a similar age through the National Curriculum, but also to an expectation of differential levels of achievement. There is no expectation that pupils of a similar age will, by the end of a year of schooling, have achieved broadly similar standards.

The emphasis in Japan on uniformity of learning experience encourages progression at a similar rate. All children are expected to attain the minimum standards prescribed and to acquire a broadly similar understanding of the curriculum specified for a particular grade – teachers are observed to spend time and effort ensuring that 'slower learners' in the classroom do not get left behind, often encouraging faster children to help the slower members of their class group (Rohlen and Letendre, 1996). In educational systems of other countries which have an expectation for all children to progress together and to achieve specified minimum standards by the end of a year in order to progress to the following grade, it is common to find some flexibility built into the system whereby pupils who do not reach the required standard repeat the appropriate school year. This is found in several European countries including Germany, Switzerland and France: by the end of compulsory schooling perhaps one quarter of children will have repeated one or more school years.[7] The system in Japan, although it has standard expectations with regard to levels of achievement for all pupils does not have a similar pattern of flexibility: it is only in the most exceptional circumstances that a pupil will be allowed additional time or to repeat a school year in order to attain the expected standard.[8] While this is entirely consistent with the values of an education system which promotes the efficacy of the virtues of effort and perseverance in achievement, yet there is clearly some need for additional help and support outside the classroom for slower pupils. This is provided by the '*juku*' system of private evening tutorials which is crucial in enabling many pupils to keep up with the progress of the class (Beauchamp, 1991). The view of many both inside and outside Japan is that without the support of the private evening sector through the years of compulsory schooling, it would not be possible to achieve official expectations with regard to standards in the public daytime (Kitamura, 1986; Harnisch, 1994).[9] The extent to which pupils use the *juku* facilities increases with age. It is difficult to obtain precise figures, but it is estimated from various sources that attendance at *juku* increases from about 4 per cent of pupils in the first grade of schooling to about 45 per cent in grade 9 (Leestma and Walberg, 1992; Becker *et al.*, 1990;

---

[7] In France, by the end of primary schooling, approximately 20 per cent of children have repeated one year of schooling and 10 per cent have repeated two years (Lewis, 1985).
[8] From discussion with school principals and other educationists in Japan.
[9] Pupils will, also however, attend *juku* for reasons other than 'catching up': it is common for bright pupils to choose to attend *juku* in order to get ahead and to meet problems of a more challenging nature (Rohlen, 1983, p.104).

Harnisch, *op.cit.*). During the first and second grade of schooling it is relatively unusual for pupils in the state sector to attend evening *juku* and none of the pupils in the classes observed was attending *juku* for additional teaching.[10]

In Japan an additional source of help for pupils from outside schooling comes from parents, many of whom – especially mothers – are committed to and involved with their children's educational development to an extent unusual in England. For the objective of uniform minimum standards to be a practical possibility – even at elementary school level – requires a combination of resources for additional help for slower learners from within and outside the classroom.

Comparison of mathematics curricula

For the elementary school pupils in Japan, the overall objectives of the mathematics curriculum stated for each year of schooling are likely to remain unchanged for a considerable period of time. They were updated to reflect the recommendations of the National Council on Educational Reform (1987) which planned for a more outward looking, international curriculum that would take Japan into the 21st century. It is unlikely that any further changes will be made to the elementary school curriculum without measured and thorough consideration of the implications: the normal practice is for the curriculum to be reviewed every ten years.[11] In contrast, however, since the National Curriculum in England was first introduced in 1989, it has undergone three major revisions. First, following complaints from teachers regarding the 'unmanageability' of the first published Curriculum, the number of Attainment Targets was reduced (the original version contained fourteen separate Attainment Targets for mathematics), and a further version was introduced into school in September 1995. Teachers were then promised that there would be no significant changes to the National Curriculum until the year 2000; however, it was announced in 1998 that existing National Curriculum

---

[10] According to the class teachers and from conversation with individual children in the sample of classes observed. Thus although the *juku* system plays an important part in the Japanese educational structure as a whole, it is not given special consideration in this study.

[11] By the end of 1995, a number of subject committees had been established in Japan to consider and make recommendations regarding desirable changes to the curriculum for the next century.

requirements would no longer apply to geography, history, art, music, or PE. (Teachers were expected to provide suitable teaching in these subjects while continuing to meet National Curriculum requirements in English, mathematics, science, information and communications and religious education.) The new revised version of the National Curriculum will be introduced into schools in the year 2000.

The mathematics curriculum in Japan states the following broad aims: "To help pupils acquire the fundamental knowledge and skills regarding numbers, quantities and geometrical figures, develop their ability to consider daily phenomena logically with insight, appreciate the advantage of mathematical processing, and to foster an attitude to willingly make use of them in life". (Course of Study: *Monbushō*, 1994)

Objectives stated in such broad terms could easily have been taken from the English National Curriculum for pupils in Key Stages 1 & 2; when the curriculum is stated for each *grade* of pupils in Japan, however, it becomes more tightly focused. The first-grade curriculum, for example, contains three more specific objectives, followed by a description of the contents of each of the three sections of the curriculum: Numbers and Computation; Quantities and Measurement; Geometrical Figures. For the purposes of reference, the content of the section relating to *Numbers and Computations* is shown in full here:

1. To enable pupils to express correctly the number and order of objects using numbers, and through these activities to help them understand the concept of number.
a. To compare the numbers of objects by an operation such as correspondence.
b. To count or express correctly the number and order of objects.
c. To know the size and order of numbers, to make a sequence of them, and to express them on a number line.
d. To consider a number in relation to other numbers by taking the sum or difference of them.
e. To know the meaning of a place value in 2-digit numbers.
2. To help pupils to understand addition and subtraction of numbers, and to enable them to use them in computation.
a. To know the cases in which addition and subtraction are applied, and to express in formula and interpret them.
b. To be able to correctly carry out addition of 1-digit numbers, and subtraction as its inverse operation.
c. To know that addition and subtraction can be applied to 2-digit

numbers as well by dealing with simple cases.
3. To enable pupils to classify and express concrete objects by counting them efficiently, dividing them into equal parts, etc.'
(Course of Study: Monbushō, 1994)

It is clear that the specific nature of the curriculum for Number &
Computation allows for little variety of interpretation: what is not apparent from the above statement but becomes clear in textbook
analysis and in classroom observation is the extent to which Number
and Computation dominates the first grade mathematics curriculum,
accounting for perhaps 80 per cent of lessons. This emphasis on the
development of numerical understanding and competency in calculation establishes a firm foundation on which the more complex and
later concepts of mathematics may be laid.

In contrast, in England the Key Stage 1 'Programme of Study' contains
three elements or 'Attainment Targets', namely:

* Using and Applying Mathematics;
* Number
* Shape, Space and Measures.

The 1995 National Curriculum included the following on the topic of
'Number':
1. Pupils should be given opportunities to:
a. develop flexible methods of working with number, orally, and mentally;
b. encounter numbers greater than 1000;
c. use a variety of practical resources and contexts;
d. use calculators both as a means to explore number and as a tool for
calculating with realistic data, e.g. numbers with several digits;
e. record in a variety of ways, including ways that relate to their mental work;
f. use computer software, including a database.
There are three major differences between the National Curriculum
of the two countries: firstly, in the breadth of the content, secondly, in
the degree of specificity of that content in terms of mathematical topics
and operation, and thirdly in the grade/stage for which it is stated.

The English National Curriculum (1995) appeared broader in content
than the Japanese National Curriculum, attaching more value to variety of mathematical method and the provision of opportunities for pupils

to acquire skills and experience, but did not specify precise concepts or operations with which pupils should be familiar or competent at applying. This led to a diversity of interpretation and considerable variety in the 'Schemes of Work' developed by classroom teachers as a basis for delivering the National Curriculum; a recent response by the government to this diversity has been the introduction of the National Numeracy framework. With the content of the National Curriculum applying to all the years in a Key Stage rather than for each year of schooling, there is no clear specification of the standard expected by the end of a year. It is thus difficult for a teacher to identify which children are falling behind – and without identifying them, no special help can be put in hand in order to enable them to 'catch up', nor can parents' assistance be enlisted to help with this process. Without a clear statement of the required standard, children and parents may be given a false sense of security with regard to progress achieved; assessment by the teacher of a child's progress may be in relation to a child's perceived ability rather than to an average or better level of attainment. The National Curriculum to be introduced into schools in the year 2000 (QCA, November 1999) is more detailed in terms of the content of the mathematics to be taught, but still lacks a degree of specificity comparable with that of the Japanese National Curriculum. The new curriculum continues to be stated in relation to a Key Stage, and not for each year of schooling.

The idiosyncratic nature of the National Curriculum and its administration may be observed from the fact that, on the one hand, the philosophy of English education allows pupils to 'progress at their own rate' and expects, even encourages, differential rates of development, but, on the other hand, does not explicitly allow slower learning pupils any additional time to compensate for a slower rate of development; nor are they routinely provided with any extra help or tuition to enable them to keep up or catch up with pupils progressing at a faster rate. It is possible that a ready acceptance of differential rates of development has a negative effect on standards, since it is easy then to accept that some children will fall behind, and it is consequently unreasonable to expect them to reach an 'expected' standard. Governmental policy in education, however, discourages the use of strategies to enable pupils to 'catch up': this was made explicit in the document on homework policy (DfEE, 1998g). While fully accepting that some pupils will grasp new concepts faster than others, it is surely important to ensure that slower pupils have the necessary opportunities for developing that understanding. For example, Haylock (1991, p.9), in discussing the problems of low-attaining children, suggests that some children will need far more practical work with concrete materials before progressing to abstract calculations. This view is also supported by Whitebread (1996, p.28) and Anghileri (1995).

In addition to its lack of specificity in terms of both topic content and expected levels of achievement, the 1995 National Curriculum may also be criticised for the inappropriateness of some of the items included. For example, it is by no means certain or desirable that the majority of pupils at Key Stage 1 should experience numbers greater than 1000 – in the observed practice of other arguably more successful countries in the teaching of mathematics, it is more important to concentrate in the early years on the significance of numbers *up to* 1000, and to leave discussion of the meaning of large numbers to a later developmental stage.[12] It is significant that in the new National Curriculum for mathematics, to be introduced into schools in the year 2000, numbers over 1000 have been omitted from the Key Stage 1 curriculum. It must be remembered that children in Key Stage 1 will be no older than seven – and in many other countries would be in only the first year of formal schooling. Observation of pupils in English classes indicated that significant numbers of pupils experienced difficulty with the concept of 'place value' in numbers with only two digits; three- and four-digit numbers would be expected to present greater difficulty. This observation is supported by the analysis of answers by English children to the objective written test in this study. Concern over the general weakness of understanding of 'place value' led to a more detailed examination of the teaching approach to the topic; this is included in Chapter 8.

The issue of calculator use by young children is not a central concern of this study. The questions of at what stage and in what ways children should use calculating tools, however, arouse strong feelings among teachers and educationists, and evidence may be produced to support rival views. Supporters in England of early use of calculators refer to the CAN project which found that mathematics standards improved among young children using calculators (Duffin, 1994), although it has not been established that such improvements are maintained in the longer term. Research by Professor Ruthven (1997, 1998) suggested that a 'calculator aware' approach from an early age could encourage pupils to develop informal methods of calculation although he does point out that "the

---

[12] See, for example, some of the mathematics schemes in use in Switzerland and some parts of Germany, such as *Mathematik* (Hohl, 1994-6) in the Canton of Zürich and *Denken und Rechnen* in Baden-Württemberg (Palzkill *et al.*, 1994).

more important feature of this curriculum may have been its active promotion of mental calculation rather than its distinctive pattern of
calculator use". Others express concern that encouraging the use of calculators by young children may introduce a dependency and restrict the
development of mental fluency and flexibility (Mullis *et al.*, 1997) and
suggest the following reasons:

- young children performing basic calculations with small numbers
  need a visual, concrete representation (Ginsberg, 1983) and the
  abstract symbolic form on the calculator screen means little to young
  children;
- while recognising that calculators are a significant aid in performing calculations involving large numbers or complex procedures,
  these calculations may be inappropriate for young children who need
  to develop confidence with simple procedures and numbers within
  their understanding;
- young children must grasp the logical structure of number (Nunes
  and Bryant, 1996) and using a calculator will not help this because
  the nature of the calculation *procedure* is entirely concealed with an
  electronic calculator;
- the 'magical' nature of calculators encourages children to have a total confidence in whatever appears on a calculator, and does not
  encourage self-checking;
- children need plenty of mental practice with numerical calculations
  in order to consolidate conceptual understanding and develop procedural competence (Geary, 1994);
- only through repeated practice and using a variety of methods will
  children develop confidence in using strategies for mental calculations which involve applying understanding of the structure of
  number. This has been observed to be a particular shortcoming of
  English children, who are likely to move straight from a counting
  strategy (involving fingers or a number line) to using a calculator
  (Bierhoff, 1996). This particular point is discussed in more detail in
  Chapter 8 in relation to mental strategies in subtraction calculations.

Recent recommendations by the Numeracy Task Force (DfEE, 1998a) that
children below the age of 8 should not normally use calculators in school[13]

---

[13] This, however, was met with opposition from some practising teachers attending a
conference to discuss the report in May 1998.

were given greater force by the governmental statement in January 1999. The National Numeracy Strategy recommends that all children in Key Stage 2 should learn how to use a calculator, although the importance of checking approximate answers mentally is also emphasised.

In Japan, use of calculators by young children in the classroom is not an issue, partly because calculating aids have not, traditionally, been of the calculator variety, and partly because greater value is placed on mental fluency and flexibility. The *soroban* which is the Japanese equivalent of an abacus was until relatively recently used as a matter of standard practice in all elementary schools. The *soroban* is arguably of much greater value than a calculator in helping young children with their calculating skills. For example, the process of addition or subtraction must be fully understood in order to use a *soroban* effectively, which then continually reinforces understanding of number structure. The process involves the moving of concrete objects or counters, and the *soroban* user is involved and in control of the computational process in a way that a calculator user is not. In contrast, the 'magical' nature of calculators renders understanding of number structure and procedural competence unnecessary and irrelevant. If children fail, through their dependence on calculators, to grasp the *logical* nature of number structure and mathematical processes at an early stage, there are serious consequential difficulties for later understanding of more complex concepts.

It is also argued here that the recommendation for young children during the Key Stage 1 years to use computer software, including a data base, is inappropriate for several reasons. First, there is evidence from a number of sources that young children develop understanding of mathematics through interaction with teachers and other pupils and the use of language (Galton, 1983; Geary, 1994; Anghileri, 1995). Secondly, much of the available software requires a degree of literacy not possessed by young children.[14] Thirdly, from a study of the available software for the learning of mathematics at Key Stage 1, it would appear that much of the software has been designed by computer experts who lack an appropriate level of understanding of children's development of mathematical concepts and processes. Much of the software encourages the use of

---

[14] In many primary classrooms in England individual children have been observed sitting in front of a computer, but lacking the necessary skills either to read instructions or to comprehend the meaning. Some were observed to resort to randomly pressing keys until by chance the correct one was selected and the program moved on; such a technique is thought unlikely to benefit mathematical development.

'guessing' as a strategy for finding the correct solution: this could dam-age children's perception of mathematics as an accurate, precise subject built on a logical structure. Fourthly, studies suggest that although Eng-lish classrooms are well-equipped with computers, these are frequently not used as effectively as possible (Lovegrove and Wiltshire, 1997).

It is also clear that the way in which computers are used by children in Years 2 and 3 varies between and within schools, depending on, *inter alia*, the availability of hard- and soft-ware, timetabling restrictions, at-titudes and personal competences of teachers. This is a further example of the lack of consistency of opportunity for children that characterises the English educational system.

In summary, it appears that the curriculum in Japan benefits from greater specification and greater precision, associated with the greater degree of central control exerted by *Monbushō* over the educational sys-tem. Relatively little deviation is permitted in Japan in comparison to the curriculum and textbook materials in England, where the advantages of greater flexibility must be weighed against the greater burden on the class teacher in interpreting the curriculum producing the detailed scheme of work, and producing the teaching materials. Greater variation in inter-preting the National Curriculum may also contribute to the greater diversity of pupil progress and levels of attainment which characterise the teaching of mathematics in England. While the greater flexibility may be helpful for higher attaining pupils, it may encourage slower children to fall behind, while providing little in the way of a 'safety net' for a catch-ing up process.

Textbooks and other teaching materials: the process

The greater degree of state control of the educational system in Japan is also apparent in the publication and use of textbooks. After receiving ap-plications from the publishers, *Monbushō* consults its team of education specialists on the Textbook Authorization and Research Council and takes decisions regarding the recommendation of suitable textbooks to the Minister for approval. Once textbooks are approved by the Minis-ter, lists are distributed to schools through the prefectural boards of education, who, in the case of schools in the public sector, decide (usu-ally after consultation with teachers although any views expressed by teachers may be ignored) which of the textbooks on the (short) approved list are to be used in schools the following year (*Monbushō*, 1994). The textbook series of a particular curricular subject, such as mathematics, will apply to all years of elementary schooling, and will normally be unchanged for at least five years. In the case of elementary school mathematics, two main series of textbooks currently predominate: the most common one being the series '*Atarashii Sansū*' (New Arithmetic) and the other being '*Sansū*' (Arithmetic). Of the three fieldwork schools in Tokyo (each in a different administrative area), two used the mathematics series '*Sansū*' and one used '*Atarashii Sansū*'. An earlier edition of '*Atarashii Sansū*' has already been the subject of some analysis and comparison with available American elementary school textbooks (Stevenson & Bartsch, 1992). This study focuses analysis on the content of '*Sansū*' but also includes examples drawn from '*Atarashii Sansū*'.

The tight control which *Monbushō* exerts over the publication of textbooks may be compared with the situation existing in England. Each of the major educational publishing houses produces a series of mathematics textbooks for use in primary schools, having commissioned (a) particular author(s) to produce the textbook materials to an agreed structure. Advertising material will then be sent to schools, teachers' centres, inspectors, and others concerned with the purchase of textbook materials; this is often followed up by a sales representative visiting schools in order that teachers may see inspection copies of new textbooks. Thus a school has freedom of choice with regard to the teaching materials used, and also there is a much greater range from which to choose. Heads and teachers choosing one of the many published mathematics schemes or text book series may supplement this with additional material from other schemes, and by worksheets and other materials produced by individual class teachers. The extent to which a new teaching scheme is piloted or tested before its market launch is variable. Equally, it is not common for teachers to have the opportunity to 'trial' a new scheme in their classes before purchasing the new scheme, and many may have insufficient opportunity to study it in detail. The lack of any rigorous trialling of new textbooks, together with a lack of opportunity for teachers to study textbooks in detail, results occasionally in a mistaken choice of textbooks – perhaps influenced by the 'glossy' appearance of the textbook on offer.

To many teachers in England, the Japanese system of textbook approval represents an undesirable level of external control, and, indeed, in Japan, many teachers may privately be critical of the existing arrangements: yet the meticulous examination of teaching material prior to governmental approval appears to result in carefully planned and logically sequenced textbooks. In England, mathematics schemes are produced under commercial pressures: it is not obvious that they can rely on evolutionary long-term testing and improvement which, to some extent, accompany an officially approved text. Moreover, whereas in Japan, each pupil will have his/her copy of the current textbook, in England, with a more individualised approach to learning, a number of textbooks will be available and used in a particular primary classroom: children will be directed to specific sections or pages of textbooks that accord with their progress through the 'scheme of work'. It is thus very unlikely that within a classroom there will be a sufficient quantity of any one textbook to enable each child to have a copy.

The nature of teaching materials

One of the many questions to be considered in relation to the difference in performance of English and Japanese pupils in mathematics is whether the teaching materials available for use by Japanese teachers are superior to those available to English teachers, and, if so, whether improving existing teaching materials would enable English teachers to teach more effectively. Weinert *et al.* (1989) have argued, following Waxman and Walberg (1982) and Fraser *et al.* (1987), that quality of instruction is a key factor in effective teaching. In this section, the content, structure, format and usefulness of published materials are considered, and the extent to which they are likely to improve teachers' knowledge and ability in teaching.

The *diversity* of textbooks available to practising teachers in England and often apparent within classrooms is a consequence of the 'free' uncontrolled nature of the publication process, and is an example of the diversity of educational provision characterising the English system. Whereas only one set of mathematics materials will be chosen and available to each elementary school in Japan, in England each primary school will normally possess sets of a number of different mathematics schemes, and teachers will draw on material relating to different topics within the curriculum as they feel appropriate for their pupils, often on an individual basis. Materials from the following series were observed in use in the fieldwork schools, and the schools had access to most of these schemes:

Ginn Maths (Hollands, R.,1993; Cambridge University Press)
Primary Mathematics (Scottish Primary Mathematics Group (SPMG)
Stage 1 (1988); *Stage 2* (1987) (Heinemann Educational)

Cambridge Mathematics (Edwards, R. *et al.*, 1995; Cambridge University Press)
Nelson Mathematics New Edition – Towards Level 1–5 (1995-6; Thomas Nelson & Sons)
HBJ Mathematics (1995; Harcourt Brace Jovanovich)
Peak Mathematics (Brighouse , A.,1981; London; Thomas Nelson & Sons)
Steps Mathematics Level 1–5 (Woodman, A., 1995; Collins Educational).

Each of the series develops its own approach to the learning and sequencing of mathematical topics: in contrast to the content of the two series in Japan, there is little in the way of agreement on sequencing of topics, or the best way of introducing new mathematical concepts. It is thus not easy to make generalised comments on the content of the textbooks available in England. The scheme which appeared to be used most frequently in the lessons for Years 2 and 3 classes in the fieldwork schools was *Ginn Maths* (1993 edition). Informal discussion with all the teachers of the classes observed in the fieldwork indicated that of the mathematics schemes currently available, this was the one preferred. Personal observation of schemes used in primary schools in other areas of England supports the view that this is a popular and widely used scheme: it is the one chosen, therefore, to form the basis of the detailed following comparison with the Japanese scheme '*Sansū*'.

With the Japanese series '*Sansū*', the content of the textbook for use with the first grade pupil, translates the content of the prescribed curriculum very carefully, step-by-step into logically sequenced chapters. The 15 chapters of '*Sansū*' are arranged as follows:

1. Introduction to numbers up to 10; counting, writing (including 0), ordering.
2. Joining and separating numbers up to 10.
3. Ordinal numbers up to 10.
4. Addition up to 10.
5. Subtraction up to 10.
6. Introduction to numbers up to 20.
7. Shapes and solids.
8. Comparing lengths, capacity area.
9. Combined addition and subtraction with numbers up to 10 (e.g. 10 – 8 + 5).

10. Addition (U + U) crossing the tens boundary (9 + 6).
11. Subtraction (TU – U) up to 20 crossing the tens boundary.
12. Larger numbers up to 100; addition and subtraction; 100-square; ordering up to 100.
13. Time: analogue and digital.
14. Making pictures with triangles; shape and space.
15. Review.

Although the content of the 15 chapters described above suggests that about 70 per cent of time is allocated to 'number work' in fact the proportion is greater, since the chapters relating to non-numerical topics tend to be shorter and to contain less in the way of pupil tasks. The above list of chapter topics does indicate, however, the logical development of progress through the curriculum, and the careful coverage of all required topics by all the pupils in a particular class. It is not possible, due to the highly individualised nature of pupils' schemes of work in England, to describe in a similar way the work that will be covered by pupils aged six. It is now widely accepted that Attainment Level 2 is expected to be within the capability of the average child at the end of Key Stage 1, and so a very general indication of topics normally covered may be obtained from examination of the content of Levels 1 and 2 Attainment Target: Number – as follows;

Level 1
Pupils count, order, add and subtract numbers when solving problems involving up to 10 objects. They read and write the numbers involved. Pupils recognise and make repeating patterns, counting the number of each object in each repeat.
Level 2
Pupils count sets of objects reliably, and use mental recall of addition and subtraction facts up to 10. They have begun to understand the place value of each digit in a number and use this to order numbers up to 100. They choose the appropriate operation when solving addition and subtraction problems. They identify and use halves and quarters, such as half of a rectangle or a quarter of eight objects. They recognise sequences of numbers, including odd and even numbers.   (DFE, 1995, p.25)

The lack of sequencing of topics becomes apparent when compared with the Japanese curriculum specified earlier – this for example, required children to develop an understanding of numbers up to 20, whereas the English curriculum ignores this intermediate stage and moves immediately to numbers up to 100. Also ignored are the vital steps involved in the stages of addition and subtraction to 'crossing the tens boundary' – if any single one of these is omitted, understanding of the essential nature of the structure of number may be affected with consequent loss of numerical competence.

Structure and format of teaching materials

Both *Ginn Maths* and '*Sansū*' schemes include teachers' resource books/ teachers' manuals, pupils' books and work sheets. *Ginn Maths* also includes 'Big Books' which are similar in format and size to 'flip charts' and are used for group demonstration, typically to a number of children seated on the 'carpet area'. In many ways the use of 'Big Books' compensates for a blackboard which is missing from many classrooms at Key Stage 1 in England.

A distinction needs to be made between pupils' textbooks and workbooks. Textbooks are those containing explanations of new concepts worked examples, and some examples for consolidation and practice by pupils, although further practice is often provided by means of supporting work sheets. Workbooks, in contrast, contain nothing by way of explanation or worked examples, but provide a quantity of examples for pupils to complete within the workbook. Whereas textbooks are used throughout the '*Sansū*' scheme, the 'Ginn' scheme uses workbooks until towards the end of the third year when a textbook approach is introduced.

The significance of the differences between the two approaches and their relationship to pedagogy is often overlooked. The textbook format is appropriate for Japanese primary classes because the whole-class approach permits the 'reading together' and discussion of the textbook explanation and worked examples. This, incidentally, improves children's reading and comprehension skills, and develops confidence in reading aloud. On the other hand, the workbook format is more consistent with the individualised approach of English teaching, but suffers from a lack of explanation. In any case, given the limited reading skills of young children, it would be inappropriate to include written explanation for reading individually.

The '*Sansū*' scheme provides one textbook to cover the mathematics curriculum for first-grade children aged six; for second-graders the curriculum is split between two books. Each book comprises 112 pages, each of full colour, with many illustrations, especially in the case of contextualised problems, and using simple language to a minimal extent. The 'Ginn' scheme includes three work books for each year, of variable length from 24 to 40 pages; a text book (60 pages) is introduced for use in the later part of Year 3. This scheme also uses colour and illustrations – these are more limited in colour range and cruder in design than those used in 'Sansū'. Both schemes include worksheets for further consolidation and practice, intended for completion on an individual basis.

Curricular content of pupils' materials

The content of *Ginn Maths* and '*Sansū*' reflect the contents of the National Curriculum for England and Japan respectively. *Sansū* 1 and *Sansū* 2 were used by the first- and second-grade pupils respectively in Japan. *Ginn Maths* 2 & 3 were used (together with materials from many other sources) by the six-and seven-year old pupils in England; for the purposes of comparing content, *Ginn Maths* 1 has also been included. Comparisons are shown in Table 5.2 below.

Although this table gives only broad topic headings, it is possible to see that by the end of '*Sansū* 2' pupils have been introduced to most of the topics included in *Ginn Maths* 1–3. This is certainly true in relation to the topics in Number (with the exception of the topic of 'fractions', which is introduced as a general concept to pupils in *Ginn Maths* Book 3, but is not introduced in Japan until the 3rd grade); in many cases, the work on Number is more rigorous and more demanding for pupils in Japan.

Structure and format of teachers' guides/manuals

The quality of the guidance proivded for teachers on the delivery of the mathematics curriculum, and the use made of that guidance, has a direct bearing on children's learning. In Japan, the teachers' manual is of crucial importance, determining the sequencing of the teaching material, the use made of the pupils' textbook, the use made of pupils' work sheets, the way topics are introduced to children, the questions asked, and the practical demonstrations made by teachers and children with

Table 5.2 *Comparison of school years in which topics are introduced: England and Japan*

	England (*Ginn Maths*)	Japan (*Sansū*)
Number	*School years*	
Classifying	1	1
One-to-one, mapping	1	1
Recognising, counting and writing numbers up to 10	1	1
Patterns	1	1
Order, ordinal numbers	1;2	1
More/less/fewer/greater/same	1	1
Addition up to 10	1;2	1
Subtraction up to 10	1;2	1
Place value up to 100	2	1
Estimation	2	–
Patterns: odd/even	2	–
Order, ordinal number up to 100	2	1
More/less up to 100	2	1
Addition up to 100	2	1
Subtraction up to 100	2	1
Place value up to 1000	3	2
Order up to 1000	3	2
Estimation	3	–
More/less	3	–
Addition up to 1000	3	2
Subtraction up to 1000	3	2
Multiplication; units by units	3	2
Fractions (half, quarter, third)	3	–
Measures		
Comparison of two measures	1	1
Time: hour and half hour	2	1
Money: 1p,2p,5p/yen	1	1
Length: cm	2	2
Length: m and cm	3	2
Weight: kg	2	2
Money; 10p, 20p/yen	2	2
Money: up to 100p/yen	3	2
Money: up to 1000p/yen	–	2
Capacity	2;3	1; 2
Time: hours and minutes	3	1; 2
Shape and Space		
Position'	1;2	1
Patterns	1;2	1
Three-dimensional shapes	3	1
Two-dimensional shapes	2;3	1
Right angles	2;3	–
Symmetry (Line)	2;3	2
Nets of cubes and cuboids	2	–
Handling data		
Classifying	1;2	–
Block graphs	2;3	2
Collecting and recording data	2.3	2
Classifying using two criteria	2;3	–
Probability	2;3	–

concrete objects. The fact that the teachers' manual is able to dominate the teaching method to such a remarkable extent, is itself a consequence of the educational aims in Japan, which relate to 'mastery learning' (Bloom, 1971). This may be defined broadly as expecting the largest number of children possible to reach the required or expected standard, and carries with it an expectation that the whole class will move forward together. With such an aim and expectation, a whole-class teaching approach is facilitated. In England, however, in contrast to a 'mastery learning' approach, the expectation is that children will achieve widely differing standards and will develop in very different rates and directions.

Teachers in England have for many years been encouraged to differentiate in their teaching according to the ability of pupils and children are typically engaged on a range of activities at different levels of difficulty. It follows that the teacher must continually adjust the teaching approach needed to meet the needs of an individual child and is thus unable to use a teachers' manual to teach a single lesson to the whole class. Indeed, it is rare for a teacher to have a personal copy of a teachers' manual; there is likely to be a single school copy and such a resource, like other teaching resources in English primary schools, is likely to be shared by all teachers. The fact that a school is likely to possess only a single copy of such a manual has marketing and publishing implications; since the number of copies sold is relatively small, it has been uneconomic for publishers to update these manuals on a regular basis.[15]

In contrast, every teacher in Japan will be provided with a copy of the appropriate teachers' manual, and will use this frequently in lesson preparation and planning; the detailed pedagogical instruction (considered in the following section) provided enables all teachers to develop pupils' understanding of mathematical concepts in carefully graded stages.

Content of teachers' manuals

Typically, a teachers' manual in Japan will follow precisely the content and structure of the pupils' textbook, with identical page numbering. Each page of the manual will include a copy (reduced in size) of the cor-

---

[15] It is too early to judge whether the publication of the more detailed framework of the National Numeracy Strategy, together with its recommendation for an element of whole-class teaching to be included in a mathematics lesson, will encourage greater use of teachers' manuals by teachers in England.

responding pupils' page, together with answers to exercises, points to be made in explanation and questions to be put to pupils. For example, in one lesson on place value to second-grade children, (see Chapter 8) the manual includes very precise instruction on the distinction that needs to be understood by all children regarding the difference between '25'and '250'; between '24' and '204', using diagrammatic equivalents of Dienes' rods, and emphasising the mathematical notation to be used and the use of zero. The topic-by-topic approach in a teacher's manual includes detailed questions to be asked by teachers of the class when introducing a new concept.

The provision of such detailed level of questioning, including different *types* or *levels* of questions, enables *all* teachers to deliver a lesson which will encourage a sound understanding of concepts. The use of questions and the expectation that pupils will provide detailed *explanations* of their reasoning allows weaker children to hear mathematical vocabulary correctly used in different contexts. Misconceptions and errors will be discussed as they arise by the whole class; teachers often ask for pupils to evaluate the response and approaches of their peers. The use of misconceptions is regarded by Japanese teachers as an important tool for learning. Weaker children, in particular, are thought to benefit from the opportunity to observe the problem solving approach of more able children, since this will enable them to increase their own repertoire of approaches.

There is no doubt that the use of such a teachers' manual affects both the nature of the preparation and lesson planning to be done by teachers and also the role of teachers within the classroom. In Japan, teachers have more time to concentrate on the delivery of the lesson, and to ensure that children are developing the appropriate understanding. In England, teachers need to spend considerable time outside the classroom in preparing a detailed scheme of work; inside the classroom their role is more of manager and facilitator with less concern for direct instruction during the developmental stage of the lesson.

The use of teachers' manuals may be seen as ensuring an adequate syllabus coverage, and standardising mathematical learning approaches. This will not eliminate variation between teachers entirely, however, since regardless of uniformity of content and teaching approaches, each teacher will bring a distinctive and individual 'gloss' to a lesson. It will, however, give teachers confidence that they are providing a sound mathematical basis for the learning of the children in their class, and enable them to question children appropriately and to encourage discussion;

many primary teachers in England lack confidence in both their own level of mathematical competence and also their ability to provide explanations of mathematical concepts to an adequate level of detail for all the children in their class.

The impact of rapid change in an educational system

Having participated in the school experience as children, every adult has a core of expectations about how teaching and learning should occur. In Japan, adults will have had a relatively uniform experience of education in terms of curriculum, teaching methods, social behaviour, school organisation and attitudes towards learning, and are thus more confident of their understanding of the educational process when their children begin to participate in it. Parents in Japan will also have had recent experience of observing their children learning the ritual-like school routines through attendance at kindergarten. Although some curricula reforms have been introduced in Japan since the reports of the National Council for Educational Reform (1987), other aspects of school life remain basically unchanged.

In contrast, the number of educational initiatives and the speed at which they have been introduced in England during the last two decades have created an atmosphere of confusion in the minds of much of the parent population – and indeed has created doubt and uncertainty among many practising teachers and education specialists – manifested in the continuing widespread lack of confidence in the educational system. In the learning of mathematics, for example, the core curriculum has undergone significant change within the last two decades, including many 'modern' topics (set theory, probability, data handling, etc.); teaching methods have changed in order to focus on investigative approaches to the learning of mathematics; and the introduction of the use of calculators has affected the value traditionally attached to the value of computational skills. Parents in England are aware that the educational system has undergone significant changes since their own experience of schooling – in terms of curricular content, nature of examinations, attitudes towards learning and teaching methods – yet lack sufficiently clear knowledge of the structure and learning patterns of the current system. As a result, parents lack confidence in their awareness and understanding of the system which inhibits their behaviour in several ways – for example, in the extent to which they feel able to assist or support their children in their learning, and also in the development of close home–school relationships. The way in which parents' feelings of inadequacy with regard to knowledge of the educational system affect their support for children's learning is often underestimated. From observation and discussion with parents of children at primary schools in England, there appears to be a considerable amount of goodwill among parents from a wide range of backgrounds to help their children in whatever way possible, yet the extent to which they are able in practice to help their children educationally appears limited. Schools must take part of the responsibility for this and should ensure that they provide parents with clear information about the learning expectations for their children and the organisational environment. Teachers also could give clearer guidelines regarding the specific help in learning that parents might provide for their children. For example, every first-grade child in Japan has his/her own set of cards containing number bonds up to 10, which can be used at home with a supportive parent to consolidate knowledge and practise factual recall. In England, however, parents' help is unlikely to be sought in a similarly specific way even though parents express willingness to do so.

At the time of writing, there are growing demands for mathematical curricular change in Japan, resulting from an awareness of the need for some greater flexibility. It is too early to judge whether any subsequent changes will be real or cosmetic, but, whatever the nature of changes made, it is to be hoped that they will result from greater levels of discussion and more sympathetic implementation than in recent years in England.

Summary

The degree of central control of curricula and teaching materials in Japan is perceived as having two major effects on the teaching of primary school mathematics: first, it encourages uniformity of educational opportunity and experience and, secondly, the provision of a sufficiently detailed scheme of work together with carefully developed teaching materials assists and supports teachers in the classroom. This provision is seen as freeing teachers from the need to develop detailed schemes and to prepare their own teaching materials, thus enabling them to pay greater attention to the delivery of the curriculum, and to show a greater level of pedagogical awareness and concern.

The responsibility of English primary school teachers includes the delivery of all ten subjects in the National Curriculum to a level and in a way that meets with the approval of head teachers, governors, Ofsted inspectors, parents, and satisfies the needs of the children themselves. The first step for any classroom teacher has been to create a detailed scheme of work for each subject for the particular year group that will meet all the necessary requirements. While this may be shared by a group of teachers, on a subject or year basis, it is a daunting task, and involves considerable replication of effort in schools across the country. The autonomy of individual teachers in England for the learning experience of their class of pupils adds to the variability of children's learning experiences between and within schools which is reflected in the variation in pupils' attainment between and within schools (Sammons *et al.*, 1995). The schemes of work devised to meet the perceived needs of the particular children at their development levels have reflected the diversity of educational provision that is apparent throughout the English educational systems and have arguably contribute to the diversity of achievement among pupils. It may well be that the workload of teachers in this respect has been reduced by the provision of a National Numeracy Strategy; it is too early to anticipate what effect, if any, that may have on reducing variation in pupils' learning experiences and on subsequent attainment.

In Japan elementary school teachers will, like primary teachers in England, be 'generalist' teachers and responsible for almost all subjects across the curriculum (the exception in both countries is music where specialist teachers are likely to be involved to some extent), yet the way that the curriculum is specified in a more detailed way for each grade and each subject means that teachers do not need to create detailed schemes of work. This is seen as having a standardising effect on teaching, avoiding expensive replication of teacher effort, and saving valuable teacher time which may be put to better use in, for example, planning lesson delivery.

In Japan, while the use of approved textbooks may be perceived as discouraging teachers' creativity and initiative, it seems clear that the use of a carefully sequenced and trialled textbook series produces a logical coherence and a step-by-step approach to mathematics teaching that may be lacking from the more topic based approach in England. It is also worth noting that if all schools within an area are using the same textbook series, the transition for pupils needing to move schools is less difficult. It is estimated that currently about 10 per cent of primary school pupils in

England move schools each year, and it is thought unlikely that this will decrease in the future.

Textbooks are supported in Japan by teachers' manuals which give a topic-by-topic and page-by-page analysis of the curriculum, outlining the conceptual processes involved in the learning of the children and identifying what questions need to be asked in order to develop a secure understanding. These teachers' manuals are seen as being a key factor in maintaining quality of teaching, by supporting weaker teachers and at the same time developing pedagogical knowledge of cognitive development in the process of mathematical understanding.

Teachers in Japan need to make fewer pedagogical decisions in order to interpret the National Curriculum and then also enjoy the benefit of greater support from the published materials. The effect of these major differences between English and Japanese educational systems in relation to curriculum and learning materials is to reduce the possibility for variation in the learning experience of children in Japan, but to allow it to increase in England. The way that this diversity of learning experience is further increased by the different approaches to teaching and pedagogy is discussed in Chapter 6.

6

Models of children's development and approaches to pedagogy

Introduction

We know that the way in which children develop mathematical knowledge is complex and that this involves a number of separate and distinct abilities. We also know that a significant proportion of children experience difficulty in developing conceptual understanding and procedural competency in mathematics. We need to understand the way in which children move forward in their learning; how they build on their existing knowledge; and how the use of language helps them. Placing the contrasting approaches to children's learning (as observed in classes in England and Japan), within the context of theories of children's development, enables us to appreciate the nature of effective pedagogy that improves progress in learning.

First, however, in order to understand the process of acquiring mathematics understanding and skills we need to draw together two strands of research which are frequently considered separately. On the one hand we have a considerable body of work involving theories of children's learning and development, dominated in the West by the work of Piaget and, more recently, by that of Vygotsky. The other strand of research has focused on the mathematical processes themselves and in detailing the underlying structure of mathematics. Yet in the learning of mathematics, where children commonly find the linking of conceptual and procedural knowledge less than straightforward in developing an understanding of the logical structure of number, we need to appreciate both these aspects and the relationship between them in order to gain insight into children's progress in mathematics.

122

Secondly, it is proposed that there are differences between England and Japan in the attitudes of teachers and educationists regarding pedagogy, and that these differences affect the choice of teaching methods and the nature of classroom practice. Whereas in Japan the concept of pedagogy is perceived as central to effective teaching and learning, in England the term pedagogy has been unfashionable for many years. The reasons for the lack of a pedagogical model in England and the effect of this lack on children's learning is examined.

Thirdly, this chapter considers evidence from research studies relating to instructional variables associated with effective teaching. We need to examine the levels of pedagogical and subject knowledge and to consider how theoretical knowledge is translated into a practical teaching model. Finally, some practical examples observed in the classrooms in England and Japan regarding activities designed to promote mathematical learning are provided in order to illustrate the different approaches to teaching and learning.

Models of early childhood development

Theories of cognitive development and learning may be regarded as falling into one of three categories which are briefly summarised:

(i) *the transmission model* which proposes that teaching is the major force in promoting development, and that cognitive development may be seen as following teaching. This approach was reflected in the didactic style of teaching that could be seen in many primary classrooms in England before the publication of the Plowden Report (1967). This model also represents the stereotypical perception of Japanese education, in which children's learning is seen as directed and tightly controlled by teachers.

(ii) *the constructivist model* which proposes that teaching should follow development, and that a child should have reached a certain level of developmental maturity before the teaching process should start. This view, which links development more to the maturing of the brain than to the effects of teaching, is ascribed to Piaget (*inter alia*).

(iii) *the compromise model* which proposes that cognitive development results partly from maturation and partly from teaching. The extent to which maturation and teaching are thought to contribute to development varies with the particular theory of learning. The work of Vygotsky, which also emphasised the importance of the use of language in learning, is included in this category.

The approach of the first model, in which the teacher is perceived as *transmitting* knowledge and controlling the rate and direction of children's learning was, to a great extent, superseded by the acceptance and adoption of a Piagetian *constructivist* model, which emphasises the maturing of the brain and experience in the environment rather than teaching. As outlined in Chapter 1, ideas on cognitive development in the last fifty years have been greatly influenced by the work of Piaget (Piaget, 1941; 1965; 1969). Piagetian theory had a significant effect on all areas of educational thought, but especially on mathematics education, partly because much of his research was concerned with understanding how children construct mathematical ideas for themselves, but also because earlier theories such as those of Thorndike (1924) and Brownell (1935) had paid sparse attention to children's constructions of understanding.

During the 1960s, the ideas of Piaget gained considerable ground and influence with educationists. A major contribution was to identify the basic concepts underlying much of the teaching of mathematics in the early years of schooling, such as conservation, transitivity, and class inclusion, which are sometimes described as 'Piagetian logical operations'. From his detailed observational studies of young children, Piaget identified four distinct stages of development among children:

(i)   the sensorimotor stage (birth to 2 years);
(ii) the pre-operational stage (2 to 7 years);
(iii) the concrete-operational stage (7 to 11 years);
(iv) the formal-operational stage (beyond the 11th year).

He argued that the order of these stages was invariant and that all children progress through them in a cumulative way, building on the previous stage and preparing for the next stage. This study is concerned with the third stage and, according to Piaget, at the beginning of this stage, a child still needs to use concrete objects in his/her concept of change. S/he uses concrete materials to create mental structures (operations) that allow him/her mentally to combine (change) objects, but has difficulty in combining two or more mental operations. In this stage, children need to deal with concrete facts and materials rather than with hypothetical propositions; it is not normally until the age of 11 or 12 that a child is capable of completely abstract thought. Piaget argued that the child moving towards abstract thought begins to construct a version of reality and that in terms of mathematical development s/he begins to construct mental mathematical structures and processes. Although each of the four stages may be defined by a particular structure of thinking, development is a continuous process, and Piaget's work on understanding the way in which children make gradual progress from the early phase of one stage to the later phase of that stage and on to the next stage has had great influence.

Piaget's second main proposition was that the child is an active participant in his/her learning and that activity and experience facilitate development. This approach to learning – often mistakenly labelled as 'learning through discovery' – has influenced much of the early years' curriculum and practice in England since 1960.

The Plowden Report (Plowden, *op.cit.*), as already mentioned in Chapter 4, was greatly influenced by the work of Piaget and observed the need, especially at primary school level, to accommodate the different ways and rates at which children mature and develop cognitively. It also emphasised the importance of 'child-centred' learning in which the needs of the individual child are the paramount focus. This Report, which had a fundamental and long-lasting effect on teaching approaches and classroom practice in primary school education in England, influenced educationists and teachers to continue the trend away from a whole-class teaching approach towards one in which children worked in small groups or on individualised schemes of learning.[1] In order to accommodate this approach, classrooms changed in appearance with desks – or, increasingly, tables – being arranged in groups of four or six, with children seated to face inwards towards each other, and away from the teacher or the blackboard. By the mid-1970s, it was rare for any primary classroom to retain the earlier more formalised arrangements of desks 'two-by-two'. As whole-class teaching became increasingly educationally and politically unacceptable, the concept of children needing to face the teacher or to be able to see the blackboard became irrelevant. Existing blackboards were frequently removed – especially from infant classrooms –

---

[1] Para. 754 in the Plowden report stated that 'In the last 20 years, schools have provided far more individual work, as they have increasingly realised how much children of the same age differ in their powers of perception and imagery, in their interests and in their span of concentration. When children first come to school they learn most effectively if they choose what they do from amongst a range of materials carefully selected by their teachers.'

and, in many cases, were not fitted to new classrooms. Through the 1970s and 1980s, many primary schools used an 'integrated day', with groups of children within a class simultaneously being engaged on a number of activities associated with different parts of the curriculum. It was common to find, at any one time, one group of children engaged on mathematics, another on handwork, another on 'creative writing' and another on 'topic work' that might involve a combination of history, geography and awareness of the environment.

Underpinning the classroom practice of this period was the assumption that children should be encouraged to be in control of their own learning; that the role of the teacher was as manager/administrator/facilitator/ adviser, and that children's natural curiosity and delight in discovery would enable them to move to the next step in their cognitive development when they were ready for it. Encouraging children to proceed to the next step more quickly than they would have done by themselves was regarded as undesirable and a potentially damaging experience for children's future cognitive development and their attitudes towards learning.

Piaget's work on the 'pre-operational stage' of children's development is also of great relevance for this study. This stage of development, which is dominated by language development, corresponds broadly to the years between three and six. It is of significance that whereas in most countries, including Japan, this period corresponds to the years of pre-schooling, in England many children begin formal schooling as they turn four, and may thus be exposed to a formal curriculum before they have reached the developmental stage at which (according to Piaget) they would benefit from it. The way in which the aims of kindergarten in Japan are more concerned with preparing children aged 4–5 years for the formal learning situation, and for developing the skills that will facilitate later learning, than with the delivery of a formal academic curriculum has been outlined in Chapter 4. This has been contrasted with the approach in England where, paradoxically, teachers appear to be under pressure to develop learning of formal skills as early as possible, regardless of a child's readiness for this. Thus while a Piagetian approach is seen to dominate educational theory in England, and children are expected to be active participants in their own learning, in practice this is in conflict with the external pressures on teachers – from parents and official educational bodies – to ensure that children's development is maximised. These conflicting messages that are conveyed to teachers may be a contributory factor in the increasingly high stress levels experienced by teachers in England during the last two decades and especially since the introduction of the National Curriculum and the associated national testing at the end of each of the Key Stages.

The 'social constructivist' model attributed to Vygotsky perhaps represents a position somewhere between the 'transmission' and 'constructivist' models. Although Vygotsky viewed children as 'active learners' in the sense that they controlled the process of constructing meaning, yet the teacher – or adult– was seen as having an important role in the learning process by helping children to make sense of their social situation and to help them to move to the next stage of their cognitive development. He argued that while some types of learning experience are acquired directly by children responding to aspects of social and physical reality, other types of learning result from interaction with adults and give children the opportunity to form general concepts that are not based on direct experience.

The Piagetian viewpoint that there are psychological structures in people's minds which explain their behaviour and are independent of their relationship to other individuals and the cultural environment was also criticised by Vygotsky who suggested that far from being internal and individualistic, cognitive abilities and capacities are formed and built up by social phenomena and interaction with the environment. He believed that: "Child logic develops only along with the growth of the child's social speech and whole experience . . All higher mental functions are internalised social relationships . . . when we turn to mental processes, their nature remains quasi-social. In their own private sphere, human beings retain the function of social interaction" (Vygotsky, 1981, p. 164). He argued that cognitive development involves the internalisation, transformation and use of routines, ideas and skills that are learned socially from more competent partners: this idea contrasts with the individualistic cognitive approach of Piaget.

Vygotsky argued that attempting to describe a child's development in terms of his/her current capability was at best simplistic and possibly misleading: "Essentially speaking, to establish child development by the level reached on the present day means to refrain from understanding child development" (Vygotsky, 1934, p.119 and that it was more appropriate and informative to assess children's capabilities in two ways; namely, their current capabilities and their future potential. The difference between the two levels, Vygotsky argued, was an indicator of what he termed 'the zone of proximal development'. Thus while Vygotsky was critical of Piagetian theory, he also criticised other approaches to teaching and learning, arguing that teaching and development, although related, are separate processes and should not be confused.

While Vygotsky's own research focused on the process of developing literacy, his ideas may be adjusted to relate to the development of numeracy: thus it may be argued that a child experiences difficulty with answering written arithmetical questions because of the need to translate the written question into an internalised mathematical structure, and that the child must be aware of his/her own internalised structure. The abilities that a child has to acquire in learning are not directly taught by the teacher; a child must become conscious of his own internalisation, but teaching, Vygotsky argued, can assist a number of developmental processes to take place that will result in learning; this led to his operationalisation of the concept of a 'zone of proximal development'. This was defined by him as: "the distance between the actual developmental level as determined by independent problem solving and the level of potential development as determined through problem solving under adult guidance or in collaboration with more capable peers" (Vygotsky *in* Cole, 1978, p. 86).

He perceived it as relating to those functions that are in the process of maturation and providing a means of understanding the process of internal development, arguing that: "What a child can do with assistance today she will be able to do by herself tomorrow" (*ibid.*, p. 87).

He insisted, however, that : "to engender a series of processes of internal development we need the correctly constructed processes of school teaching" (Vygotsky, 1934, p.134), and was, therefore, more aware of the need for the development of appropriate instruction to assist the learning process than Piaget. He criticised Piaget for giving undue emphasis to the content of children's thinking and neglecting the functional aspect. Bruner summarised Vygotsky's argument for 'scaffolding' saying that the teacher: "serves the learner as a vicarious form of consciousness until such a time as the learner is able to master his own actions through his own consciousness and control. When the child achieves that conscious control over a new function or a conceptual system, it is then that he is able to use it as a tool. Up to that point, the tutor in effect performs the critical function of "scaffolding" the learning task to make it possible for the child, in Vygotsky's world, to internalise external knowledge and convert it into a tool for conscious control" (Bruner, 1985, p.25).

Vygotsky's view was, in brief, that the two distinct forms of development – from the processes of maturation and learning – were mutually interdependent, and that cognitive development involved both maturational processes and learning through teaching. The argument that through teaching a child a specific task the child learns important structural principles which raise the child's potential for performing other activities, has important implications for teaching in the classroom.

A widely-held perception of Japanese education is that it depends on a 'transmission' form of learning, in which teachers direct and control the learning of children in the classroom. Yet observation in this study of classroom teaching in Japan suggests that, in reality, the approach is closer to Vygotskian ideas. This was demonstrated in two main ways; first, the strong emphasis given to problem solving, and secondly, the help given to children in moving them forward individually to the next stage of understanding. The first of these – the emphasis on problem solving – has been observed on by other authors, notably by Stigler who described a typical Japanese mathematics lesson as comprising: "presentation of the problem; students attempting to solve the problem on their own; class discussion about the solutions that the students came up with; and students working alone on further practice problems from the textbook."

He continued: "This sequence of activities is prototypical of the Japanese lessons we have observed. The teacher almost always begins the class by posing a problem, and the rest of the lesson is oriented to understanding and solving that problem" (Stigler *et al.,* 1996, p.221–2).

Although this description was written in relation to fifth-grade lessons, it also may be used to describe the first- and second-grade lessons observed. Pupils were asked to contribute their own thoughts and ideas, which were collected together by the teacher before any discussion or evaluation of alternative approaches took place.

Nagasaki (1998, p.8), writing about mathematics teaching says: "In order to foster mathematical ways of thinking in whole-class teaching in a mixed-ability class, instruction that appreciates students' various ideas in problem-solving has been advocated" and quotes from an earlier paper (Nagasaki & Becker, 1993) that: "Generally the teacher develops the lesson around one single objective (e.g. a topic of behavioural objective) and class activities are focused on it. The main role of the teacher is that of a guide, not a 'dispenser of knowledge'. The activities and sequence of events in a lesson are commonly organised to draw out the variety of students' thinking."

The last quote demonstrates the way in which teachers in Japan aim to move individual pupils along the continuum of development, by having a detailed knowledge of the exact point of each pupil's present understanding and his/her zone for potential development, and by using the pupil's own ideas and contributions to the lesson.

Teachers in Japan thus create a situation in which individual children who need more help in moving to the next stage of development are provided with that help – within the lesson, sometimes at the end of the lesson by means of extra, individual help from the teacher, or sometimes from home. It is recognised – even encouraged – that parents will give additional help within the home environment in enabling their children to progress to the next stage. This is possible not only because it is culturally acceptable for parents to support their children in their cognitive development, but also because parents are well-informed – by the curriculum and by the class teacher – as to the precise nature of the next stage of development to be reached and the next skill to be acquired, whether this is in the learning of mathematics, the acquisition of fine motor skills required for handwork or the co-ordination and gross motor skills required for PE.

Understanding the structure of mathematics

The second strand of research relates to understanding the structure of mathematics and the learning process involved. The application of more generalised learning theory to the development of mathematical understanding began in the 1920s with the behaviourist approach of Thorndike (1924). This was criticised in the 1930s by Brownell (1935) and others who argued that an understanding of basic mathematical concepts was a prerequisite for effective instruction and that a behaviourist approach tended to divide the curriculum into a large number of fragmented parts which might be taught separately, thus ignoring the inherent and underlying structure of the discipline of mathematics.

The structure of the discipline of mathematics was given greater consideration and focus in the theories of Ausubel (1968), Bruner (1960, 1966) and Gagné (1965). In particular, Gagné's research on task analysis helped to produce a framework for organising principles, concepts and skills involved in the foundation of mathematics. While the influence of task analysis remains important in the specification of relationships between different mathematical principles, contents and skills, the focus has broadened from that of the more restricted behaviourist objectives to include an awareness of cognitive processes, and in more recent years has been concerned with "what children actually do when they solve mathematics problems" (Romberg and Carpenter, 1986).

A theory of instruction developed by Case (1983), based on work by Pascaul-Leone (1970), concerned the limitation of the working memory in the development of mathematics. He argued that instruction should be prevented from exceeding the working memory of the pupil, chiefly by simplifying the learning strategy and breaking it down into a number of discrete steps.[2] This theory, which has been successfully applied in the teaching of a number of mathematical topics with which children are known to have difficulty, includes the following steps:

- identify the task;
- assess the strategies used by children at all levels of performance;
- order the strategies into a developmental sequence, and develop instruction on the same sequence bringing pupils from one level to the next;
- provide sufficient practice at each stage so that the procedure becomes automatic.

One obvious shortcoming of such a theory is that it may involve the teaching of strategies that are highly individualistic and thus not necessarily accessible to all children. We know that children are ingenious and innovative at developing their own strategies for problem solving, and that one individual child may have a range of sophisticated strategies for use in different situations, while another may have very primitive strategies. We need to ensure that all children have access to calculating strategies that are efficient, simple, and are widely applicable in a range of situations.

As research in the West has continued to increase understanding of children's learning, so children have increasingly been viewed as active in their own learning and not merely passive recipients (Wittrock, 1977; Steffe *et al.*, 1983). Others have suggested that children are capable of developing for themselves a great deal in the way of ingenious approaches and constructions in understanding mathematics (Resnick, 1983); that

---

[2] More recent work (Bull and Johnston, 1996) has shown that although children's arithmetical difficulties had often been attributed to a short-term memory deficit, in fact when reading ability was controlled, processing speed was the best predictor of arithmetical skill level, from which the conclusion was reached that arithmetic difficulties among young children may be attributed to a 'general speed of processing deficit' rather than to a short-term memory deficit.

they come to schools with a great deal of mathematical knowledge and understanding (Ginsburg, 1977); and that much of this mathematical knowledge that children bring with them to school is largely ignored by teachers (Aubrey, 1994b). While it is also true that children in Japan begin formal schooling with significant amounts of mathematical knowledge and understanding, teachers of first-grade children begin with the earliest concepts of the structure of number and ensure that all have grasped a fundamental understanding of this before progressing to procedural applications.

Understanding children's strategies in approaching mathematical problems is a prerequisite for developing appropriate instruction. Much can be learned about children's strategies from analysing the errors made in applying arithmetical procedures such as addition and subtraction. This is a complex and difficult process, attempted in relatively few research studies: notable contributors are mentioned here. Early pioneering work by Murray (1939), for example, on the relative difficulty of basic number facts for children in the early years of schooling, analysed the frequency of errors made in the four arithmetic operations by over 2000 children aged seven.[3] The process of subtraction is accepted as causing greater difficulty to young children than the process of addition, and the analysis of subtraction errors has been the focus of greater research interest (Brown and Burton, 1978; Clements, 1980; 1982; Brown and Van Lehn, 1982). One approach (Brown and Van Lehn, *op.cit.*) viewed errors made as analogous to pupils forgetting part of an algorithmic rule and in 'repairing' the omission creating an error. Analysis of subtraction errors was taken further by Van Lehn (1990) with his development of a generative theory of errors which suggested that some errors or 'bugs' arose from problems of memory, others from problems of interpretation and some from computation.

In general, there is now a greater realisation that mathematics instruction must take into account how the learner thinks about mathematics, and that this affects the selection and sequencing of curriculum material. The question remains, however, as to how instruction might best be designed to reflect our understanding of sequencing. "We currently know a great deal more about *how* children learn mathematics than we

---

[3] This research established, for example, the relative difficulty of single digit addition involving the digit 0; subtraction involving 9 in the subtrahend; multiplication involving 0 (except 0 x 0), and division where the quotient was 1 (e.g. 6 ÷ 6; the most difficult division of all was 1 ÷ 1).

know about how to apply this knowledge to mathematics instruction" (Romberg and Carpenter,1986, p. 859).

The importance of numeracy

It is common for the view to be advanced in England that the world of work has been so transformed by technology that 'numeracy' has become a redundant skill and that children need only to think in a broad mathematical way. But developing skill with numeracy – or procedural competence – can only progress after conceptual understanding in mathematics is secure, and testing of numerical skills is a very practical way of testing mathematical understanding (Geary, 1994). The structure of numbers is probably the first example that children meet of a logical structure which is consistent in the way in which rules are obeyed. It is important for their future understanding of the rules of logic and their ability to apply invariant rules to a wide range of different situations that children understand the fundamental structure and principles of number (Baroody, 1987a).

In order to be confident that children understand the *counting system* of number, we need to be satisfied that they understand each of the following three conditions: that counting displays the use of a one-to-one relationship; that a stable order is maintained; and that the last number counted may be used as a description of the whole. Only when these basic criteria are satisfied may it be assumed that there is any understanding of the significance of counting: we do not assume simply because we hear children reciting numbers that they understand the counting system (Gellman and Gallistel, 1978; Ginsberg, 1983). When children learn that five objects may be represented, regardless of the nature of the object, by the single character '5' they are developing a basic understanding of the symbolic, abstract representation of a type commonly used in the number system (Anghileri, 1995).

It may be argued that children in Japan have a distinct advantage over English children in the development of basic counting skills since the number-name system is regular and centred on a base-ten system. For example, 14 is heard as the equivalent of 'ten-four' and 278 as 'two-hundred-seven-ten-eight'. The likely benefit of using a regular number-name system is discussed in detail in Chapter 8 in the context of place value; it is sufficient here merely to say that the various sources of evidence together suggest that the benefit is relatively minor. We need to be clear, however, that children understand the *structure* of number in the context of place value and that the implications of using a base-ten system are fully understood. The rules of a 'base-ten' system also affect the four operations of arithmetic (Baroody, 1989). Children need to appreciate the commutative nature of the operations of addition and multiplication, and the non-commutative nature of subtraction and division. They need to appreciate the relevance of the same rules to algebraic forms[4] of the four operations. And, most importantly, they need to understand that these rules may be applied in a wide variety of situations: they need to develop the skill of analysing the nature of contextualised word problems and of recognising the category of arithmetical operation required for the solution of the problem (Geary, *op. cit.*). In some education systems, children are encouraged to create their own examples of contextualised word problems in which the solution involves the application of a specific arithmetical operation. When children are performing these tasks, they are doing far more than grasping the little bits and pieces of numerical facts; they are applying analytical skills to the solving of problems in a logical way and applying the rules of logic carefully learned. It could be argued that the use of number is unnecessary to the development of this understanding of the principles of logical thought; instead children could be presented with a more abstract generalised form of rules. This would, however, present children with a far more difficult task conceptually, since the task of manipulating a situation involving the generalised case (that is, with non-numerical symbols) requires a more sophisticated level of development than dealing with the specific case (Baroody, *et al.*, 1983; Hiebert, 1986; Schmittau, 1993).

Besides encouraging a rudimentary understanding of logical principles, the development of competency in numeracy also aids the development of other important facilities such as memory and concentration. When children are being encouraged to 'learn their number bonds' or at a slightly later stage to 'learn their tables', they are not simply learning facts which may or may not be useful to them throughout their lives, they are developing a particular type of memory facility. Research studies have established that there is often an association between difficulty with 'fact retrieval' and some memory defects (Richman, 1983, p.103). Improving

---

[4] The term 'algebraic form' is used to describe calculations or problems of the type $a + ? = b$; $? \times a = b$ etc. The more traditional use of the term 'algebraic form' to refer to problems involving letters rather than numbers is here referred to as 'generalised arithmetic'.

their facility in fact retrieval will also enable children to apply more easily and quickly the mathematical concepts they have acquired and the procedures they have learned.

Attitudes to pedagogy

It is argued that in the field of mathematics teaching there is a greater need for pedagogy than in other curricular subjects, and that the lack of a pedagogical approach to the teaching of mathematics in England effectively restricts the options that are, in practice, open to classroom teachers. In contrast to the attitude prevailing in England, an awareness of the need for mathematical pedagogy is apparent in the observation of Japanese teaching and is seen to influence teaching methods and classroom practice. The different attitudes to the need for pedagogy are paralleled by the different frameworks and theories of learning underpinning the teaching of mathematics in England and Japan. The ready acceptance of the need for pedagogy and the application of pedagogy in the teaching of mathematics is consistent with the holistic approach to educational theory and practice which characterises the Japanese model.

A pedagogical approach to learning requires an acceptance of, first, a *capacity* for learning among all human beings and, secondly, a belief that the *process* of learning is broadly similar among all types of people (Simon, 1981; Stones, 1979). The influential Committee into the Education of Young Children (Plowden, 1967) was rightly concerned to promote the learning of individual children; it did so, however, by emphasising the differences between the rate and nature of learning capabilities in children. From arguing that these differences were so fundamental that each child had a unique educational need, the conclusion was drawn that every child required a teaching approach specific to his/her needs. Primary school teachers were encouraged to pay attention to the individual learning needs of each child; this developed, however, into an expectation that each child would be provided with a carefully monitored individualised programme of learning. As teachers increasingly provided a series of individualised tasks at an appropriate level of difficulty the development of a general classroom pedagogy became marginalised and irrelevant.

In contrast, approaches to teaching and learning in Japan began from a different starting standpoint. Greater emphasis was given to the common aspects shared by people in society rather than their differences.

While differences among Japanese people in terms of ethnicity and language do exist, it may be argued that there is currently a perception of greater homogeneity in these respects than is to be found in England. It may also be argued that in terms of expectations of social behavioural standards and the holding of moral values, there is a greater degree of commonality in Japan than in England where there is little consensus over such matters. For example, the way in which pre-schooling in Japan prepares children for the experience and requirements of formal schooling assumes a common agreement on the behavioural expectations of formal schooling that does not exist in England. It is perhaps easier in Japan, therefore, for an approach to teaching to be based on what children have in common as shared experiences, rather than their individual differences – which provides the necessary underpinnings for an acceptance of pedagogy. Further, Japanese society in general – and schools in particular – demonstrates the belief that achievement is not dependent on the level of natural intelligence, rather that progress in understanding and resulting attainment results from individual efforts (Rohlen and Letendre, 1996; Shields, 1991; Cummings, 1995). The view that effort is the greatest determinant of success means that little importance can logically be attached to psychometric scores; the relative lack of interest of teachers in the IQ scores of their pupils has been commented on elsewhere (Shields, *op.cit.*). Cummings (*op.cit.*, p.129) says: "Japanese teachers are less ready to concede that there are inherent differences in ability, or even that the environments from which students come have indelible effects. They further reason that inadequate effort stems from inadequate teaching."

While testing retains an important function in Japanese education, particularly during lower and upper secondary schooling when the pressure of competition becomes apparent, it serves as an indication of children's absolute levels of attainment, which are not set in the context of their perceived levels of intelligence. Within the state *elementary* school system in Japan, there is not the competition between schools comparable to that created by the government in England with its publication of 'league tables' of National Curriculum test results and 'value-added' measurements.[5] At present there is no national system of testing at the elementary school stage in Japan, and so it is not possible to assess the

---

[5] At the upper secondary school stage, however, publication of *hensachi* test scores required for admission indicate a school's academic standing in the educational hierarchy.

extent of variation between pupils or schools. A leading Japanese educationist expressed the view that there is thought to be little difference between elementary schools; variation was thought to be greater at the level of the individual teachers.[6]

The comment by Cummings that "They [the teachers] further reason that inadequate effort stems from inadequate teaching" indicates the extent to which Japanese teachers take responsibility upon themselves for their pupils' progress: if a pupil fails to reach the expected standard, the blame is shared between the teacher, the parents and the pupil. This could scarcely provide a greater contrast with the attitude in England which expects the standards attained by pupils to vary considerably and although teachers in England demonstrate high levels of commitment to their pupils and their progress, it is rarely suggested that teachers should bear responsibility for below-average standards of some of their pupils.

In Japan, the desire to provide a relatively uniform experience for all children regardless of school location and teacher variability, combined with a belief in the qualities of effort, perseverance and self-discipline as over-riding factors in levels of individual achievement, created a climate in which the importance of pedagogical considerations were, and continue to be, appreciated. Teaching is viewed as a science or craft which can be learned, and in which teachers can continue to improve. Thus in Japan the idea of pedagogy has become central to the achievement of effective teaching and learning.

Evidence for the central role of pedagogy within the educational system in Japan is provided by, for example, the willingness of those engaged in the transmission of learning to spend time and effort in considering and discussing with others ways in which the effectiveness of teaching and learning can be increased; by sharing ideas; by participating in the giving and observing of 'demonstration lessons'; and by considering a wide range of possible approaches to improving conceptual development. In England, although in-service training (INSET) is provided by local authorities ('opted-out' schools make their own arrangements for such provision), this will frequently be provided in respect of current government initiatives, or changes to the curriculum – for example, on how to make adequate arrangements for the delivery of ICT (Information and

---

[6] From private correspondence with Dr Nagasaki, of the National Institute for Education Research, Tokyo, 1998.

Computing Technology) to each child, or on the role of school governors.[7] It is only rarely that teachers have opportunities to participate in demonstration lessons or detailed discussion of possible teaching approaches of particular mathematical topics.

The need for pedagogy in the teaching of mathematics

The development of an understanding of the structure and processes of mathematics is, it is argued, fundamentally different from the development of understanding in other disciplines. Learning in mathematics is widely accepted as being more 'cumulative' in development and acquisition than other subjects, in that a sound understanding of a particular stage or concept is a prerequisite for transition to the next stage of understanding; mathematical development, to a greater extent than elsewhere, builds upon previously acquired understanding and competence (Boden, 1977) – the analogy of building a wall, layer by layer, may be appropriate. The sequencing of topics within the mathematics curriculum is thus of particular importance. In contrast, it is possible to teach, and for pupils to acquire understanding in, other curricular subjects such as history or geography, using a topic-based approach in which topic ordering is less important. Equally, an effective teaching approach to the humanities may be regarded as analogous to completing a jigsaw, in which the frame is first fixed in place before attention is given to the remaining detail.

Another important difference in the teaching and learning of mathematics relates to the fact that whatever the level or difficulty of concept being introduced, relatively complex – and usually abstract – thought is required. It is widely accepted that children frequently experience difficulty with new and complex concepts; hence a degree of 'scaffolding' – in Vygotskian terms (Cole, 1978) – is helpful in order to move pupils forward from one stage of understanding to the next. Learning in mathematics can be greatly facilitated by the breaking down or fragmentation of a new process or operation into small individual steps which, when mastered individually, may be combined to lead gradually and cumulatively to the understanding of a new idea.

Thus the field of mathematics teaching may be in greater need of pedagogy than the teaching of other subjects which depend to a greater extent

---

[7] See, for example, INSET provided for Greater Manchester LEA.

on creativity and to a lesser extent on understanding of complex logical processes. Teachers need to have more knowledge of the science of teaching mathematics before they can begin to adapt this to the particular needs of the classroom.

Contrasting pedagogical approaches

Following the publication of the Plowden Report "which having dipped eclectically into the pluralistic, often self-contradictory field of progressive education, posited a theory of teaching which distinguished between progressive and traditional teaching practices" (Bennett, 1988, pp. 19), an 'ideal-type' progressive teacher was seen as encouraging children to be active in their learning, engaged in exploration and discovery, and interacting both with the teacher and with each other (Galton *et al.*, 1980). Teaching styles were categorised broadly into only two types, labelled severally as 'progressive-traditional', 'informal-formal', and 'didactic-exploratory'; in reality, however, such a simplistic categorisation is misleading since teaching styles may well contain a mix of different approaches.

More recent studies have tended to focus not on teaching styles but on the nature of classroom interaction; effective teachers were identified as those who used a questioning whole-class approach to teaching, in such a way that children's learning was directed and 'managed' (Galton *et al., op. cit.*). The problem remained, however, of identifying the *specific* teacher behaviour within an enquiring style which facilitated achievement and development. A further problem related to the teacher variability in effectiveness; that while some teachers using a questioning approach to teaching were effective, others were not. Thus during the 1970s and 1980s in England, there were no clear directions for teachers as to what teaching approaches encouraged achievement; the only clear message was in relation to the importance of meeting the *individual* learning needs of children.

The responsibility of primary school teachers for translating the broad, generally-stated demands of the National Curriculum into a workable practical manual, tends to create a sense of 'ownership' of the documents produced. Teachers are thus naturally more defensive of the structure and content of their lessons than they might be if an external body were to be responsible for producing the level of detail required. Teachers' self-esteem has suffered through the clear perception of the lack of public confidence in their professional skills (to which the government and HMCI have undoubtedly contributed); the sensitivity of teachers to out-side criticism is further increased by this ownership of schemes of work.

In contrast, primary school teachers in Japan have experienced less in the way of change with regard to the content of the curriculum, school organisation and teaching methods than English teachers. Even though the recommendations of the Reform Council (1987) were intended to effect wide-ranging changes on the educational system, in practice the educational system has shown a degree of resistance to significant change.[8] While primary school teachers in Japan are, like their English counterparts, to a large extent 'generalist' teachers and responsible for learning across the curriculum, they do not have the responsibility for planning the year/subject curriculum or scheme of work, since this has a higher degree of specification by *Monbushō* (*Monbushō*, 1989). This has two notable effects on the delivery of the curriculum; first, it encourages uniformity of pupil experience (which has earlier been identified as a cornerstone of the Japanese educational system) and, secondly, it frees teachers from time-consuming and worrying responsibilities, enabling them to pay greater attention to the delivery of the curriculum within the classroom and to be more aware of pedagogical concerns.

Knowledge needed for teaching

Background

Although it has long been accepted that teachers need two types of knowledge – *what* to teach and *how* to teach – in England there have been relatively few attempts to specify these with greater precision. Some educationists argued that teaching was an art rather than a science, and

---

[8] Although the Reform Council was established by Prime Minister Nakasone who wished for a complete overhaul of the educational system and was ambitious in his ideas for major reform, the Council failed to reach agreement on many of the substantive proposals, with the result that the reforms recommended were greatly reduced in scope. The reforms actually introduced were on an even smaller scale and were relatively slight in comparison to Nakasone's original ideas (Reform Council, 1987; Schoppa, 1991). Some small moves were made towards 'internationalisation', and a little flexibility was introduced to school organisation (for example, the frequency of Saturday schooling was reduced) and the curriculum, although there was a powerful lobby to prevent changes which were perceived as endangering standards (Lincicome, 1993; Marshall, 1994).

as such was not subject to the applications of generalised laws. The different perceptions of teaching as an art or a science were summarised by Stolurow (1965) in his now famous question "Model the master teacher or master the teaching model?" In recent years the concept of the 'master teacher' has influenced the format of teacher-training in England to the extent that teacher-training students now spend the majority of their time in schools under the supervision of a 'mentor'– an experienced teacher who has a similar role in training to that of the '*Meister*' in the German apprenticeship scheme of the nineteenth century (Weinert *et al.*, 1992).

But although it may be possible to perceive teaching as an art form, yet teachers need, first of all, detailed knowledge of the science of teaching. Research demonstrates that teaching expertise increases with experience; experienced teachers are able to perceive the structural aspects of a classroom teaching problem more readily than novices, and to be flexible in the solutions they apply. They are able to draw on a broad base of knowledge both for advance planning and preparation of lessons and to adapt as and when demanded by the situation (Leinhardt and Greeno, 1986). Experienced and effective teachers demonstrate not only a high level of subject matter knowledge – what to teach – but also procedural instructional knowledge which requires long-term training (Berliner, 1992). The knowledge possessed by experienced, effective or 'expert' teachers has been analysed and categorised into four areas by Weinert and Lingelbach (1995) as follows:

- subject-matter knowledge;
- instructional knowledge;
- diagnostic knowledge;
- management knowledge.

and is given separate consideration below.

Subject-matter knowledge

This refers to the content of the knowledge to be taught; however, it also needs to be readily available and accessible in a well-organised form (Grossman *et al.*, 1989). Teachers who do not themselves fully understand a particular topic within the curriculum will not be able to identify or help with pupils' misconceptions or misunderstandings, nor will they be able to assess the extent of pupils' learning and progress (Bennett *et al.*, 1984). This is of particular relevance to the teaching of mathematics generally, since it is known that young children frequently have difficulty with understanding new and often complex concepts. There are additional reasons why it is likely to be a problem in the teaching of mathematics to young children in England; for example, only a small minority of primary school teachers in England has a mathematical qualification beyond the minimum requirement ('O' level or GCSE). Secondly, mathematics has been a notoriously unpopular subject in England for decades and it is quite acceptable to profess an inability in numeracy (or any other aspect of mathematics) that would be unthinkable in relation to literacy. Thirdly, many teachers in primary school today were themselves educated during the post-Plowden era when the emphasis was on children being in charge of their own 'discovery' learning, and are thus unlikely to have experienced any significant degree of 'active' teaching which arguably would have improved both the depth of their mathematical competence and their ability to convey the necessary sequenced steps to their pupils. Research in England has also shown that only a minority of primary school teachers feel confident in their ability to teach all subjects of the National Curriculum (Bennett and Dunne, 1989; Bennett and Carre, 1991).

In contrast, primary school teachers in Japan are likely to possess a much sounder base of subject knowledge; the educational system requires all pupils to continue with the study of mathematics throughout the years of schooling (Monbushō, 1994). Ninety-five per cent of young people now remain at school until 18 to complete upper secondary schooling (Monbushō, 1997); all intending teachers will have graduated from secondary school before proceeding to university or teacher training, and will have studied a compulsory course in basic mathematics during upper secondary schooling. By the time of the Second International Mathematics and Science Study (SIMS) it was estimated that over 50 per cent of young people in Japan reached a standard which was at least the equivalent of 'A' level Mathematics compared to approximately 10 per cent of young people in England at that time (Cresswell and Gubb, 1987). More recently, reference has been made to Japan achieving the 'double' in mathematics attainment, namely, the overwhelming majority of young people attaining a standard regarded elsewhere as 'elite' (Reynolds and Farrell, 1996). Beauchamp commented: "Perhaps most significantly, the Japanese have persuasively demonstrated that mass education does not have to be purchased with diluted standards." (Beauchamp, 1991, p.34)

The combination of significantly higher average standards in mathematics at all stages of schooling and the fact that mathematics is a subject for all pupils in full-time schooling up to the age of 18 has succeeded in producing a generation of teachers with a sound base of subject knowledge (Shimahara and Sakai, 1995).

Instructional knowledge

This includes knowledge of teaching strategies; procedural knowledge relating to structuring the curriculum and sequencing topics within it; methods for achieving instructional goals and how to choose between them; planning, monitoring and evaluating achievement; knowledge of how to adapt a prepared lesson to a particular teaching situation that might arise. Instructional knowledge is especially important for the teaching of mathematics to young children when the development of conceptual understanding is both essential and a complex process. Further, given the linearity of development and understanding in mathematics, the sequencing of topics must be organised in such a way that children are presented with only very small steps in understanding, and only those representing the next stage of their cognitive development (Rosenshine, 1979; 1987). It is all too easy for teachers to overlook the need to break down a topic into very small stages, or to fail to appreciate the number of different concepts involved (Bierhoff, 1996).

For example, it is common for children in Year 3 of primary schools in England to be faced with the calculation of two-digit addition and subtraction sums involving the application of vertical algorithms as the next step after using Dienes' rods to develop an understanding of place value up to 100. Children of a similar age in Japan, however, will be introduced more gradually to an approach involving vertical algorithms; and will be required to master each of the following stages:

U + U up to 20, not crossing the tens boundary
U + U up to 20; crossing the tens boundary
T + T up to 100
T + U up to 100
TU + T up to 100
TU + U up to 100, not crossing the tens boundary
TU + U up to 100; crossing the tens boundary
TU + TU up to 100, not crossing the tens boundary
TU + TU up to 100; crossing the tens boundary
[T=tens; U=units]

For several reasons, teachers in Japan are more likely than English teachers to possess the instructional knowledge which will enable them to break down the learning process into a number of small steps, as demonstrated above. First, they will themselves have been taught to approach calculation in a similar way; secondly, the instructional material in children's textbooks will use the same standardised approach; thirdly, the appropriate teachers' manual will provide detailed instruction for the teachers on the best way of developing conceptual understanding (see Chapter 5); and fourthly, from observation of the schools visited in Japan there appeared to be a great deal of discussion among practising teachers regarding instructional knowledge.[9]

Diagnostic knowledge

An essential ingredient of an effective teacher is his/her ability to have a specific, thorough and detailed knowledge of the abilities of every pupil in the class; his/her strengths and weaknesses as a learner; levels of attainment across the curriculum; to identify those points of difficulty in moving to the next stage of cognitive development; to be aware of misconceptions and the nature of errors made in mathematics; and to be able to provide help and support to enable any pupil to overcome his/her learning difficulties.

Fieldwork observation provided considerable evidence to support the view that English primary teachers are highly professional in the way in which detailed records are maintained on the progress of individual pupils on every aspect of each subject in the National Curriculum. Not only are detailed written records maintained, but teachers in discussion were able to specify exactly the mathematical attainment of any individual child who was the subject of discussion and relate this to his/her cognitive development. Equally, there was evidence that teachers were able to diagnose the particular learning problems of individual children, and were observed during lessons assigning them tasks which were designed to solve or lessen the problem. In spite of the diagnostic skills and careful selection by teachers, however, children appeared to make relatively

---

[9] There may well be substantial and important differences in the instructional knowledge for mathematical learning imparted to students during their period of teacher training for primary schools in England and Japan; analysis of the content of teacher training is, regrettably, beyond the scope of this study (and would require a high degree of bilingualism and biculturalism for comments of any analytical value to be made).

little progress in developing understanding. The reason for this was observed to relate to the combination of two circumstances. First, due to the highly individualised nature of learning that was the observed practice in English primary classrooms, the amount of time teachers were able to devote to children for individual interaction and explanation of the particular task was limited (Galton and Simon, 1980; Croll and Hastings, 1996). In the ORACLE project (Galton, Simon and Croll, 1980), teachers were found to spend an average of 1 minute 20 seconds interacting with each individual pupil during the lesson.

Secondly, children were observed to have difficulty in comprehending the nature of the written instruction in the mathematics textbooks or worksheets. Many children need teacher interaction and discussion to make progress in mathematical understanding (Vygotsky, 1966); the difficulty for many children was observed to be compounded by the poor reading skills and levels of concentration of the children. Children who have difficulty acquiring mathematical concepts are most in need of teacher help; many of them also have poor levels of literacy.[10]

In Japan, a major reason for favouring a whole-class teaching approach is to maximise teacher–pupil interaction and instruction time (Rohlen and Letendre, 1996). Even with a whole-class approach, teachers were observed to pay detailed attention to the progress of children on an individual basis, and to demonstrate detailed knowledge and understanding of the learning capability of each child. Teachers were careful to include weaker children in questioning, to call upon them to give oral explanations, and to demonstrate solutions to the whole class. For example, in one first-grade lesson, in which children individually demonstrated their 'subtraction stories' in booklet form, the teacher was careful to call upon children of all abilities to contribute; after showing their booklets to the class and reading their subtraction story, children were applauded. At the stage of a lesson when children were engaged on individual written consolidation and practice, teachers would be seen giving weaker children additional support, and immediately checking on their understanding.

One of the schools in Japan selected for observation had been designated the 'maths research school' in the neighbourhood, and was thus particularly concerned with effectiveness in teaching mathematics. Once

---

[10] Many children also appeared to have an inadequate or incomplete understanding of earlier mathematical concepts which would increase the chance of misconceptions at the following stages.

a term a mathematics lesson to each class was observed by all the class teachers and the school principal. Part of the preparation for such a demonstration lesson, which was taken by the regular class teacher, included careful description of the level of mathematical attainment of each pupil in the class, and the anticipated stage and nature of difficulty anticipated for each child in relation to the mathematical concepts involved in the demonstration lesson. A copy of the background information relating to each pupil in the class was provided for every observer. Every demonstration lesson was routinely recorded on video, and was the subject of extensive discussion and analysis at a staff seminar the same afternoon. During such a demonstration lesson, careful notes were made by observing teachers as to the precise progress in learning achieved by individual pupils; of particular concern was whether the topic had been presented with optimum clarity and effectiveness. It is suggested that the advantages of demonstration lessons are considerable both for teachers demonstrating and for those observing. Weaker teachers learn by observing skilful presentations by more capable or experienced teachers; demonstrating teachers benefit from the comments and suggestions of others; and, if all class teachers are routinely involved, demonstrating becomes a normal part of teaching culture (Shimahara and Sakai, 1995). The ensuing discussion concerning the explicit nature of misconceptions and misunderstanding of individual pupils helped to make all teachers more clearly aware of the problems involved in the effective teaching of mathematics, and the ways in which such problems might be successfully addressed.

This apparent contradiction in which Japanese teachers display greater knowledge of, and concern with, the developmental progress of individual children while maintaining a whole-class approach to learning is explained by the fact that due to the quality of the teaching materials available (see Chapter 5), less time and effort is needed for the preparation of the lesson to all children. In contrast, while teachers in England appear to be more concerned with progress of children on an individual basis, in reality the time and effort taken to prepare work schemes and detailed lesson plans adversely affects the attention that teachers can give to individual problems.

Classroom management knowledge

For a teacher to have the capability of being effective in the classroom a high level of knowledge regarding many aspects of classroom organisa-

Aspects of Japanese elementary school life (photographs taken by the author)

A first-grade girl outside school. She is carrying a school rucksack and a yellow school hat. School uniform is not worn (except in private schools), but since she is in her first term of schooling she has a name tag attached to her T-shirt which also gives her class number.

First-grade pupils (observed by the author) attach differently coloured magnetic counters from their individual 'sansu setto' to their own small magnetic boards, and arrange them in groups of ten.

First-grade children serving lunch to other members of their class. The servers wear white overalls and white hats. Children's individual table mats are laid out on desks in preparation for lunch.

A mother (from a rota of parents) supervising children crossing a road on their approved route to school carries a yellow flag as a warning to motorists.

A first-grade girl plays a 'pianika' which requires hand-to-eye co-ordination as well as synchronised breathing.

Each first-grade pupil grows a plant in a pot. The growth of the plants is recorded regularly.

Handwork activities include modelling in clay or 'nendo'.

All first-grade pupils are taught how to swim. These pupils are having their first lesson in the school open air swimming pool. The class teacher is in the water giving instruction.

First-grade pupils in standard P.E. kit in the sports hall. Behind them can be seen racks of balls which are used frequently in sports lessons to develop co-ordination and concentration. The hats worn by all pupils for P.E. are reversible (red/white) and are often used to denote membership of competing teams.

These two girls in the third grade are standing in front of the racks provided for the storage of outdoor shoes; here the racks are for the shoes of children in the third grade, first kumi.

A first-grade girl demonstrates her subtraction problem to the rest of her class.

A boy in the third grade demonstrates his solution to a problem that had been posed to the whole class for consideration.

A first-grade boy demonstrates a possible arrangement of 17 magnetic counters on the board.

In the playground at break time.

tion and management is required. This includes knowledge of how to maintain discipline and how to deal with inappropriate behaviour; how to minimise interruptions to teaching; how to maximise 'time on task'; how to organise teaching materials; how to arrange classroom furniture, etc. (Weinert *et al.*, 1992; Marshall, 1994).

Longitudinal research work by Weinert *et al.* (*op.cit.*) has established that the four areas of knowledge identified above were good predictors of several criteria of successful teaching. In one study in which teacher knowledge was related to mathematics achievement after one school year, the four predictors accounted for 72 per cent of the variance in achievement (Weinert and Lingelbach, 1995). Research by Helmke and Schrader (1988) suggested that in addition to the four types of theoretical knowledge that teachers needed, 'executive teacher competencies' in such aspects as supervision, control, evaluation and correction of pupil activity were also needed. Only when these 'executive' skills are exercised will teachers be able, through their successful behaviour, to translate their expert knowledge into effective instruction applied to specific goals, which is yet capable of adaptation to meeting changing situational demands. The way in which teachers' expert knowledge may be translated into effective teaching is considered later in this chapter.

There have for some years been a number of research studies concerned with investigating teacher effectiveness and its relationship with instruction. The findings of many early research studies were, however, disappointing since they were often either so general as to be self-evident or diverse and contradictory. Compare, for example, the generality of the conclusion that instruction is effective when: "learners are motivated; tasks match learners' aptitudes; learners have sufficient opportunity to match the learning task to the learning goal; learners can use external criteria to assess their progress" (Thorpe and Schmuller, 1954) with the comment that: "large class, small class, TV instruction, audio-visual methods, lecture, discussion, demonstration, team teaching, programmed instruction, authoritarian and non-authoritarian instructional procedures, etc., all appear to be equally effective methods in helping the student learn more information or simple skills." (Bloom, 1966, p. 217.)

Research evidence from these early studies was inconclusive and provided little in the way of meaningful insight. During the last twenty years, however, further research has resulted in a large number of studies which have been more tightly focused on particular aspects of classroom practice, and are thus of greater value. The findings of these studies were summarised notably by Rosenshine (1979); Romberg and Carpenter (1984) and Brophy and Good (1986). Waxman and Walberg produced a 'Review of Reviews' (1982) which compared and summarised the results of the assessments available at that date. Since then, other valuable contributions to knowledge of 'which factors contribute to effective teaching' have been made by Fraser *et al.* (1987) Mortimore *et al.* (1988); Weinert *et al.* (1989); Gipps (1992); Croll and Hastings (1996); Alexander (1995). The important work by Weinert (the Munich study), which involved a longitudinal study of pupils in fifth and sixth grades over a two-year period, investigated the impact of instructional quality and classroom management variables on cognitive and affective pupil outcomes. Instructional variables chosen for the study and for subsequent analysis were linked to the key categories identified by Brophy and Good (*op.cit.*). These in broad terms (examined in more detail in Chapter 7) may be summarised as:

- quantity and pacing of instruction;
- whole class v. small group v. individualised instruction;
- giving information;
- questioning the pupils;
- reacting to pupils' responses;
- handling of consolidation and practice (seatwork and homework).

The Munich study involved multilevel analysis of the interaction of different instructional variables; however, the partial confounding of instructional variables with contextual variables indicated that a causal modelling technique should be used in order to give a clearer identification of the effect of instruction on achievement. The effects of social and cultural influences on educational achievement were also recognised in the Munich study, and the importance of understanding the nature of these influences was stressed. The results of the complex analysis of the data from this study suggested that, if achievement is defined narrowly in terms of test results at the end of the research period, then the factors with the greatest causal effect on this (apart from pupils' achievement in the pre-test at the beginning of the research period) were clarity of instruction, use of instructional time, and individual supportive contact. The factors suggested are, however, rather broad and non-specific; for the purposes of later comparison and analysis, the descriptors used by Brophy and Good are more helpful. The categories identified by Brophy and Good are considered in greater detail in the following chapter, together with the findings of other research studies in relation to these specific categories; the classroom practices observed in Japanese and English classrooms are then considered in the context of the agreed research findings of what constitutes effective teaching practice in these identified categories.

Pupils' learning observed in mathematics lessons

The educational experience of children in Japanese and English classrooms was observed to reflect, in many ways, different attitudes to pedagogy and learning already described. A few of the major areas of observed differences are identified below, but much of the detail is provided in Chapters 7 and 8.

In the primary classrooms visited in England, for the overwhelming majority of mathematics lessons, children were seated in a group but were working individually.[11] No examples of whole-class instruction were observed to take place. This is consistent with the observations of others who have regularly visited primary classrooms in England. It would thus be reasonable to expect that much of children's learning occurred when they were working on their schemes of work. In fact, the work set for children was, in many cases, unlikely to encourage learning, being either at an undemanding level involving only repetition of known facts, or beyond the capability of the individual child. Very few activities were observed in which children were required to think in a way that would facilitate learning. Children aged six in Year 2 classes were observed working on, *inter alia*, the activities summarised in Table 6.1.

The list of activities in table 6.1 , which includes only a selection of those observed in Year 2 classrooms, perhaps serves to demonstrate not only the diversity of the range and types of activities set by teachers, but also the extensive range in terms of mathematical difficulty. Whereas some children in Year 2 were not able to count correctly using a number line or other concrete teaching aids, others were set tasks which required a conceptual understanding and competence with numbers larger than

---

[11] Professor Galton in his report on the ORACLE Study (Galton *et al.*, 1980) described children working everywhere *in* groups but not *as* groups. More recently, he has referred to the low incidence of 'genuine collaborative work' to be found in English primary classrooms, in spite of the seating arrangements being such as to benefit only this type of work (Galton, 1998).

1000 (although major misconceptions were observed with regard to number structure beyond 1000).

In many cases there was little evidence that children were making progress in mathematical understanding as a result of the activities they were set. While teachers had clearly spent considerable time and effort in planning the lesson, in preparing the organisation of the materials required for the different activities involved, and in explaining to children the nature of the activity to be performed, these preparatory efforts were not sufficient to guarantee that any actual learning subsequently occurred. Tasks were judged to be either insufficiently demanding, providing only simple repetition of previously practised activities, or were too demanding and were well beyond the reach of children without teacher assistance. From the lessons observed, the problem of setting a task at exactly the right level of mathematical difficulty which would, by providing a sufficient cognitive challenge, enable children to move to the next stage of understanding, but, at the same time, was within their reading and conceptual comprehension so that they could proceed without teacher assistance, became very apparent.

This further underlines the point previously made, namely, that given the nature of mathematical learning, in which each 'layer' of understanding must be secure before the next is laid upon it, and also the conceptual difficulty that many children have with proceeding to the next developmental stage in mathematics, the requirement for teacher assistance in explanation/demonstration/discussion is greater than in relation to mathematical learning in other areas of the primary school curriculum.

Teacher assistance in the Japanese classes visited was observed to be of a different type. While children were involved in their own learning, the decisions on learning objectives were taken by the teachers, who engaged in extensive interaction with the children to ensure that conceptual understanding occurred. Pupils participated energetically and demonstrated their enthusiasm for mathematical learning, which contrasted with the more relaxed and occasionally lethargic atmosphere of English classrooms.

For purposes of comparison, a few examples of activities observed in Japanese classrooms are given in Table 6.2. In general, all children in a class were set a common activity at any one time. Due to the way in which a whole class progressed together, and the sequencing of the textbook content, a smaller range of topics was observed than in English classrooms.

Reference has already been made to the particular complexities associated with learning in mathematics – namely, the distinctive 'linearity' of mathematical learning and development, and the fact that many children find difficulty with developing an understanding of mathematical concepts. Given these particular complexities, the problem of setting tasks at an appropriate level for children's cognitive development is especially acute for teachers in mathematics: tasks, apart from those set for purposes of reinforcement and consolidation, should be sufficiently demanding in nature to 'move children forward', but not so demanding as to be beyond children's reach.

The comparisons given above between the two systems of activities in mathematical learning, although few in number, would suggest that teachers in the Japanese system are more successful in providing activities which are, firstly, at a level commensurate with children's developmental stages and, secondly, sufficiently challenging in nature to enable children to develop further understanding of a particular mathematical area.

Summary

The foregoing brief examples have demonstrated that there are fundamental differences between English and Japanese attitudes to cognitive development and learning. In England, the approach to primary education and learning recommended by policy and educationists and practised by teachers has reflected a 'child-centred' theory of development in which a high degree of differentiated learning has been encouraged and expected. This has produced a situation in which little formal instruction in mathematics occurs, yet many children are without the skills that would enable them to learn from the activity selected for them. There is little evidence that teachers are able to translate their theoretical knowledge into a practical teaching model. Teachers have become expert class managers and are adept in drawing from a range of teaching materials in order to provide a suitable range of learning activities, yet to a large extent lack both the pedagogical knowledge and the subject knowledge of the structure and sequencing of mathematics that is necessary for effective instruction. Teachers in England have, additionally, been subjected to considerable curricular change which has added to difficulties of instruction.

Children in England who begin school with significant levels of mathematical knowledge and skills in place are able to build on this effectively and to make fast progress. Children without these skills and lacking mathematical experience, often a reflection of their home background, may not be provided with the support or instruction to enable them to develop, and may fall further behind their peers, thus widening the gap in attainment. Dore summed up the problem when writing his new introduction (1997) to 'The Diploma Disease' (which when written in 1976 was highly critical of the methods of Japanese schooling): "I was not aware when I wrote the book how much a 'child-centred' pedagogy, stressing spontaneity and pleasurable discovery as the main source of the desire to learn, however good it might be for the bright ones, could, in fact, when combined with egalitarianism and the belief that it was more important to boost a slow learner's self-confidence than to insist on standards of correctness, cheat the slow learners by depriving them of the discipline which alone can get them through the tough slog to competence." (Dore, 1997, p.xxii)

In Japan there is a greater awareness of the value of effective pedagogy. Japanese teachers are helped in their knowledge and application of pedagogy by the logically sequenced teaching materials and teachers' manuals described in Chapter 5. They are also likely to enjoy a greater level of subject knowledge than English teachers, due to the curriculum structure of high school and the consequent need to study mathematics until the final year of schooling. Although this study has established that when children in Japan begin school their mathematical skills are likely to be less than those of English children of the same age; we have also seen (in Chapter 4) that children beginning school in Japan are likely to have the necessary skills for learning in place, developed from their experience of kindergarten and the home. Teachers in Japan are able to take advantage of the learning and behavioural skills already acquired and to use their pedagogical knowledge to take children forward to the next developmental stage. This involves a detailed understanding of each child's present developmental stage. In addition, the curriculum needs to be divided up into very small individual steps, all carefully sequenced to continue in a logical developmental pattern, and for teachers to have adequate subject and pedagogical knowledge of this. The extent to which this is, first, an explicit theoretical aim and secondly, a practical reality in the two systems of primary schooling is examined in Chapter 7 on 'Teachers and their Teaching in the Classroom'.

Table 6.1 *Examples of Year 2 pupil activities observed in English classrooms*

Activity followed by Comment

1. Comparing single digit numbers for bigger/smaller; finding the total of the two numbers.
Children were unable to proceed with the work since they were not able to read the words 'bigger', 'smaller' or 'total'.

2. Throwing two dice and adding together the scores seen; recording total scores in a 'tally chart'.
This was carried out with teacher assistance and supervision; children were helped with addition. Ticks for scores in tally charts became confused since the paper used for the purpose was unlined.

3. Throwing two dice and describing orally which number was larger and which was smaller.
This activity was conducted with the help of a Special Teaching Assistant (STA).

4. Subtraction involving 'tens and units (TU – TU), with decomposition due to 'crossing the tens boundary'.
Children fell into two sharply divided groups. Either they were capable of performing all the calculations correctly or they appeared to have no concept of place value and decomposition. The children who were not able to cope with the calculations (normally not covered in Year 2 except with able children) were observed to be mainly 'off-task' throughout the time allocated to this activity, but received no teacher help since the attention of the teacher was fully engaged with other pupils.

5. Adding together single digits by combining Unifix cubes.
Children found the total of the Unifix cubes by counting all the cubes in the rod for each sum. On no occasion was any child observed to count on from either the longer (larger) or shorter (smaller) addend, nor was this approach demonstrated by the teacher to any of the children. No children displayed any knowledge of 'knowing' their number bonds. When three children were questioned individually as to the sum of 5 + 3, each gave the (correct) answer after counting all on their fingers.

6. Dienes' rods were used to develop understanding of place value; for example, 56 was shown as '5 tens and 6 units' and written as such in a table provided.
Children were able to complete this relatively undemanding activity, and appeared to have some understanding of place value, which was being reinforced and practised by this activity. On questioning, a boy volunteered that he 'knew' up to 100, but then proceeded to count '10 tens and 1 unit' as 110.

7. Adding and subtracting 10 and multiples of 10 (e.g. 7, 17, 27, 37 etc.).
Children had difficulty in reading the instructions due to poor reading skills; once the message and the process had been comprehended, most were able to answer some of the

Table 6.1 (continued)

---

questions. The example in the book said, 'This is an adding machine. 10 is added to every number' with an illustration showing '6' being 'put in' and '+ 10', and '16' emerging at the other end. More difficulties were also experienced in reading and comprehending slightly different questions later on the same page, for example: "3 + 10 = 13   13 + 10 = 23   23 + 10 = 33   Continue pattern up to 93."

---

8. Using Dienes' rods to calculate TU + TU without crossing the tens' boundary
Children had great difficulty in putting, for example 2 tens and 3 units on the board provided, followed by 4 tens and 2 units, and then counting the total number of tens and units. Apparently this was not the first occasion these children had practised this activity, but it appeared that further explanation, demonstration, discussion and practice would be required to consolidate any development in understanding of place value.

---

9. Which of three numbers is closest to a given multiple of 10? e.g. which of the numbers 157, 164, 260 is nearest to 160?
Children were especially poor at this activity, due in part to the confusing sequencing of topics within the published scheme. Since the immediately previous topic had required children to 'round to the nearest 10' (e.g. 57 to 60, 32 to 30), several children thought that both 157 and 164 were nearest to 160 as these numbers would have been rounded to 160 as the nearest multiple of 10. This demonstrated an imprecise understanding of the term 'nearest'.

---

10. Sequentially adding 10 to 1000.
Children succeeded in arriving correctly at 1090, but with the next addition of 10 wrote down '2000'. After discussion and checking with a calculator, they were able to correct it to '1100', but the next step of '1100 + 10' took them to '1200'. Mistakes from other misconceptions became apparent later when the '10' and '20' were written in the units column. Numbers greater than 1000 are conceptually too difficult for many children aged 6 – 7 years of average ability; in National Curriculum terms this is Level 3 material and would normally be encountered at Key Stage 2.

---

11. Snakes and Ladders – counting on up to 100.
Competence in 'counting on' was unreliable; one boy 'counted on' 6 from 85 and arrived at 93 (it is possible, however, that this was deliberate 'cheating', since there was no adult supervision). Children were not encouraged to use addition strategies as an alternative to counting on.

---

12. Throwing three dice and forming the largest possible number with the digits seen.
Children were able to perform this activity successfully, but were not able to 'say' the numbers correctly; one girl, for example, read '213' as 'two hundred and thirty one, which suggested that her understanding of place value might be insecure.

Table 6.1 (continued)

---

13. Finding different combinations of three digits to give a required single digit total (e.g. $5 = 3 + 1 + 1$).
While this activity was within the cognitive capability of the group of children working on this task, the inadequacy of their social behaviour prevented them from completing more than one question.

---

14. Completing algebraic forms of two-digit addition up to 10 (e.g. $? + ? = 6$).
One boy wrote: $4 + 2 = 6$, $3 + 5 = 6$. When asked how he had worked out the latter sum, he responded 'in my head'. 'How did you work it out in your head?' 'I just counted in my head'. When asked how he had worked out the '2' in the previous correctly-written sum, the response was that the teacher had written it in. He declined an invitation to try any further 'sums' since he was 'waiting for the teacher'.

---

15. Drawing shapes with a specified number of sides (3 – 8) on isometric ('dotty') paper.
Most children were able to draw a triangle and a quadrilateral correctly – some with a ruler as instructed.- but beyond that had great difficulty. It was clear from their discussion amongst themselves they lacked an accurate concept of a 'side' and had no strategy for identifying a 'side'. When subsequently 'sides' had been identified, two children were unable to count them correctly.

---

16. Addition up to 20 using a number line.
In one class where this activity was observed, children were able to perform this task adequately. In another class of children of a similar age, children were unable to use a number line correctly for the purpose of 'counting on'. In neither case were children encouraged to use any strategy other than counting. In a similar activity involving subtraction, children were not able to answer the sum '7 – 7' because '0' did not appear on the number line.

---

17. Using counters for single-digit addition.
Children used a 'count all' strategy; e.g. for '5 + 8', 5 counters were put out, then 8, and then all 13 were counted. No child was observed to use a 'count on' strategy, starting from either the larger or smaller number. There was no attempt to remember number bonds, nor to use any 'derived fact strategies'.

Table 6.2 *Examples of first- and second-grade pupil activities observed in Japanese classrooms*

Activity followed by *Comment*

First-grade

1. Visual contextualised addition up to 10

Pupils were provided with a worksheet showing a basket and were asked to draw some apples in it. They were then instructed to draw some more and the teacher discussed with them how they might write a sum to describe it (eg 'At the beginning there were 3, 2 were added later, altogether there were 5' might be written as 3 + 2 = 5). Children wrote and verbalised their own contributions on the board. One girl who wrote '1 + 45' corrected herself when she saw the other examples on the board.

---

2. Practising non-contextualised written addition with numbers up to 5

After the first contextualised question (one child meets three other children; how many altogether?) had been read aloud together, the teacher demonstrated how the solution might be written as a sum. Children then worked individually on other similar questions, involving practice only with numbers up to 5. All made progress on this activity, although the pace varied. One girl wrote 1 + 2 = 2, looked at it carefully and corrected herself. One pupil was seen counting on his fingers, others were not apparently using any concrete materials or other aids. The teacher insisted that questions be set out correctly, one figure to each square.

---

3. Writing addition stories (up to 100)

The teachers demonstrated a card she had made that opened up. The number '2' on the first page was followed by a picture of 2 red tulips on the next page; these were followed by the number '3' and a picture of 3 pink tulips. Finally, 5 tulips were shown, and the story was written in words as '2 red tulips plus 3 pink tulips makes 5 tulips'. 'Answer 5'. Making the card involved taping 2 sheets of paper together; pupils managed this without difficulty and, using their own wax crayons, made their own cards, and demonstrated them to the class towards the end of the lesson. Their cards involved a range of sums and objects. The teacher asked the other pupils not to talk while a child acted as 'teacher'. Use of correct vocabulary was stressed by the teacher.

---

4. Numbers between 10 and 20

Introduction to these numbers constitutes a distinct stage in Japan in developing understanding of number structure. After discussion of a visual demonstration on the board, pupils use the materials in their own Sansu Setto to arrange 17 cubes, stickers etc on their magnetic board. Subsequent discussion led to the fact that it is convenient to group 10 objects together. This is essential for later work on place value.

Table 6.2 (continued)

Second-grade

1. Practising subtraction: two digit numbers minus one digit numbers
39 children in the class demonstrated an ability to complete the subtraction calculations at speed and with accuracy. One child in the class had difficulty and worked very slowly (he had been observed twelve months earlier when his learning difficulties were clearly apparent). [a] This activity was provided for consolidation and practice, however, rather than progressing to a new stage of understanding or development.

2. Contextualised subtraction problems: two digits minus two digits.
The children were required to contribute oral answers to problem situations presented by the teacher to the whole class, and involved the understanding and application of 'comparison and difference'. For example, in the problem 'There are 23 pencils and 31 pencil tops; how many would be left over?' children were invited to first write the sum needed (31–23). When some children wrote it the wrong way round, the following discussion enabled children to comprehend better the nature of the problem and the mathematical approach required. (All children except one in the class of 40 were able to answer 31 – 23 correctly). All children were able to write the sum required correctly for the next problem which was 'I have 15 sheets of origami paper and I want to make 24 cranes (birds). How many more sheets of paper do I need?' It appeared that during the discussion, demonstration and explanation of the earlier example, in which the teacher and all the pupils were involved, a significant number of children had progressed to the next stage of their conceptual understanding of the nature of subtraction problems, so that they were able to distinguish accurately between the subtrahend and the minuend in a contextualised word problem. This stage is known to cause difficulty to a large proportion of children in the early years of schooling; evidence from TIMSS (Mullis et al., 1997) suggests that a significant minority of English pupils fail to appreciate this by the age of 14.

3. Introduction to the concept of measurement, using non-standard units.
The whole-class discussion, led by the teacher, focused on comparisons of distances between rabbits and a carrot, and the characteristics of suitable objects/units of measurement of these distances, leading to use of a cm. ruler. One girl experienced difficulty in cutting out the cm. ruler provided in each pupil's textbook (every pupil had a personal copy), but once this was achieved, all pupils were able to copy follow the teacher's demonstration of 'how to measure using a ruler'.

4. Place value with numbers up to 1000. [b]
Following extensive teacher demonstration and discussion of the meaning of 'hundreds, tens and units', which involved visual aids similar to Dienes' rods (also incorporating the use of distinguishing colour), the oral/verbal reading of the mathematical notation, and the use of mathematical notation to write numbers heard orally (particular attention was given to those three-digit numbers including a zero), most children were able to write

Table 6.2 (continued)

---

numbers such as 213, 204, 820, 408 etc. in correct mathematical notation. By calling on the weaker children to write the numbers on the board, the teacher was able to correct mistakes and clarify understanding before the end of the lesson. The content of this lesson related to a concept which is known to cause difficulty to children of weaker mathematical understanding, and misunderstanding persists among a proportion of children throughout their schooling (Keys et al., 1996).

Notes: (a) The boy described here was by far the weakest out of the 104 second-grade Japanese children observed. During the first period of fieldwork he had appeared unable to concentrate on the lessons, and was observed playing with pencils, turning over pages in books, attempting to distract his neighbour, and not paying attention to the development section of lessons. He lacked the fine motor skills that others of his age possessed, and was unable to form *hiragana* characters with any clarity. The teacher gave him additional help from time to time, but not at the expense of the other children in the class. In England he would have been identified as having special educational needs; would have been 'statemented' and would have received the benefit of a Special Teaching Assistant for the majority, if not all, of his time in school. During the first period of observation I was concerned that he would fall increasingly further behind as time passed, and that he would be one of the failures of the Japanese educational system. Twelve months later, by the time I returned to the class (with the same teacher), his progress had been impressive. While he had not yet attained the average standard, he was able to participate adequately in the majority of the learning activities with the rest of the class, and to take part in demonstration to the whole class. He was no longer an outsider, and was able to relate socially to the other children in a way he had been unable to do the previous year.

(b) The topic of 'place value' is discussed in greater detail in Chapter 8.

7

Teachers and their teaching in the classroom

Introduction

Education is a product of the wider context within which the classroom is set, and reflects societal values and attitudes towards learning. Yet within the framework of influences from outside the classroom, decisions taken by the teacher at the classroom level are of paramount importance in determining the educational and learning experience of each and every individual child. There is ample evidence that instructional quality affects academic achievement (Alexander, 1995), and that progress made by pupils varies considerably between schools and classes.[1] Classroom experience is of particular importance in respect of progress in mathematics which is acknowledged to be less subject to influence from social and cultural factors than progress in other areas of the curriculum (Rutter *et al.*, 1979; Mortimore *et al.*, 1988).

Evidence in relation to an effective teaching model is examined together with the variables which other research studies have identified as affecting 'what the pupil learns' within the classroom. The term 'effectiveness' in relation to teaching is very rarely defined (Croll and Hastings, 1996; Medley, 1979)[2] and in contrast to many non-educational contexts where it would have a specific definition, it is frequently used

---

[1] Analysis of the KS1 and KS2 results from the recent SATs in primary schools in England provides evidence of a remarkable degree of disparity between schools' average attainments – see paper by Marks (1998).

[2] School effectiveness is defined more frequently than effectiveness in teaching – see for example, Sammons *et al.* (1994).

in a very general way. Effectiveness in teaching is interpreted here using the broad definition proposed by Berliner, namely, that "teachers get most of their students to learn most of what they are supposed to learn" (Berliner, 1987, p.94). This definition is built on the assumption that the classroom experience of pupils affects their learning outcomes; a view supported by the range of 'process–product' research into the effect of instructional variables on pupil achievement which has already been mentioned in Chapter 6. While the degree of replication and control over entry variables required for an experimentally and statistically valid project is beyond the scope of this book, the evidence from a large number of research studies in relation to the importance of instructional variables and effective teaching helped to define the area of interest and enabled the classroom observation to be highly focused. The evidence from the written objective tests used in this study (see Chapter 3) show that Japanese children made more progress in mathematical competency (as measured by the tests) between the ages of six and seven than did English children of a similar age. While these tests provide relatively simplistic measures of attainment and progress, and take no account of many other factors (for example, whether teaching has achieved other educational or learning progress in addition to those in the intended area), they provide *prima facie* evidence to suggest that Japanese teachers are more effective in achieving mathematical development than English teachers.

If the main influence on children's mathematical learning results from decisions taken by teachers at the classroom level, we need to examine in what areas these decisions are made, and whether they are consistent with a particular teaching model. A constructivist view of learning believes that children develop conceptual structures to make sense of what they hear and see (Steffe and Gale, 1995), but although the approach provides a framework for thinking about mathematical learning it does not provide a model for teaching (Simon, 1995). If, however, we regard the function of teaching as assisting children in building their conceptual structures and helping them to increase the complexity and level of these structures, then this is consistent with a Vygotskian view of teaching (Vygotsky, 1962). The way in which teachers effectively perform this function in the teaching of mathematics is examined through consideration of classroom variables affecting the teaching of mathematics under the following headings, namely:

- management and climate of the classroom;
- teachers' attitudes towards cognitive and social development and

teaching methods used;
- teaching approaches to instruction, including strategies for calculation;
- nature and use of teaching materials;
- expectations in relation to minimum standards for all children.

Clearly each of these headings includes a number of different factors. For example, teaching approaches to instruction include:

- quantity and pacing of instruction;
- teaching methods; whole class v. small group v. individualised instruction;
- giving information; questioning the pupils; reacting to pupil responses;
- consolidation and practice (seatwork and homework).

(Brophy and Good, 1986)

Additional factors that are inter-related to teaching instruction include, for example, the emphasis given to oral work and to written consolidation; the level of interaction between teachers and pupils; and whether or not lessons tend to follow a particular format. Children's learning is also affected by the attitudes of teachers regarding the importance of developing conceptual understanding and procedural competence and by the attitudes of children themselves, as indicated by their levels of participation.

The effect of teachers' and parents' expectations on the standards achieved by children also needs to be considered, and to what extent there is a concept of a minimum acceptable standard for children's achievements. Teaching methods and forms of instruction used to promote the development of slower learning children will be compared, together with the arrangements made for children who fall behind to 'catch up' with the rest of the class, since the different arrangements affect the diversity of children's attainment.

Examination of the major factors reflecting children's mathematical development is based on fieldwork observations of classroom practice in Japan and England and is supported by discussions with teachers and other educationists in the two countries. The relative importance of the specific differences between the practices observed are broadly identified; finer detail is given in Chapter 8, where the teaching of two specific mathematics topics is examined. However, first, in order to contextualise the actions and decisions of teachers at the classroom level, we need to provide some background information on the characteristics of English and Japanese primary teachers, and to examine whether there are fundamental differences between them as professional groups that would encourage different classroom approaches.

Teachers' backgrounds and roles

All classroom teachers in England and Japan must have the appropriate level of training and qualification, although there are some differences in the nature of the educational training. In England, the majority of primary school teachers have obtained a Bachelor of Education degree[3] qualification (B.Ed.), although some will have studied their specialist subject(s) for a degree followed by a one year post-graduate certificate of education (PGCE). Teaching has been a graduate (or equivalent) profession since 1975, but some who qualified before this date hold teachers' certificates. In Japan, elementary school teachers are likely to have studied education at university for four years after graduating from high school: the remainder will have attended junior college for two years[4] (*Monbushō*, 1994). In both countries, teacher education courses include an element of teaching practice, and qualification depends on assessment or examination (Mullis *et al.*, 1997).

Primary school children are more likely to have a female teacher in England than in Japan – the proportions of pupils aged eight and nine in the TIMSS samples taught by a female teacher were 75 per cent and 61 per cent for England and Japan respectively (Mullis *op.cit.*).[5] With regard to the age distribution of teachers, it appears that there are greater proportions both of younger and older teachers, in England than in Japan, as is shown in table 7.1.

---

[3] Entrants to maintained sector nursery and primary schools in 1994 included 57 per cent with a B.Ed and 43 per cent with a PGCE qualification (Statistics of Education, Teachers, 1997, Table 7a).

[4] Chart XXXVIII in 'Education in Japan' (1994) indicates that 74 per cent of elementary school teachers had a Bachelor's degree. Another study of Japanese elementary teachers found that 68 per cent had a BA of whom 70 per cent had majored in elementary education (Stevenson *et. al.*, 1986).

[5] Other available data suggest that the difference between the predominance of female teachers in primary schools is more marked: in 1996, 80 per cent of teachers in nursery/primary schools in England were female compared with 56 per cent of elementary school teachers in Japan in 1994 (*Monbushō*, 1994; DfEE, 1998d).

Table 7.1 *Age of teachers: England and Japan*

Age of teachers (years)	England (%)	Japan (%)
less than 30	16	12
30–39	19	40
40–49	49	44
50 and over	16	11

Source: Mullis *et. al.*, 1997, Table 5.2.

Table 7.2, which relates mean scores obtained by 9-year old children (taught by these teachers) in the recent TIMSS mathematics tests to length of teaching experience of their class teachers, suggests some positive correlation between length of teaching experience and pupils' achievement.

The figures in the table, however, do not suggest that pupil achievement is a linear function of teaching experience – rather a curvilinear relationship is suggested by the Japanese data, in which effectiveness in teaching appears to decrease when teaching experience is more than twenty years. This is consistent with the research findings of Barnes (1985) and is discussed by Weinert *et al.* (1990) who suggest a number of possible reasons for this, including teacher 'burn out'.

With regard to the conditions of employment of teachers, it is notoriously difficult to make valid cross-national comparisons of salaries, first, due to the variable exchange rate (for example, during the first period of fieldwork in 1995 £1 = 130 yen; by early 1998 this had changed to £1 = 240 yen, representing an increase in the relative value of sterling of over 80 per cent), but also due to the differences in the costs of living in the two countries, and differences with regard to expectations of living standards. Available evidence suggests that there may be some slight advantage in the salary scales of Japanese teachers compared with those of English teachers: in 1992, for example, the yearly salary of an elementary school classroom teacher in Japan ranged from about £12,000 to about £27,000, according to experience, but in addition, substantial allowances may be paid for family, commuting, housing, adjustments for areas with high costs of living, and many others. These allowances could be worth the equivalent of a further £10,000 (*Monbushō*, 1994). In comparison, in England, salary scales for primary school teachers in 1994 were similar to those prevailing in Japan in 1992, and ranged from £11,600 to £31,300 (DFE, 1994a). However, the cost of living appears higher in Tokyo than in London: taking all the evidence into account (and the

Table 7.2 *Teaching experience and pupil achievement: England and Japan*

No. of years of teaching	England		Japan	
	% of teachers	Mean score of pupils	% of teachers	Mean score of pupils
up to 5	19	504	11	589
6–10	14	513	10	585
11–20	34	513	31	601
more than 20	33	521	21	596
All teachers (pupils)	100	513	100	597

Source: Mulllis *et al.*, 1997, Table 5.3.

available evidence is far from conclusive) suggests that there is not a great deal of difference between the salary levels of the teachers.

If it is correct that in terms of measurable quantities, such as age, experience, qualifications and wage levels, there are broad similarities between the occupational groups in the two countries, are there differences in aspects of the qualitative variables such as teachers' expectations, attitudes and values? While detailed consideration of these aspects lies outside the scope of this study, informal discussions with class teachers in the two countries indicated that teachers in both countries had broadly similar aspirations, priorities, and problems For example, in both countries the levels of commitment to teaching and to the progress of individual children were observed to be high; teachers' stated priorities were to help children to maximise their progress in academic attainment and also to become responsible members of society. Nothing was seen that conflicted with the view that teachers worldwide are in the classroom not for personal gain or ambition, but in order to do a worthwhile job well, and to make a small contribution to the development of the next generation.

There are, however, differences between teachers' attitudes towards their additional responsibilities (other than classroom instruction and management). For example, data from the TIMSS study show that teachers in England spend more time than teachers in Japan on administrative tasks such as marking, recording, assessment, and preparing the documentation associated with developing schemes of work (Mullis, *op.cit.*, Table 5.5). Teachers in Japan appeared to spend more time than English teachers outside lessons (during short lesson breaks, at lunchtime and sometimes at the end of the school day) in giving individual help to a few children who appeared in danger of falling behind the rest of the class, thus preventing disparity in levels of attainment from becoming embedded. The administrative burden on teachers in England is acknowledged to be considerable – especially since the introduction of the National Curriculum – and it is regrettable that one consequence of this is to reduce the time available for teachers to spend with pupils outside lessons.

Comparing the relative status of teachers within the social scale of society is, like comparing conditions of employment, problematic. It appears that the greater value attached to education by Japanese society in general enhances the status of teachers and the consequent desirability of entering the profession of teaching.[6] In earlier generations in England, teaching was perceived as a means of achieving upward social mobility for children from relatively modest backgrounds; achieving the status of schoolmaster/mistress carried with it a certain respect. Decline in the status of teachers during the last two decades has led to a situation in which the occupational group is held in low esteem both by its own members and the wider society. While teachers in England have lacked control over training courses and admission to teaching, which is an important condition for professionalisation of an occupational group (Jackson, 1970; Johnson, 1972; Whitburn, 1995a),[7] this is also true for teachers in Japan where training courses are the responsibility of *Monbushō* and admission to the profession is controlled at the prefectural level. It is possible, however, that practising teachers in Japan have enjoyed the opportunity to be closely involved with the training of teachers for a longer time than in England. Certainly the way that each of the four 'teacher training' universities in Tokyo is attached to a primary school situated on the same campus encourages a level of involvement and a close relationship between teacher training establishments and schools. While the 'mentoring' scheme introduced for the training of teachers in England in recent years transfers a great deal of the responsibility from the training institution to experienced classroom teachers, it is far from clear that those teachers appointed as 'mentors' – many of whom have a full-time teaching commitment – have the time or opportunity to provide training at an adequately detailed level (Kerry and Mayes, 1995; McIntyre and Hagger, 1996).

---

[6] One author writes that "in Japan the word 'teacher' carries a connotation of reverence and indebtedness". (Ozaki, 1978, p. 284).

[7] Progress towards the establishment of a General Teaching Council for England and Wales has been made by the Labour Government since May 1997.

One further aspect of teacher training should, however, be mentioned. This relates to the *breadth* of knowledge that is necessary for primary school teachers in both England and Japan. As generalist teachers they are required to cover the whole curriculum (the possible exception is music). Four areas of knowledge have been identified (in Chapter 6) as necessary for teaching, namely; subject matter, instructional, diagnostic and management. Clearly, the amount of time that can be devoted towards the development of subject matter knowledge in mathematics during teacher training is limited, and so teachers' mathematical knowledge is largely a reflection of the knowledge acquired during their own schooling. In England, it is a requirement for primary teachers to have gained a 'C' grade or better in GCSE Mathematics (or equivalent) but relatively few entrants to the profession are thought to have higher mathematical qualifications. While in Japan it is equally true that only a small proportion of entrants to the profession are likely to have studied mathematics as a major subject during their training (estimated to be of the order of 10 per cent), all entrants to the profession will have graduated from upper secondary school or high school, where mathematics remains a compulsory subject until the final year of schooling.[8] The level of difficulty of mathematics in the final or twelfth year of schooling in Japan has been estimated as approximating to that of current 'A' level syllabuses in England (HMI, 1991). Many entrants to elementary teacher training in Japan thus begin with significantly greater levels of mathematical competence than entrants to teacher training in England. While subject-matter knowledge is acknowledged as representing only one part of the pedagogical knowledge required, yet it must affect teachers' self-confidence in their ability to teach mathematics competently. The lower levels of subject-matter knowledge among many entrants to teacher training in England result from the comparatively early specialisation which is a characteristic of the English educational system. It could be argued that the introduction of a requirement for all intending teacher trainees to continue with the study of mathematics beyond GCSE would enhance their later teaching capability in mathematics. Such a requirement, however, would undoubtedly be unattractive to many intending teacher-trainees and could also adversely affect the supply of teachers.[9]

---

[8] Mathematics I is required for all students; other mathematics courses are optional in upper secondary school.

[9] The educational systems of many other countries require a larger number of subjects to be studied throughout schooling – often five or six are required in the final years of schooling.

Causes of differences in learning

We need, therefore, to look further than differences between the teachers themselves, in order to discover reasons for differences between progress in learning. We need to consider, for example, what is known about the relationship between what the teacher does and what the pupil learns. Much of the available evidence on this relationship – sometimes termed the 'process-product paradigm' – is reviewed by Waxman and Walberg (1982) who, on the basis of 35 variables or 'empirical indicators', constructed a 'process model of teaching' which grouped the many variables together under four broad constructs:

1. cognitive and motivational stimulation, including, teaching materials, questioning, interaction, pace and quality of instruction, teaching methods, control and structuring;
2. pupils' engagement, including length of active learning time, participation, time on task, and teacher use of time;
3. reinforcement, including practice, monitoring, diagnosis and evaluation, use of praise;
4. management and climate, including atmosphere, flexibility, classroom management, discipline, attention to pupil needs.

The authors assumed that the causal direction is from stimulation, to engagement, to reinforcement and back to stimulation, with the management and climate construct referring to the way teachers control the activities and atmosphere of the classroom and being supportive rather than direct influences on learning. While this model may have strengths in analysing the 'process' of teaching and learning, a major weakness lies in the fact that many classroom variables are inter-related with each and every one of the 'constructs'. While their review of the evidence relating to variables affecting teaching/learning has usefully informed this study, it is felt that a more relevant analysis of classroom variables is achieved by using the classification of variables outlined in the introductory section of this chapter.

Management and climate of the classroom

While the elementary school classroom in Japan is likely to reflect aspects of wider cultural and educational values, it is important to stress at the outset that many of the stereotypical perceptions of schooling in Japan were not observed in elementary schools during the periods of field-work. For example, the standard Westernised perceptions of Japanese schooling stress emphasis on rote learning, pressure of examinations, didactic-style teaching, emphasis on discipline, achievement at the expense of understanding, and general lack of creativity (Cummings, 1980). In reality, classroom observation revealed the exceptional *liveliness* of the elementary school classroom, the *active participation* of children in lessons; their response to the skilled questioning of the teachers; the willingness of the children to evaluate their own ideas, and, above all, the sheer *enthusiasm* of the children for learning. This is not to suggest that liveliness and active participation were not also to be observed among English pupils – it is simply that such characteristics came as more of a surprise in Japanese classrooms. This observation is consistent with the comments of Lee *et al.* (1996, pp.157–8) in which the stereotyped image of Japanese elementary school is reported as an "inaccurate description of what occurs today". They report that when showing videos of Japanese classrooms, viewers are surprised and shocked by the liveliness of the children and the vigour of the lessons. They observe that "Japanese elementary classrooms maintain a boisterous, engaged atmosphere while simultaneously getting children to do significant amounts of academic work".

The physical environment

Common features often shared by Japanese and English elementary schools include relatively modest standards of low-level school buildings, surrounded by a playground. In Japan, school buildings are often made of concrete, but painted a beige or sandy colour, in contrast to the brick-built English schools; playgrounds in Japan have a sandy surface rather than tarmac. The most noticeable difference on approaching a school is the relatively large size of Japanese schools, which, especially in inner-city areas, often cater for 120 or more children in each of the six years of elementary schooling, thus producing an overall size of 700–800 pupils. Primary schools of this size are rarely found in England; 'all through' primary schools which include an 'infant' as well as a 'junior department' are likely to have no more than two parallel classes in a year group. Where the local density of population in England produces three or four parallel classes in a year, a primary school will tend to have autonomous and separate 'infant' and 'junior' departments (corresponding to the years of Key Stages 1 & 2), perhaps on different sites, thus reducing the overall numbers of pupils on a single site. The Japanese schools visited, in accordance with their greater size, were likely to have three floors of classroom accommodation, with the first- and second-grade classes situated on the ground floor and thus having easy access to the playground, and with older pupils on the upper floors. In only one of the fieldwork schools in England was there an upper floor which was used for teaching purposes; the other schools were single storey buildings which had been altered as demand for places varied with the needs of the local population.

Classrooms in the fieldwork schools in Japan tended to be larger in floor area than those visited in England, commensurate with the greater average class size in Japan. The provision of other facilities showed some differences; whereas all schools visited in both countries had a large indoor area which served the dual purpose of school assemblies and sports/gymnastics lessons, these were larger in the Japanese schools, reflecting the greater number of pupils to be accommodated. Wall bars and ropes for climbing were seen in English schools but not in Japanese sports halls, which were more likely to be equipped with sufficient balls of a football type for each child in a class. These were used to practise co-ordination, precision, accuracy and control. Schools in both countries attach importance to encouraging primary school age children to learn to swim; however, whereas each of the fieldwork schools in Japan had its own outdoor swimming pool, in the English schools arrangements were made to transport pupils to local indoor swimming pools for instruction.

Before school and during the breaks, the yard or playground surrounding a Japanese school was observed to be well-used: children energetically played football, volleyball, rode uni-cycles, used climbing equipment and swings, played with skipping ropes, or ran about with friends. In contrast, children in England appeared to be less active in the playgrounds. Before the beginning of morning schooling clusters of mothers within the playground perhaps unintentionally discouraged children from playing games, but even during other breaks, English children were more likely to stand or sit about chatting with their friends than to engage in boisterous or energetic games. Occasionally a small group of boys was seen playing with a football; no girls were observed participating in this activity, or any other ball games. Supervision of children in the playground was less obvious in Japan than in England: although one responsible adult (not a teacher) was often present in the playground, s/he observed but was not seen to intervene. Teacher and other play supervisors responsi-

ble in playgrounds in England were observed to have a higher profile, and
to intervene more in pupil–pupil situations. The incidence of undesirable activities such as scuffles, verbal arguments, bullying or possessive-
ness in Japanese playgrounds appeared in observation to be rare and was
certainly less than that observed in English playgrounds. The influence
of Japanese pre-schooling in encouraging children to develop co-operative, considerate and social behaviour (*shūdan seikatsu*) may be seen in
the quality of playground interaction and the capability of children to
resolve their own difficulties.

Procedures for entering school have already been described (Chapter
4); in English schools this was formalised with teachers supervising the
'lining up' of children after a bell had been rung, and their marching in
a crocodile into school, while in Japan children were free to enter school
in their own time. In both countries, children used a side entrance rather
than the main entrance reserved for visitors: in Japan, both entrances
were likely to be more spacious than in England, accommodating shoe
racks (for visitors as well as teachers and pupils) and umbrella racks for
the rainy season. While corridors and all common areas were correspondingly larger in Japanese schools in order to accommodate the greater
number of pupils and staff, the walls were, like those of the English
schools, covered with displays of art work, poster displays, information
for parents, and hand work (Hendry, 1986a). Wall displays were also part
of the classroom culture in both countries: however, in Japanese classrooms and corridors, any display of children's artwork or handwriting was
likely to contain a sample of work from *each* child in the class, rather than,
as is common in England, selecting the *best* for display purposes. This is
consistent with different expectations; namely that in Japan all children
in a class will produce work of an expected level and quality, whereas
considerable diversity in levels and quality of achievement among children is expected in England, with the work of the 'best' or 'highest'
achieving children often being singled out for praise and display.

Classroom organisation

The arrangement of classrooms in both countries indicates careful planning by classroom teachers, yet this planning is based on differing sets of
principles and considerations (see Appendix F for examples). The larger
Japanese classroom had clearly designated separate areas around the
classroom walls for the storage of rucksacks ('*randoseru*'), mathematics
sets ('*sansū setto*'), musical instruments (often '*pianikas*' – a cross between

a keyboard instrument and a recorder), modelling sets (*'nendo'*); shoe bags, sports bags, and, at the appropriate time of year, swimming bags were hung on labelled pegs outside each classroom in the corridor. Within the large undivided classroom space, desks were arranged in 'twos' within rows, with all desks facing the large blackboard. The arrangement of desks was, however, frequently changed during the course of a school day: for example, into groups of four for activities of a handwork nature; into groups of six for lunch; or pushed back against one wall for the purpose of cleaning the room (by the children under the supervision and help of the teacher every day following lunch), and also, on occasions, for musical activities involving movement. Desks (labelled with the child's name) had a shelf underneath for the storage of textbooks, exercise books, pencils etc.; individualised cushions (which also doubled as protective 'earthquake hats')[10] were placed on chairs (also labelled).

In contrast, a classroom for six-year-old children in England was likely to be divided up by shelves to waist height into a number of separate corners: for example, the carpet area, the book corner, the handwork area, the computer corner. Tables (without storage facilities) were usually arranged in groups of four or six, with chairs facing inwards for all activities/ lessons. In several classes each child kept his/her books in a 'work box'; these were stored together on shelved units. Pencils tended to be kept in a jar on each group of tables and shared by the pupils in the group.

Many English classrooms for children at Key Stage 1 do not have a blackboard. Occasionally a flip chart was used by the teacher for demonstration to children seated on the 'carpet area' – this, however, appeared to be a relatively unsatisfactory substitute since it is far more limited as a teaching aid. Each Japanese classroom, however, had a large blackboard which was used frequently for demonstration and explanation during the development section of a lesson to the whole class. These blackboards had the added property of being magnetic; this property was used extensively in both teacher- and pupil-demonstration of concepts and examples involving magnetic concrete materials. In addition, small

---

[10] During one first grade lesson observed, an unexpected fire practice took place. On hearing the bell all the children – who had been in school a matter of weeks – immediately and silently turned their cushions inside out revealing the fire-proof nature of the material. These became 'hoods' which were tied under the chin using the ties that had previously attached the cushions to the chairs. They proceeded silently into the main playground, accompanied by the teacher who had put on her 'hard hat' from her cupboard. The whole school lined up and was addressed by the school principal on the importance of correct behaviour in such practices, before returning to lessons.

portable blackboards marked with small squares were used from time to time in teaching; these were placed on the ledge in front of the main blackboard when needed.

One aspect of teaching facilities in which English schools are clearly superior is in the provision of computing facilities, which are a requirement for every primary school. In only one of the Japanese schools visited were computing facilities available; these were provided centrally in a computer room timetabled for use by fifth- and sixth-grade pupils on a whole-class basis. While computer facilities are regularly used on an individual basis by six- and seven-year-old children in England, there were no comparable examples of Japanese children of this age using computers in schools. This finding is consistent with the evidence from the TIMSS survey which indicated that 38 per cent of primary schools in Japan had no computers, and only 22 per cent had at least 1 computer to 50 children. In England, 90 per cent of schools had a computer for each class of 30 children, and the remaining schools had 1 computer for between 30 and 50 children (Martin *et al.*, 1999, table 5.1). Another study suggested that more computers were available to pupils in England than in almost any other country, with the provision in primary schools being almost six times as great as in Japan (Lovegrove and Wiltshire, 1997).

Seating arrangements

As mentioned in the previous section, children in England are likely to conduct their mathematics lessons (in common with all other lessons) seated in informal groups: there is considerable evidence from different research studies showing that in such informal grouping the 'time on task' of children is likely to be reduced. This is discussed by Croll and Hastings who comment that: "In every reported case, children have spent a markedly greater proportion of their time actively engaged with their individual work when seated in rows than in their normal groups." (Croll and Hastings, 1996, pp. 34–5.) They go on to observe that, in the studies examined, the classes in which pupils were least 'on-task' when seated in groups gained most in terms of 'on-task' time when seated in rows, and that the between-class variation in 'on-task' time was much less for those seated in rows. It is clear that seating by rows does not encourage pupil-pupil eye-contact in the same way that seating by groups does; it is a less 'sociable' arrangement and there are fewer sources of distraction. Two studies, by Axelrod in the United States and by Wheldall in England, established that proportion of 'time on-task' decreases significantly when children are seated in groups around tables (Axelrod *et al.*, 1981; Wheldall *et al.*, 1981). These studies also demonstrated that quality of work was affected when children sat in groups. Seating around tables, it is suggested, leads to more disruption, less on-task behaviour and less desirable teaching behaviour; other seating arrangements are thought to be preferable when independent work is expected (Wheldall and Glynn, 1989).

Other studies examining the effects of seating arrangements within the classroom on time 'on-task' considered the effect of mixed-gender or same-gender seating arrangements, finding that time 'off-task' and class disruption rates decreased when children were seated in 'mixed-gender' pairs (Wheldall and Olds, 1987). This point is relevant to this study because in Japan pupils were deliberately seated by the teachers to be as far as possible in mixed-gender pairs. The precise reason for the effect described, however, is unclear – Croll and Hastings suggest that it may be due to the "discomfort of being seated next to an opposite-sex classmate" or it is "the fun of chatting with a same-sex mate that leads to less time on-task". In classes in England, seating arrangements appeared to be largely independent of gender: the grouping of children at different tables was more likely to be on the basis of perceived ability. Children of approximately similar levels of ability, according to the teachers' perception, would be seated together, thus encouraging greater differentiation of achievement, rather than the arguably more egalitarian grouping in which groups contain a mix of children of perceived levels of ability, with all groups having approximate parity in achievement. Occasionally, groups in English classrooms would be organised on the basis of friendship groups; it was observed that with this grouping, children of the same gender tended to choose to sit together.

The above research evidence relating to the effect of seating arrangements on 'time on-task' is widely recognised, yet the findings appear to have had no impact on classroom practice and organisation in England, illustrating the failure for evidence from accepted research studies to be translated into practical applications (Weinert and De Corte, 1996).

Classroom behaviour and discipline

Within the Japanese classroom, children demonstrated consistent patterns of behaviour, both in terms of social interaction and in the learning situation. It is taken for granted that there are correct procedures or rituals to be observed, from arrival at school and the changing of shoes, stacking of umbrellas and storing possessions correctly to the way in which children stand up behind their pushed-in chair to answer questions (White, 1987; Peak, 1991; Benjamin, 1997). The concept, however, that there is a 'correct' way to do things is appears to be alien to the English culture, perhaps being perceived as a denial of individual freedom and choice.

In Japan, providing opportunities for individual children to address the whole class is seen as an important part of the learning experience. Through this, children are encouraged to develop self-expression, self-confidence and a level of articulation that is important for effective communication in later life. Children in Japanese classes – even the first-grade children who had been in school for only six weeks – displayed capability in this and clear knowledge of the ritual associated with pupil-demonstration in the way in which they stood up, pushed their chair in behind their desk, walked up the side aisle to the front of the class, where they conducted their demonstration or explanation clearly and audibly. On occasions, teachers reminded children to speak in a loud voice so that all the class might hear; this is an important teaching point since it encourages children to listen to each other, and the need for the teacher to repeat the explanation is unnecessary. In contrast, English teachers were observed to repeat any answers to questions from individual pupils so that the rest of the class might hear, often amplifying or elaborating whilst doing so. This carries with it the clear message that only that which is said by the teacher is important and belittles the value of individual contributions, rendering it unimportant and unnecessary for children to listen to each other. Learning to listen to each other is a necessary part of appropriate classroom behaviour in Japan which reinforces the importance attached to the cohesion of the class or '*kumi*', and the desirability of children supporting each other and co-operating with each other in the business of learning.[11]

Standards of *expected* behaviour were not dissimilar in the two countries; teachers demonstrated a common desire to promote responsible behaviour among their pupils in which consideration for others was

---

[11] While acknowledged experts on the Japanese educational system have described the use of *han* or smaller groups within a *kumi* (Hendry, 1986a; Fuson and Kwon, 1991; White, 1993), no use of *han* was observed during either of the two periods of fieldwork in Japan which informed this study. The reason for this is unclear; it is possible that since the fieldwork was conducted at a relatively early time in the school year, the smaller groups had not at that time been constructed.

paramount. There were clearly observed differences, however, in the *actual* standards of behaviour and there was a marked contrast between the handling of behavioural difficulties which is crucial to an understanding of the different attitudes towards learning.

Within the Japanese classroom, only a few isolated incidents of children deviating from the standards of expected behaviour were recorded. In general, these were ignored by the teacher – usually another child would intervene to assist the child experiencing difficulty. This also shows the influence of Japanese pre-schooling experience during which teachers will gradually have used peer pressure to address behavioural problems and discipline. On only two occasions was a pupil (or in one case, two pupils who had been disputatious) observed being reprimanded individually by the teacher. On one other occasion a first grade girl was in tears at the beginning of a lesson (the reason for her unhappiness was unclear), but had calmed herself by the time the teacher arrived. Other authors have analysed in detail this approach to developing responsible behaviour among pupils which minimises teacher intervention and which has been carefully encouraged by teachers during pre-schooling (Tobin *et al.*, 1989; Lewis, 1995). When individual Japanese pupils had experienced behaviour problems, these were often considered by the whole class during the important 'reflective' period ('*hansei*') which ended each school day. Lewis (*op.cit.*, pp. 91–2) has commented on the way that teachers "relied on the gradual, cumulative effect of children's self-examination, rather than on direct intervention, to bring about discipline". This critical self-reflection time provided an opportunity for reviewing the events of the day, whether good or bad, from a slightly distanced perspective. During these sessions, the comments of the children were remarkable for the degree of maturity displayed and for their understanding of the feelings of other children (Lewis, *op.cit.*). Some children volunteered suggestions as to how they might better have handled difficult situations, or identified occasions when they might, with benefit, have remained calmer. For example, several children observed that they could have been of more help to the girl who had been in tears. Other children, at a lower level of reflection, simply identified events during the day that had caused them particular pleasure or enjoyment. All individual contributions from children, which were made freely and in an informal way, were acknowledged by the teacher but were not the subject of comment or analysis. One teacher took the opportunity to remind children of the importance of being kind to each other, which included not talking while their friends were addressing the class.

Such reflective periods are perceived of as making an important contribution to attitudes of Japanese children towards learning, since it is
only through reflection that children learn to be responsible for their behaviour and to be aware of a range of behavioural possibilities. They
gradually become aware that it is possible for themselves as individuals
to have control over their behaviour, and that they can be responsible
for their achievements in many different areas. It is doubtful, however, that without the preparation for learning and behaviour that is
provided by pre-school experience ('*yōchien*' or '*hoikuen*') in Japan, it
would be possible for first-grade children to develop such relatively mature reflection of their behavioural patterns. In contrast, examples of
unsociable behaviour were observed in every lesson in England. Such
incidents might be trivial – such as the taking of another pupil's pencil,
but frequently teacher intervention was required to resolve – temporar-
ily – the pupil–pupil conflict. Sometimes, the pupil who had suffered (his/
her book or other belongings had been taken, or another pupil refused
to share) protested to the teacher and initiated the teacher intervention;
at other times the teacher would observe two or more pupils arguing and
would take the initiative in intervening to resolve the argument. The
degree of classroom conflicts varied between classrooms but was a common and regular feature of all the fieldwork classrooms. There were many
observed examples within English classrooms of petty bickering and
squabbling among children – over ownership of small items, the taking
of turns and sharing equitably – that children appeared incapable of re-
solving themselves. The intervention of the teacher appeared the only
method for the resolution of such differences; some of the incidents may
well have been a ploy to gain the attention of the teacher. This is extremely wearing for teachers and sends messages to pupils about what is
sufficiently important to merit the teacher's attention. The amount of
time and effort spent in dealing with such trivialities was unfortunate and
detracted from achieving the main learning objectives. It is clear that
unless pre-school education focusses on developing the 'expected' behaviour necessary for successful learning in primary schooling, teachers
will waste precious time and effort in compensating for this.

Teachers' attitudes towards cognitive and social development

In Japan, using an implicit Vygotskian social-constructivist approach to
teaching and learning, teachers accept responsibility for helping children

to develop conceptual structures necessary for the understanding of mathematics. Within the classroom it was observed that teachers viewed cognitive and social development as being inextricably linked and interdependent. In contrast, classroom practice in England has for many years been influenced by the view that children should take responsibility for their own learning, and that children's learning is highly individual in nature. An assumption that cognitive and social development will progress differentially is consistent with this view.

In accordance with this approach, teachers in England seek to promote maximum development in children at the individual level. The way in which teachers spend substantial amounts of time and effort in devising highly differentiated schemes of work, maintaining highly detailed recording systems for each child, and diagnosing problems of individual children can only provoke feelings of admiration for the levels of dedication and commitment they evidence. The expectation of differentiation both in the rate and nature of children's development which during the last thirty years has underpinned attitudes in England towards learning has, however, made the use of a whole-class teaching approach practicably impossible as well as theoretically undesirable. This is regrettable since class teaching is of acknowledged benefit in the teaching of mathematics. It is particularly valuable for those weaker children who, without proper instruction and a high degree of pupil–teacher interaction, have difficulty in developing conceptual understanding. Teachers' attitudes towards their role in developing mathematical understanding among all children are, not surprisingly, reflected in the teaching methods they use.

Teaching approaches to instruction

Quantity of instruction

Evidence suggests that 'quantity of instruction' is a major variable affecting the effectiveness of teaching (Waxman and Walberg, 1982; Brophy and Good, 1986) yet identifying this is not as straightforward as might initially be imagined. If mathematical instruction is defined broadly to include all learning during lesson time in mathematics in order to quantify it we need to know:

- number of weeks in school year;
- number of mathematics lessons timetabled per week;

- length of each mathematics lesson as timetabled;
- actual length of mathematics lessons;
- amount of lesson time occupied at beginning and end of lesson by management and administration;
- amount of time lost through interruptions;
- amount of time lost during lesson by management and administration;
- level of pupil engagement/ 'time on-task'.

The effect of these variables on the time spent by pupils in mathematical learning is examined in this section. It has been suggested that the time devoted to mathematics instruction is greater in Japan in comparison to other countries, and that this is a major factor in explaining the greater achievement level (Robitaille and Travers, 1992). Several writers have commented on the apparently greater length of the Japanese school year, which at 240 days was considerably in excess of the number of days required in some Western countries (US Department of Education, 1987; Robitaille and Garden, 1989). By 1994, however, the argument that the greater length of the Japanese school year explained superior performance in mathematics had been effectively disproved (Stedman, 1994), and since then the school year in Japan has been effectively shortened, especially for elementary school children. As a result of the implementation of the recommendations of the report of the Reform Council (Reform Council, 1987) regarding the gradual reduction of Saturday schooling in 1995, elementary school children were allowed one Saturday free each month; this was increased to two Saturdays free per month in 1996.[12] In terms of hours of lessons for mathematics, in 1995, the Monbushō required that the first and second grades respectively should have 136 and 175 lessons of Sansū (Arithmetic) in total (Monbushō, 1995a). Since a lesson in Japan is defined as a class period of 45 minutes, this gives 102 hours and 131 hours through the year for each grade respectively. In comparison, it was recommended in England (Dearing, 1994) that pupils in the Key Stage 1 years of schooling should receive 3½ hours of mathematics each week. This gives a total of about 137 hours during a year of 39 weeks, thus greater than that for Japan.[13]

---

[12] Marshall (1994) reported that 642 test schools were experimenting with no Saturday schooling and a further number of schools had dropped Saturday school every other week.

[13] In the autumn of 1996, a survey of 400 schools by the NFER (Harris and Henkhuzens, 1998) found that the range of time allocated to the teaching of mathematics each week varied between schools from 60 to 450 minutes at KS1 and from 80 to 480 minutes at KS2.

More recently, it has been recommended that each primary class should "teach a daily mathematics lesson, with a high proportion of these devoted to numeracy" (DfEE, 1998a).[14] These figures suggest that primary school pupils in England are likely to spend as much time, if not more, than their Japanese counterparts in the study of mathematics. This is supported by the evidence from the TIMSS study (Mullis *et al.*, 1997, Table 5.4) which showed that the average number of hours mathematics was taught every week to pupils aged nine was 4.6 and 3.7 hours in England and Japan respectively. Thus one of the reasons often suggested to explain the superior performance of Japanese pupils in terms of mathematics attainment, namely, that more time is allocated to the study of mathematics in Japan, is refuted, and reasons to explain the difference in performance must be sought elsewhere.

Observations in Japanese and English schools were consistent with these figures. In Japanese schools, the timetables for both first and second grade pupils included four mathematics lessons, each of a standard 45 minutes.[15] In the English schools visited, timetables appeared to be more flexible in nature, and the pattern of lessons observed was more variable. Mathematics lessons lasted for between 30 and 75 minutes, and took place between three and five times a week. Mathematics lessons in both Japan and England were designed to take place, as far as possible, during the morning session although one class teacher, in accordance with her preference, had introduced a 'maths day' once a week into the timetable. The desirability for relatively young children to concentrate on a single subject for a whole day seems pedagogically questionable, but the example serves to illustrate the degree to which children's learning experience, within the English system, is affected by views of individual teachers rather than the educational system.

In addition to considering the amount of timetabled time for mathematics lessons, we need to examine 'actual' lesson time, and the efficiency with which that lesson time was used. Analysis of the lesson observation forms shows that in English classes 22 per cent of lesson time was classified as 'No activity recorded', compared with 7 per cent of time in Japan. From observation, more time was lost at the beginning and end

---

[14] Initially, publicity from the Numeracy Task Force, which was the body responsible for producing the report 'Numeracy Matters' recommended the introduction of a daily 'Numeracy Hour'; after some confusion as to whether an hour referred to 60 minutes or 45 minutes, the latter was accepted as being more suitable for young children.

[15] Examples of time-tables for first- and second-grade classes in Japan are included in Appendix G.

of lessons in England than in Japan. Lessons in Japan were observed to start punctually, with a formal beginning provided by two children (on a *tōban* system rota) calling the class to order, following which the teacher was able to begin teaching. This was facilitated by the fact that children had their books and equipment ready to hand; if these were not already on top of their desks in anticipation of the lesson, they were quickly and easily extracted from the 'drawer' underneath the desk. In contrast, on average ten minutes was lost at the beginning of a lesson in England due to a few 'stragglers' who needed to be reminded of the nature of the lesson and the equipment required. There was less variation in the amount of time lost at the end of a lesson; in most cases the same two children would draw the lesson in Japan to a formal close, before children disappeared for their short between-lesson break. This break, which followed every lesson, is thought to be valuable since it not only allows children a time to be energetic and 'let off steam' after their intense concentration, but it also provides a clear demarcation of lesson time and enables children to return ready to refocus their attention and concentration on the next lesson. In England, children remained on their activity until the end of a lesson that might be followed by the single mid-morning break or the lunch break; it was also possible that a lesson on a different curricular subject followed straightaway.

The rate of external interruptions to lessons showed a great difference. During all the lessons observed in Japan, there was only once an intrusion from the outside – and the reason was to deliver a message to me. This is an indication of the priority given to the activity of *teaching*; and evidence of the view that the quality of pupils' learning should not be put at risk by other less important considerations. In contrast, external interruptions were a regular feature of English lessons, averaging three interruptions for each lesson observed, which frequently resulted in the departure of individual (or groups of) children for a variety of reasons. Although these interruptions had a less disruptive effect than they would have done in Japan (children were, in the main, engaged on individual work and pupils could easily be extracted without adversely affecting other children), the *frequency* of interruptions, often for relatively minor administrative reasons, suggested that the activity of teaching was not given a high priority. Due to the frequency of the interruptions, it was clearly very easy for an individual child to have reduced time on mathematics, and to fall behind in his/her development of understanding and competency without the teacher necessarily being aware of this or able to provide additional 'catch-up' time.

The amount of instruction actually received by children in the English classes observed is difficult to quantify. Since the teachers observed gave relatively little direct instruction, the majority of children obtained most of their mathematics instruction from textbooks or other published sources. The amount of instruction they were thus able to obtain from textbooks depended on a number of factors – for example, the level of their literacy and comprehension skills and whether those were commensurate with the complexity of the instruction. On many occasions children were observed with a textbook page in front of them but on being questioned regarding the nature of their task, were unable to read the words of the text. Literacy competence is clearly only the first requirement; even once this has been established at an appropriate level, the next step relates to children's ability to comprehend the meaning and relevance of the mathematical text. Observation and questioning of children in English classes again revealed that this caused further difficulty, with several children being so perplexed that they resorted to copying the work of a neighbouring child.

With the 'actual' lesson time, significant differences were also recorded in relation to the rate of pupil engagement or 'time on-task'. Recording this accurately has clear methodological difficulties: the method used during the fieldwork was to time-sample on a five minute basis, recording the number of children who were clearly 'off-task' i.e. gazing around the room, chatting to their neighbours, sharpening pencils, waiting for teacher attention, and so on. This is easier to record when children are seated in a more formal arrangement than when a grouped arrangement is used. It may also be subject to misinterpretation – for example, children apparently gazing around the room may in fact be deep in thought. Data on this should thus be treated with care, but analysis of observational forms used throughout the lessons suggested that, on average, 21 per cent of children in English classes were 'off-task' at any point in the lesson, compared with 5 per cent of children in Japanese classes. This latter figure is consistent with the figures from the study of elementary lessons by Stigler *et al.*, (1987) which found that less than 4 per cent of Japanese children were 'off-task' during lesson time.

Combining the 'off task' figures with the proportion of 'lost' time suggests an 'on-task' rate of 88 per cent for Japanese pupils and about 62 per cent for English pupils. These figures for English pupils are consistent with data collected by Tizard *et al.* (1988), which suggested that children (in England) were 'on-task' for 61 per cent of time observed, and those in the study by Axelrod *et al.* (1979) which recorded 'on-task' rates of 62 and 63 per cent. Thus the timetabled lesson time for mathematics in England is significantly reduced when effective 'on task' time is considered, and the apparent advantage enjoyed by English pupils with the greater time for mathematics disappears. In addition, the higher figures of English children 'off task' at any one time suggest that their levels of concentration were poorer than those of Japanese children, which is likely to have an adverse effect on their learning progress.

Teaching methods

Teaching methods used in primary schools may be classed broadly into four main groups:

- a whole class approach;
- collaborative pair or small group work;
- individualised learning;
- a combination of the above.

Research in England has tended to recommend a suitable 'mix' of individualised learning, strategies for group work, and whole-class approaches (Alexander *et al.*, 1992), sometimes referred to as 'middle range' strategies (Croll and Hastings, 1996). Yet studies of *actual* classroom practice in England suggest that in recent years the overwhelming majority of lesson time has been spent apparently in pair or small group work. Pair or small group work is often recommended because it is perceived as increasing pupil–pupil interaction, developing co-operation and mutual respect, removing the stigma of possible failure from weaker pupils, and enabling new insight to be developed. Galton, reporting on a study of junior schools (Galton, 1996b), stated that 78 per cent of all lesson activity was observed to take place in small groups (4–8 children) and a further 10 per cent took place in pairs. However, the same study also found that while children were seated and were apparently working in groups, for only 14 per cent of the time they were seated together were they actually *working* together. This would suggest that while the disadvantages resulting from a grouped seating arrangement would apply – such as reduced 'time on-task' – none of the possible advantages of collaborative group- or pair- work would be gained.[16]

---

[16] Brophy and Good (1986) comment on the negative correlations found in several studies between achievement and time spent on independent 'seat work' without continuing teacher supervision.

It was clear from the study by Galton and others (Galton *et al.*, 1991) that little time was devoted to a whole-class learning approach for the teaching of mathematics. Yet this approach was identified by Haylock (1991) as having distinct advantages for the teaching of mathematics. For example, whole-class teaching may be seen as more 'teacher effective' since the teacher needs to plan only a single lesson for the whole class, in contrast to an individualised or small group approach which requires a number of lessons to be planned and managed by a single teacher. If only a single lesson needs to be planned (and this can be assisted by a highly specified curriculum and a high-quality teachers' manual), this frees more teacher time for the planning of classroom organisation and effective lesson delivery. It is suggested that the greater complexity of small-group instruction involving differentiated lessons and assignments makes disproportionate demands on the teacher, who, in addition, has a more difficult task in monitoring progress and providing assistance (McNamara and Waugh, 1993).

Another major advantage of whole-class teaching is that it permits a higher level of teacher–pupil interaction to occur, which has been shown by a number of studies to be an important factor in children's learning. The small-group nature of classroom activity in reality consists of individual work, the majority of teacher–pupil interaction taking place on an individual basis. Thus, although teachers in English classes were observed to spend the majority of their time interacting with pupils, since this was conducted almost entirely on an individual basis, children spent only about one minute in every hour in interaction with the teacher. Croll comments, ". . . however much teachers increase their individual interaction from its already high level, there can only be a very small impact on any individual child's experience of one-to-one interaction with the teacher." (Croll and Hastings, *op.cit.*, p.20)

Yet the importance of interaction is a key feature of Vygotskian principles of learning which argued that the role of the teacher is crucial in assisting children to progress from one level of understanding to the next (Vygotsky, reprinted in 1987; Rieber and Carton, 1987). The role of the teacher in 'accelerating development' of children's understanding was also emphasised by Alexander (1995). Both Vygotsky and Alexander have stressed the importance of language for analysing problems and clarifying structures. Vygotsky argued that young children need to vocalise their thoughts in order to conceptualise a problem, and that the demonstration and use by the teacher of clear, precise language in explanation and discussion is likely to facilitate children's ability to conceptualise and analyse. Alexander also stressed the importance of making "teacher–pupil talk focused and cognitively challenging".

In summary, the advantages of a whole-class interactive teaching approach for developing understanding in mathematics are as follows:

- all children have the same instruction;
- teacher–pupil interaction is maximised;
- each step can be fully explained;
- misconceptions can be clarified through questioning and discussion of answers;
- children can learn from the answers given by others;
- children can be confident that they are making similar progress to others;
- children can see that they are not alone with any difficulty;
- mathematical vocabulary can be correctly used in context;
- there is a minimum standard to be achieved by the whole class;
- children can be encouraged to help and support each other in their learning; this has important implications for class unity.

It is acknowledged that effective whole-class interactive teaching requires a major level of pedagogical skill, especially in providing challenging work (on the same topic) for faster learning children who may finish the set task quickly. However, only if a significant proportion of a lesson is devoted to a whole-class interactive approach can children be provided with adequate amounts of direct instruction for developing understanding of new concepts in mathematics. The extensive use of a non-whole-class teaching approach restricts the amount of direct instruction that can be provided, which in turn adversely affects children's development of mathematical understanding. Examples from the fieldwork observation in English classes are described here to illustrate this.

At the beginning of mathematics lessons in England, children were typically summoned to sit on the 'carpet area'. There they were addressed all together by the teacher: occasionally this section of the lesson included some oral/mental questions, or some teacher demonstration using a 'flipchart' provided for that purpose. More commonly, this section of the lesson was used to give children instructions as to their learning activities for that particular lesson, rather than for instruction which might develop understanding in mathematics. Typically, four ability groups were formed within a class group – although this varied from three to six – and were provided with tasks at different levels of difficulty, and often on different mathematical topics. Teachers had clearly spent a great deal of time in preparation and planning in order to provide activities at appropriate levels of difficulties for the various groups of pupils; this is undoubtedly more demanding than preparing a single lesson for the whole class. In most lessons observed, as each group received its instructions for a particular activity, they departed to begin work – although their degree of application was highly variable and sometimes insubstantial before the teacher was able to give them further attention. It was noticeable that, for quite understandable reasons, teachers tended to start with more able groups (who would be more capable of organising themselves and their activity) and work down, so that the least able group was the last to leave the carpet. While this process enabled the teacher to provide the weakest group with greater help and more detailed instruction as to the nature of the task set, it also reduced the amount of time available to these children for learning and making progress on their individual tasks. In a typical lesson lasting for an hour, as much as twenty minutes could be occupied in detailing the tasks set for each group, with the result that by the time the last group had been instructed, the children in the first group were already at the stage of needing individual help and were frequently 'off-task' with frustration. The success of this approach in which the teacher acts as a facilitator rather than as an instructor and is more consistent with the Piagetian model of cognitive development, depends on children being sufficiently self-reliant and self-motivated to organise their activities efficiently.

Teaching methods observed in Japan, in contrast, included a large element of whole-class instruction. The view that *all* children merited similar levels of attention, consideration and teacher time was expressed by teachers and is consistent with their observed reluctance to spend lesson time on behavioural difficulties of individual children, who would then receive disproportionate amounts of teachers' time and attention. Inherent in the basic aim of equality of educational opportunity and uniformity of educational experience is the precept that it is only fair that children should receive equal amounts of teacher time and attention. Lee *et al.* comment: "All children are believed to have an equal right to an education, and Japanese schools seek to provide all children with equal opportunities to realize this right. With the whole-class method, all children receive the same type and amount of instruction." (Lee *et al.*, 1996, p.167.) One lesson was observed in Japan in which a class was divided up into groups, but the groups were not constructed on the basis of ability, nor were they engaged on different tasks of variable difficulty. This occurred in a school which unusually had a 'specialist maths teacher' on the staff. On this occasion we divided the class into halves, with half being taken into another classroom. There they were split into two further groups, who engaged collaboratively on numerical games under the supervision of the specialist, while the classroom teacher worked in parallel with her half class in her classroom. Both teachers carefully monitored the participation and competence displayed by individual children in their groups. All the activities selected required active oral participation of all the children but involved no writing or recording of number. Each group appeared to be at the same level of competence and were engaged on similar activities. The level of pupil–pupil interaction within the groups was high and the children (who had at that time been in school for only a few weeks) showed awareness of the social skills and level of co-operation appropriate for a collaborative group activity.

Whole-class instruction is a possible and appropriate method of teaching mathematics to young children in Japan because the relative uniformity of their pre-school experience and the 'levelling up' of skill levels during the years of pre-school education establish a certain commonality of experience and capability by the beginning of formal schooling, which can be built on by the class teacher. At the same time, the rules and rituals of social behaviour which have been established during the pre-school years mean that children, when they begin the years of statutory schooling, have the skills necessary for learning – namely, the ability to listen to instructions, explanations and questions; to answer questions properly and in a manner which enables all to hear; to concentrate for extended periods of time; to memorise auditory or visual patterns; to have the fine motor skills necessary for co-ordination in writing; and to consider the needs of others in the classroom, even if this entails waiting for slower pupils to acquire understanding of new concepts.

Even though children in Japan will have had training in these skills, teachers still need to appreciate differences between children's existing capabilities on beginning school. Teachers in Japan showed a detailed awareness of each child's level of conceptual understanding and were concerned to use the most effective approaches in the introduction of new conceptual ideas. They took advantage of every opportunity for pedagogical discussion with other practising teachers and more theoretical educationists, to exchange ideas, and to engage in mutual classroom observation in order to hone their teaching skills yet further. Their recognition of the extent to which the effectiveness of teaching skills can assist or hinder development in learning, and the need for the teacher to help children to move forward to the next stage of development, is consistent with the ideas of a Vygotskian-constructivist model of learning.

Lesson format

In both countries, the mathematics lessons had a distinct format which was adhered to consistently. The stages shown in the box overleaf were typical of lessons observed.

It was noticeable that the level of pupil participation was higher in Japanese lessons and that opportunities were provided for pupils to express their thinking on a particular problem. This is consistent with the observations of Stigler (Stigler *et al.*, 1996, p.224) and is discussed further in the following section on teaching content and methods used in the lessons observed.

Giving information and lesson structure

The beginning of a typical lesson in England has already been described. During this time, the attention of the children was observed to be variable, perhaps in part due to the way in which the children were confined to the carpet area and often sat in different ways (legs crossed, legs outstretched, or kneeling) which further reduced the available space and increased discomfort. The short beginning with the pupils together sometimes included 'mental' questions, or a reminder of an earlier topic. For example, one session relating to the Attainment Target of 'Shape and Space' included a brief discussion of different shapes, during which the names of shapes and solids were listed on the flip-chart, although without any reference to concrete examples that would have assisted children in their knowledge.

The main purpose of gathering children together on the carpet area, however, was to give instructions regarding the the remainder of the mathematics lesson. Children displayed widely differing levels of application in tackling their associated activity with correspondingly diverse levels of success. Given the highly differentiated nature of the individual tasks set and the variable rates of progress, it would have been remarkable if all children were able to accomplish their tasks within the same time span provided by the length of the lesson. In fact, little importance appeared to be attached to completing the task set or coming to a

---

England

Stage 1 Carpet area Instruction 10–20 minutes. Instruction provided regarding learning activities for groups of children differentiated by ability. Children depart in groups to begin activities.

Stage 2 At tables. Remaining lesson time . Children engaged on allocated activity, usually working individually although examples of collaborative pair work were observed. Teachers give individual help. Children continue until end of lesson.

Japan

Stage 1 Seated at desks. Introduction and development section 15–20 minutes. Formal beginning. Teacher introduced topic, developed through questioning, discussion, teacher- and pupil-demonstration.

Stage 2 Practice. 5–10 minutes. Application of development section – usually written practice, but sometimes practical activity.

Stage 3 Points arising. 5–10 minutes. Discussion of written practice. Pupils' demonstration.

Stage 4* Practice. 5 minutes. 'Extension activities', with some pupils making faster progress. Uncompleted worksheets taken home.

Stage 5 Summary. 5 minutes. Summary of main points. Formal ending to lesson.

* Stage 4 did not occur in all observed lessons.

---

conclusion; instead children were told when it was 'time to put their books away'. On a few occasions, children were recalled to the carpet and asked to report back and make an assessment of the progress they had made – in most cases, however, this was beyond the capability of such young children who were able only to describe what they had done, repeating their original instructions. A further factor which limited the success of the 'reporting back' phase was the unwillingness of other children to pay attention to the reporting back of others. This partly reflected their tiredness at that stage of a mathematics lesson (which in some cases had lasted for over an hour); their desire for a break was made clear by their fidgeting and talking to other pupils. It also illustrated the reluctance of pupils in English classes to listen to the oral contribution of other pupils.

In contrast, the highly interactive nature of the whole-class approach in Japanese classrooms was carefully constructed to involve a combination of teacher demonstration, questioning of pupils, and pupil demonstration. This is supported by observations of Stigler who found that nearly three-quarters of lesson time in Japanese classes involved interaction with the teacher (Stigler *et al.,* 1987). From observation in this study of first- and second-grade classes in Japan, the beginning sector of a lesson always involved extensive *teacher demonstration,* often using concrete materials, interspersed with skilled questioning of children. The topic of subtraction, for example, was introduced through the idea of a number of fish in a tank being removed by children with a net (see Figure 8.1). Magnetic fish attached to the board were physically removed by the teacher in the first demonstration, although at a later stage of the lesson children were expected to visualise their removal mentally.

A Vygotskian approach to teaching and learning was demonstrated by Japanese teachers when they helped children to a higher stage of understanding in subtraction. For example, second-grade children, who already had a competence with simple subtraction problems, were asked to consider the contextualised problem: "There are 21 pieces of candy; eight children are given one each. How many pieces will be left over?" This subtraction problem was at a higher level of difficulty for two reasons: firstly, it involved the concept of 'comparing' and, secondly, the subtraction involved 'crossing the tens boundary' with numbers larger than 20. The demonstration, begun by the teacher and completed by children, was highly detailed and sequenced. First, the teacher placed 21 stickers (to represent the candy) on the board, carefully counted out by the class. Next, the teacher drew 8 children on the board, and then invited 8 children (who were counted carefully by the class) to the front. Then another child was instructed to take stickers from the board and to give one to each child, who then attached his/her stickers to one of the children drawn on the board. The teacher then asked the question 'How many stickers are left over?' A girl carefully explained her reasoning and her calculation of $21 - 8 = 13$. Another child (a boy who the previous year had not been capable of participating in class work) was called upon to write the answer [*kotae* 13 *ko*] on the board which he did correctly (and was applauded).

By this careful demonstration, the teacher had helped the children to increase the complexity and level of their conceptual structures for understanding subtraction. The way that the children had been involved in the 'comparing' concept ensured that they understood the 'subtraction' nature of the problem. Once this had been established, the numerical calculation of 21 – 8 presented no problem since the concept of 'decomposition' was already clearly understood and could be correctly applied.

Teachers in Japan frequently used the technique of modelling the demonstration which was then emulated by pupil demonstration. Knowledge and understanding was steadily built through teacher-modelling and, as children became more confident, teacher-demonstration was withdrawn and the demonstration handed over to children. For example, in a first-grade lesson on addition up to 10 which was entirely oral in nature, the teacher first used magnetic bricks on the board to demonstrate '3 + 2 = 5'. After discussion of vocabulary used, children were asked to choose and to hold up objects from their desk to demonstrate the sum. One girl held up three notebooks and two sheets of origami. They were then instructed to go around the classroom to find a range of objects to demonstrate '3 + 2'. Through the *range* of demonstration with different objects, children came to understand the inflexibility of the sum regardless of the nature of the objects involved, which is a fundamental attribute of number structure.

The next stage of the lesson extended understanding of 'five' by altering the position of the five bricks to demonstrate the other possible ways of 'making five' (e.g. 4 + 1 = 5, etc.). This was followed by further pupil demonstration. The lesson was concluded with children drawing their own choice of 5 objects to demonstrate a sum – umbrellas, straws, rabbits, cats, mice, grapes and flowers were a few of the objects drawn. The extension of the initial demonstration of '3 + 2 = 5' to other number combinations for five provides another example of teachers helping children to extend their conceptual structures.

Other examples of building conceptual structures occurred in 'subtraction' lessons; once 5 – 2 = 3 had been established using fish swimming away, the teacher demonstrated the way '5' might be separated into '2 and 3' and might be joined together again. By developing this idea, she linked together the two processes of addition and subtraction, and showed that subtraction was simply the inverse of addition. Understanding of this concept is necessary for procedural competence with the algebraic form of addition and subtraction (eg 3 + ? = 5; 5 – ? = 2). It is known that English children often have difficulty with questions in an algebraic form and it may be that it would be helpful to pay greater attention to developing an awareness of the relationship between addition and subtraction through 'separating' and 'joining'. There was also a gradual transition from the use of concrete materials in a new problem to an abstract form; only when a problem had been demonstrated with concrete materials, was the question (*shiki*) written in symbolic form followed by the answer (*kotae*). For example, in the simple subtraction problem:

'There are three cakes; one was eaten. How many are left?

[*Keeki ga sanko arimasu. Ikko tabemashita. Nokoriwa nanko desuka?*]

This was demonstrated first by three stickers on the board and, secondly, was shown diagrammatically:

Only then was it written as a question: (*shiki*) : 3 – 1
Answer   (*kotae*)   2
3 – 1 = 2

and read aloud as: "Three subtract one makes two "[*san hiku ichi wa ni*]. The use of this diagram to show the relationship of the two parts to the whole helped to develop children's understanding by presenting the same idea in another way, and also reinforced their understanding of the relationship between addition and subtraction.

Careful and repeated questioning accompanied all the demonstrations observed; the skilfulness of the questioning was thought to be central to the success of the teachers in taking the class forward in understanding of new mathematical concepts. This is examined in the following section.

Questioning the pupils

The value of questioning in developing learning has been recognised for over one hundred years.[17] It is also accepted that the nature of the questioning affects development of understanding. Dillon and Schmeck (1985) and Tobin *et al.* (1989) stress the importance of the logical sequencing of questions for developing understanding, but they also distinguish between 'lower level' questions (which require the recollection of facts and/or procedures) and 'higher level' questions (which relate to pupils' abilities to apply or explain concepts), pointing out that the use of a greater proportion of higher

---

[17] "The teacher should explain nothing that can by judicious questioning be elicited from his pupils" (Livesey, T., 1888, in Moffatt and Paige, *How to Teach Arithmetic*).

level questions is often associated with improvement in pupils' performance. Brophy and Good (1986), on the level of questioning, suggest that if questions are at a level of appropriate difficulty then about 75 per cent correct answers and about 25 per cent incorrect or incomplete answers should result; this, it is suggested, will stimulate the evaluation of learning and the development of accurate generalisations, leading to fuller conceptual understanding.

In addition to using an appropriate 'mix ' of types of questions, teachers also need to select the mathematical examples used in questioning with care. Children are quick to make generalisations, and the examples reflecting a 'particular case' should be avoided (Charles, 1980). In asking questions, educationists agree on the benefits of increasing the 'wait time' for a response to a question; while this is shown to improve pupil response on all types of questions, the gain is greater with responses to higher level questions. The likely gain from increasing 'wait time' must be carefully balanced, however, against the need to maintain the pace of lessons.

All the Japanese lessons observed included extensive use of questioning by the teacher, which included both 'lower level' and 'higher level' questions. Perry *et al.* (1993) have commented on the powerful influence of the questioning of Japanese teachers of first-grade pupils on their mathematical thought; other writers have also commented on the frequency with which Japanese teachers pose questions involving a degree of conceptual difficulty (Redfeld and Rousseau, 1981).

Lessons typically began with an oral section involving the whole class, during which pupils were frequently asked to contribute their own ideas on a problem posed by the teacher. Stigler and Perry (1990) have drawn attention to the more reflective attitude of Japanese teachers, who were observed to develop problem-strategies of pupils by focusing on a few problems – sometimes a single problem – for an entire lesson. First-grade children were less likely to be asked to concentrate on a single problem for a whole lesson, but in one second-grade lesson the problem "which rabbit is nearest the carrot?" occupied pupils throughout the lesson. This problem led to a consideration of the concept of measurement, and pupils were asked to make suggestions as to what objects they might use for measuring distances.[18] Children's individual ideas received the same

---

[18] The *Atarashii Sansū* teachers' manual suggests that the following questions are included: "Which is the rabbit nearest to the carrot?" "Why?" "How can you find out?" "What can you use for measuring the distances?" "What is your neighbour using?" "What other things on your desk can you measure in the same way?" "What other things in the classroom can you measure in the same way?" "What can you not measure in the same way?"

level of welcome by the teacher, regardless of their appropriateness or otherwise, but, through careful questioning, pupils were able to evaluate their relevance and effectiveness and to establish the principles of comparability and invariance of units. Children were encouraged to investigate the practicalities of measurement by using their chosen measures: in doing so, they discovered the impracticability of some suggested measures (great merriment was also caused by some children attempting to measure how wide others in their class could open their mouths).

Even with the first-grade children, the level and nature of questioning used by Japanese teachers was varied. Examples of questions from teachers included the following:

Addition: There are 6 apples and 3 apples. How many altogether? [*Ringo ga rokko arimasu. Sanko ga arimasu. Awasete nanko desu ka?*]
Subtraction: There are 8 doves. If three fly away, how many are left? [*Hato ga hachi wa imasu. San wa tonde ikuto nokori wa nan wa deshō ka?*]
In measurement: How long are your fingers?
    How wide can you open your mouth?
    How long is a m? cm? mm?
    Can you measure a face?

The extensive uses of oral questioning and demonstration also helps to develop understanding of precise mathematical vocabulary. The difficulty and complexities of mathematical language for young children were recognised by the Japanese teachers and the importance of understanding language and vocabulary together with their relationship to mathematical operations was stressed. In one classroom a poster included all the 'addition' words (*awasete; minnade; zenbude; fueruto*). In a 'subtraction' lesson all the 'movement' words were discussed; going (*ikimasu*), jumping off (*tobimasu*); eating (*tabemasu*); going home (*kaerimasu*).

It was clear from observation that teachers in Japan were careful to call on 'non-volunteers' and well as 'volunteers' to answer questions and to demonstrate or provide explanations to the class. One teacher was observed to be exceptionally skilful in the way in which she directed questions of a simpler variety to a slower learning pupil, in order to involve him more in the lesson and to increase his self-confidence. Other children in the class were notably supportive of others providing demonstration or explanation – it was not uncommon for spontaneous applause to follow an individual demonstration.

In English classes, there were relatively few opportunities for questioning pupils, either collectively or individually. Any collective questioning took place while the pupils were seated together on the 'carpet area' at the beginning of a lesson. Higher-level questions were unlikely to be asked, and children were more likely to be posed questions requiring factual recall of number bonds, or those requiring only one-word answers. It was rare for children to be asked to elaborate on an answer, or to explain their reasoning. Opportunities for questioning individual children were even fewer; while teachers spent the majority of lesson time circulating among pupils, this was spent largely in checking on progress and clarifying instructions as necessary.

Japanese teachers were careful to use examples of misconceptions to develop *all* children's understanding further. When one first-grade boy wrote a sum on the board as '$3 = 1 = 2$', the teacher did not correct him but instead said to the class "What's wrong with that? Let's think". The value of the process of self-correction is generally recognised; this situation was of interest because the teacher sought to involve the whole class in considering the nature of the error and the misunderstanding, in order that all the pupils by learning from it would develop their conceptual understanding and avoid making the same mistake themselves at some future point.

Another example of a teacher using a misconception to develop children's conceptual structures arose in a first-grade class in the practice of subtraction with numbers up to 10. Achieving procedural competence with the algebraic form had been the teaching aim of the lesson, and children were involved in written practice involving the completion of questions of the type '$8 - ? = 2$'. The teacher realised that there were a number of children who, although they had no difficulty with the mathematical concept involved in the algebraic form, had incorrectly answered the question '$7 - ? = 0$', giving '0' as the answer. The difficulty that many children have with applying operations which involve '0' has been established by several earlier research studies (Murray, 1939; Clements, 1980; 1982; Van Lehn, 1990). Quickly summoning the whole class to attend, she posed them all the question, and asked seven of those children who had thought the answer was '0' to the front of the class where they formed a line. She was able easily to demonstrate, by asking the children to leave the room until there was none left in the line, that the number needed to 'take away' was '7'. Understanding was thus achieved without embarrassing any of the children who had made the error – in fact, they had clearly enjoyed taking part in the visual 'people' demonstration. She had been able to move a number of children forward to an important next stage of their understanding and to correct a common misconception by involving children in the demonstration.

Once first-grade children had achieved understanding and some competence with the process of subtraction, one lesson was spent with every pupil constructing his/her own 'subtraction story book'. This was carefully modelled first by the teacher who then showed the children how to fold their paper to make a 'book' and discussed each page of the 'book'. All the children then worked enthusiastically – and noisily – to create their own subtraction problems. At the conclusion of the lesson, a number of children demonstrated their 'books' to the class. These included the statement of the problem first in words and, secondly, illustrated, before the problem was shown solved pictorially and then in words. This was the first occasion in a mathematics lesson that children had been required to construct their own word problem to fit a particular mathematical situation; it was an important lesson since children were required to do this on many later occasions. The ability to construct a problem to fit a particular mathematical format is regarded as an indication of conceptual understanding linked to procedural application, and also reflects the emphasis given to problem solving (Stigler *et al.*, 1996, p.229). Several teachers in Japan commented that only when children were able to construct their own word problems to fit a particular mathematical operation could they be certain that children had fully understood a concept. (Examples of some children's word problems are given in Figures 8.4 and 8.5)

Mental calculation

The strong emphasis on oral work in Japan relates to the importance attached to mental calculation. During the developmental sections of lessons when oral responses to problems were the standard pattern, children were encouraged to use mental methods – first, for factual recall and then to use this to develop strategies for mental calculation.

In fact, first-grade Japanese children were observed to make few mistakes in their factual recall of number bonds up to 10. The deliberate emphasis in the early mathematics curriculum given to the importance of 'ten' helps children to develop mental strategies with numbers greater than ten (Crump, 1992; Benjamin, 1997). Japanese children within the first few weeks of beginning school learn all number bond combinations for 10, and practise these so that factual recall is almost instantaneous.

The extracts in Figures 7.1 and 7.2, from *Sansū* and *Atarashii Sansū* for the first term of the first grade show visually the construction of ten, the way it may be separated into different number combinations.

In the English classes children appeared to have very little in the way of strategies for mental calculation, and from observation and questioning of individual children it was clear that many children did not have accurate knowledge or recall of number bonds up to ten. Many depended on counting strategies – either using their fingers or other concrete materials, or using a number line. Many children in Year 3, however, were incapable of using a number line correctly for the purposes of simple addition and were observed to begin counting on the first number. Further, it was clear that many children had either not mastered or had not been introduced to the technique of counting on from the larger addend which can speed up the use of a counting strategy (Fuson, 1986a).

When knowledge and recall of number facts up to 10 is secure, children in Japan are next introduced to numbers between 10 and 20. This forms a separate and distinct stage.[19] Whole-class discussion focuses on the 'best way' of arranging concrete manifestations of such numbers (often using magnetic counters) and children themselves develop the idea of placing 10 counters together as a single unit. This is a vital foundation for the later introduction to place value (see Chapter 8).

With addition and subtraction calculations involving 'crossing the tens boundary', the idea of bridging through ten is used in Japan.[20] For example, the addition involved in '8 + 3' is viewed as '8 + 2 + 1', thus reinforcing the importance of adding to 10. Similarly, the subtraction '14 – 8' is thought of as '10 – 8 + 4' thus reinforcing the importance of subtracting from 10, and, at the same time, providing an important strategy for any mental calculation of this type.

Consolidation and practice

After discussion and sharing of ideas, a typical lesson in Japan continued with further demonstration of the application of the new concepts. In the case of concepts involving arithmetical operations, the use of sym-

---

[19] Numbers between 10 and 20 do not appear to receive special consideration in England; children are more likely to progress in one step to 'numbers up to a hundred'.
[20] This has now been formally included in the list of acceptable calculating strategies for use with pupils in England and Wales by the documentation produced by the Teacher Training Agency (1998), *Initial Teacher Training National Curriculum for Primary Mathematics*.

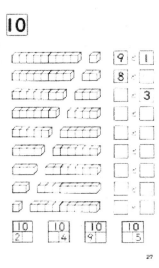

Figure 7.1 *Sansū 1, p. 27*

bolic notation and abstract mathematics sentences was introduced only after considerable discussion and demonstration of examples with concrete materials and contextualised word problems.

Ample consolidation and practice was provided, often using duplicated work sheets for this purpose. Children were observed to work with remarkable speed and confidence through a number of sequenced work sheets. In one memorable lesson on the topic of subtraction, the teacher, with fifteen minutes of the lesson remaining, placed copies of ten different work sheets around the room, and although a requirement was that children should have one sheet marked correct before they proceeded to the next (another teacher was present in this lesson to assist with the marking), several children completed all ten work sheets before the end of the lesson, while other children requested permission to take the other home to complete (and sped around the room collecting them as needed for this purpose).

On average, six different activities – related to the same learning objective and involving all children – were recorded as having taken place during the lessons observed which is slightly less than the number reported in another study (Rohlen and Letendre, 1996). Although a large number of different activities was observed in each lesson in England, these were undertaken by different children. It was rare for each pupil to be involved in more than a single activity or task each lesson.

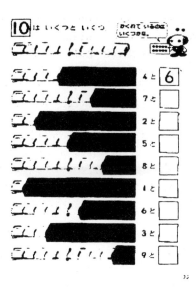

Figure 7.2 *Atarashii Sansū 1, p.22.*

Expectations in relation to minimum standards

There is no doubt that the expectation in Japan that all children will reach the minimum standard provides a powerful motivating force for parents and their children. By examining their child's text books parents can acquire a detailed knowledge of the syllabus for a particular subject, and the standard that is expected. Because all children in one class are following the same curriculum, it is relatively easy for parents to realise if their child is falling behind, or failing to achieve the required standard. Parents may provide support and help themselves at home each evening; they also have the possibility of arranging for their child to attend *juku* in a particular subject as necessary. While *juku* evening classes are privately funded and commercially organised, the fees are deliberately set at a level to be within the budget of an average family. *Juku* are acknowledged to perform an essential role in helping pupils to attain the required standard by the end of a school year; repetition of a grade, unlike in many other countries, is virtually unknown.

In England, it is much more difficult for parents to be aware when their child is failing to reach an appropriate standard. For many years, with learning in primary schools being child-centred to the extent that many children have determined their own rate of learning, the concept of an 'expected' standard has been unacceptable. Recently, however, it has been accepted that 'expected' levels of attainment are 2 and 4 for the end of Key Stages 1 and 2 respectively, although the rationale to support this is not clear. It is now possible, therefore, for parents in England to know when their child has failed to reached the 'expected' standard at the end of Key Stage 1. Were parents to have a clearer idea of standards expected at an earlier point, however, the chances of being able to help their child to 'catch up' (if necessary) would be increased. While the quality of teacher–parent communication is excellent in many schools throughout England, for many years teachers have been encouraged to assess a pupil's progress in the context of their expectations for that particular child rather than in the context of 'expected' standards, and the transition is not easy.

Expectations with regard to standards are particularly important in the context of lower attaining pupils, and no discussion of mathematics teaching would be complete without consideration of the provision and support for slower learning children or those who are lower attainers. In Japan, approximately 99 per cent of elementary school children are in mainstream education, with the remaining 1 per cent being taught either in special schools or in special units within mainstream schools (*Monbushō*, 1998). As has already been made clear, the expectation is that this 99 per cent will be taught in mixed ability elementary classes by their generalist class teacher, and all will achieve the required minimum standard. There is no provision in Japan for the use of teaching assistants within the classroom and, in general, it is unusual for any other adult to participate in the delivery of a lesson.[21]

In discussion, Japanese teachers stressed the importance attached to monitoring at the individual level the understanding and competence of *all* individual children in the class. No special support or additional help, however, was provided for weaker children. Teachers were frequently observed to spend a few minutes at the end of a lesson with a weaker child, or one who was perceived as being in danger of falling

---

[21] By chance, however, in two of the observed lessons it happened that two teachers were present. In one of these lessons, the additional teacher – who had lost her class from the previous year due to changes in pupil numbers – was deployed as a 'marker' of the children's written practice, while the classroom teacher gave additional help to slower or weaker children. In the other lesson – in a school which had a 'specialist' maths teacher – the development section of the lesson was delivered by the 'specialist'; during the 'written practice' section of the lesson the two teachers performed similar roles in circulating and providing help or checking answers.

behind. In general, however, the teaching approaches used in developing mathematical understanding were designed to help the progress of all children, including those who might well be regarded as slower learners or having 'special educational needs'.

In England, the nature of the support for slower-learning pupils is complex. First, the percentage of primary age pupils educated in 'special schools' is similar to that in Japan; nationally the figure is about 1 per cent, although this varies between LEAs from under 0.5 per cent to over 2 per cent (*Monbushō*, 1994; DfEE, 1997a, p.45; DfEE, 1998e). There is also a move to increase the inclusion rate of children with identified 'special educational needs' (SEN) into mainstream schools; the official view is that 'they should join fully with their peers in the curriculum and life of the school' (DfEE, *ibid.*, p.44). In order to facilitate the education of an increasing percentage of children within mainstream schooling, many teaching assistants work within classrooms alongside the class teacher to provide help and support for slower children and those with particular learning difficulties.[22] Children with identified 'special educational needs' now form approximately 19 per cent of the primary school population.[23] In the present continuum model of 'special needs', the final stage involves the construction of a 'statement' of the specific educational need of a particular child, together with a plan by an educational psychologist (DFE 1994b). About 1.4 per cent of pupils in mainstream primary schools currently have a statement of 'special educational need' (DfEE; 1998b; Table 6.2). Such statements are likely to recommend additional support and help for a child within the classroom setting for a child in mainstream schooling.[24] Some children are recommended for full-time classroom support; a minority with behavioural difficulties are additionally recommended for support during non-contact time in lunches and other breaks.

There is a further percentage of children in mainstream classrooms with identified 'special educational need' who may be receiving support

---

[22] These teaching assistants are given a variety of names, including Special Support Assistant (SSA); Special Teaching Assistant (STA); Learning Support Assistant (LSA), and have a range of qualifications.

[23] This varies significantly between LEAs; it is also by no means clear that the assessment of special educational need is consistent between – or even within – LEAs (DfEE,1998e, p.44).

[24] Data on this are limited, but in one Outer London Borough an average of 14 hours of classroom support per statemented child was recommended.

from a teaching assistant but who do not have a statement of need. In many schools, a learning support assistant (or similar) may be provided for a proportion of lesson time for each class in order to provide additional general help for slower-learning children (often but not necessarily SEN). Tasks and responsibilities of support staff will be directed and organised by the classroom teacher, and vary according to the priority of needs perceived by the teacher.

These arrangements reflect the policy of maximising the inclusion rate of children into mainstream education. One main aim of the 'Code of Practice' (1994), which has been given additional emphasis in recent documentation (DfEE, 1997a) was to avoid a segregational approach to special educational needs, in which pupils are removed from their peer group. Yet in many cases the reality of classroom practice may introduce a form of segregation in which a child with a 'statement of need' works individually with his/her support assistant, and thus is effectively isolated from his/her classroom peers. Interaction with other pupils is reduced – as is interaction with the class teacher, who is likely to respond to the existence of a support assistant by spending more time in interaction with unsupported pupils. It is also a source of concern that those children with the greatest difficulty in learning are, to a large extent, dependent for their developmental progress on the skills of those without teaching qualifications or pedagogical knowledge. The low pay scale of teaching assistants means that most are untrained and unqualified in educational matters, although they may well have desirable personal qualities and attributes. Many schools make considerable efforts within their restricted budgets to provide training at an appropriate level for support assistants, often taking advantage of INSET provided by the LEA. The extent and level of in-service training for support assistants, however, appears highly variable between LEAs and is provided on a piecemeal basis.[25]

Pupils who are low attainers in mathematics and who are identified as needing special educational consideration are likely to be low achievers across the curriculum (Haylock, 1991). This may well reflect a specific lack of learning skills, for example, an inability to focus on a particular task for any extended length of time or a weakness in the ability to listen to instructions and to follow them through. The concern here, however, is with difficulties in relation to the learning of mathematics,

---

[25] Many involved directly with education expressed the view that there is a need to extend the current provision for training of support assistants.

although this may well be aggravated by weakness in reading skills. In many of the lessons observed in England, children who were apparently 'off-task' were, on being questioned, simply unable to read the text and the instructions. Evidence from other studies suggests there is a significant gap between average reading skills and textbook language (Rothery, 1980).[26] The extent to which mathematical progress is restricted by reading skills may be aggravated by the use of often complex language or difficult vocabulary used, especially in the contextualisation of word-problems (Clements, 1980).[27]

Other mathematical difficulties occur with the reading and writing of symbols, which, as with letters, must be written the correct way and in the right order. It is necessary to learn, for example, that numbers go from left to right but place value from right to left. As might be expected, children with problems of dyslexia often have further problems in mathematical development connected to this (Joffe, 1981). 'Mirror writing' is common among six- and seven-year old children in England, in both letters and numbers.[28] Only one occurrence of this was observed in Japan where this does not seem to be a problem. While reasons for this difference may be complex, there is no doubt that Japanese children were provided with detailed instruction in the correct writing of both *hiragana* and numbers in a way that was not observed in England.[29] Similarly, Japanese children do not appear to make errors by reversing figures in numbers with two or more digits (for example, 71 and 17); it may be that this reflects the need to be aware of the direction of writing.[30]

---

[26] Haylock's study (1991, *op. cit.*) showed that among the boys who were low attainers in mathematics, a higher proportion had poor reading skills than amongst the girls. This may relate to the significantly greater proportion of boys identified as having special needs (Boys : girls ~3:1).

[27] This study showed that a quarter of the mathematical errors made by 12-year olds arose from difficulties in reading or comprehension.

[28] For example, '$\varepsilon + \varepsilon = 6$' and '$6 + 6 = 21$'. Examples of mirror writing were noted on 13 of the written tests by the seven-year-old children in England out of a total of 108.

[29] Whole-class instruction on the correct writing and use of pagination was observed. Children practised making the correct strokes in the air in front of them, as modelled by the teacher. At the next stage, precision in writing was encouraged by the use of paper with a square provided for each character.

[30] In Japan, the content of mathematics textbooks is presented in horizontal rows from left to right, in accordance with Western convention. Language textbooks – and most other writing – are presented in vertical columns, moving from right to left (and working from the back page of a book to the front). While this might, arguably, be perceived as a possible source of confusion, in practice, children coped admirably.

Table 7. 3 *Teachers' views of low-attaining pupils in mathematics: percentages of teachers expressing views on low-attainment in mathematics*

	Per cent
The child has been low attaining in maths from the first year in school.	82
The child is low attaining in most areas of the curriculum.	79
The child's reading skills are poorly developed.	77
The child is equally poor in all aspects of mathematics.	74
The child's language skills are poorly developed.	70
No. of children sampled.	215

Source: Haylock, 1986, pp. 205–6.

Haylock's study of low attainers in mathematics[31] supports the view that children who are low attainers in mathematics are likely to have a wide range of difficulties (see Table 7.3); the factors associated with mathematical failure are thought to be equally wide. While there is a great deal of research evidence relating to the characteristics of low-attaining pupils in mathematics and the nature of their difficulties, there is less evidence relating to teaching approaches which are successful in improving their standards of attainment. One study, however, has produced evidence to show that lower-attainers benefit from being taught in a mixed-ability group or class and that gains in understanding result from the opportunity to observe how pupils of average and above-average attainment use problem-solving techniques and apply a range of calculating strategies (Slavin, 1987; 1990). Also it has been shown that lower-attaining pupils benefit significantly from higher levels of interaction (Haylock, 1991); whereas high-attaining children may be capable of independent work, using individualised work schemes and organising their own materials, this is a problem for lower-attaining pupils. In mathematics, it is argued here, concepts are understood more thoroughly and completely if they are developed gradually through a professional teacher directing the discussion by means of skilful questioning. Pupils who are potentially 'low attainers' are then provided with the opportunity to develop learning strategies together with others, to benefit from the insights of others, and to have their misconceptions and errors of understanding corrected (as well as those of others). Lower-attainers with limited reading skills benefit from problems being read aloud and discussed by the

[31]Of pupils aged 9–10 years.

Table 7.4 *Observation of teaching characteristics: Japan and England*

Characteristic of effective teaching	In Japan	In England
High incidence of teacher-pupil interaction	√	×
Structured development of lesson	√	×
Emphasis on use of language	√	×
High levels of pupil participation	√	×
Higher level of questioning used	√	×
High percentage of time on task	√	×
Non-grouped seating arrangement	√	×
Full integration of low attainers	√	Variable
Focused, narrow curriculum	√	×
'Overlearning' with ample consolidation and practice	√	×
Steady, unhurried pace	√	×
Careful sequencing of topics	√	×
Breaking down topics into small steps	√	×
Genuinely collaborative group work	Rare	Rare

whole class. They can increase their confidence, both mathematically and orally, by hearing mathematical concepts discussed and contributing to that discussion.

In summary, table 7.4 identifies the characteristics of mathematics teaching which research studies have shown to be successful with children of all ability levels (including low attainers) (Galton and Simon, 1980; Brophy and Good, 1986; Mortimore *et al.*, 1986). The extent to which they were observed is contrasted with characteristics of Japanese and English classroom practice observed during fieldwork.

This demonstrates the extent to which observed classroom practice in the teaching of mathematics in Japan reflects those characteristics which are known to be associated with effective teaching, for pupils of *all* levels of attainment. In contrast, in England, although the importance of these characteristics is widely acknowledged, they tend not to be incorporated into observed classroom practice. Instead, the English classroom practice widely uses a teaching approach which is known to be successful among children of above-average attainment. Such children, with high levels of motivation, will be successful and achieve relatively high rates of learning. Weaker children in the English system, however, with relatively poor levels of concentration, reading and organisational skills are likely to find independent learning difficult and demotivating. Progress is made particularly difficult for weaker children, therefore, by a system which emphasises the value and importance of individual independent learning; this may be an unrealistic goal for many children. Ironically, those children who are able to attain the goal of independent learning, are those who, in any system, are likely to make excellent progress and attain high standards. Thus although the English primary educational system is apparently egalitarian in principle with its allegiance to single-track mixed ability teaching, in practice the methods used favour the higher-attaining pupils. Or, as it has been said, 'Creating egalitarian structures, for example, will facilitate egalitarian outcomes only if the participants use those structures in egalitarian ways' (Robinson *et al.*, 1992).

Summary

Each aspect and stage of the transmission of mathematical understanding in Japan demonstrates an appreciation and awareness of the process of mathematical learning in young children. Observation of the lessons provides evidence that Japanese teachers recognise the need to develop conceptual understanding first, then to establish confidence and understanding of specific mathematical vocabulary and finally to develop procedural knowledge and application. All aspects of classroom practice in Japan appeared to be the result of careful planning designed to maximise effectiveness of teachers and their teaching. The same level of care appeared to have been taken with regard to teaching styles, seating arrangements, provision of mathematical equipment and the format of lessons. The emphasis given to teacher-pupil interaction, to oral work, and to the need to clarify misconceptions is a further indication of this care in developing pupils' understanding. This holistic approach produces an almost seamless overall method in which teachers help children to move forward to the next stage of understanding, and the risk of children failing to make satisfactory progress is minimised. The minimising of this risk also benefits from children's pre-school educational experience and the cultural attitudes of teachers and parents which have been discussed in Chapter 4. These include the development of qualities seen as facilitating progress and achievement – namely, effort and perseverance – and the emphasis on the importance of a co-operative rather than competitive learning atmosphere in the classroom environment.

In Japan, the importance attached to consideration of problems is perhaps surprising, given the common perception that Japanese children spend much of their time in rote learning of basic number facts. This was a major difference between the teaching approaches and the lesson content in the English and Japanese classes observed, and reflects the way that greater attention is given by Japanese teachers to developing children's thinking. Whole-class discussion of problem-solving approaches and strategies is thought to be of particular benefit to weaker children in developing their understanding. The emphasis given by teachers to the need for children to develop their own word-problems is thought to be particularly valuable in establishing a sound link between conceptual understanding and application of the related procedure, and at the same time ensuring that all children fully understand the associated mathematical language and its correct use.

In contrast, although observation of classroom practice in England demonstrates teachers' high levels of concern for their pupils' development and also their detailed knowledge of individual pupils' capabilities, teachers were observed to act primarily as managers or administrators in the classroom. They were not able to employ a direct teaching approach because the wide range of attainment rendered a whole-class approach inappropriate and children needed to be given differentiated activities commensurate with their particular developmental stage. At the same time, this limited possible teacher–pupil interaction and increased the burden of classroom management of a number of different activities. The need to construct a detailed scheme of work, to develop lesson materials and to prepare a large number of plans for a single lesson – together with the organisation of relevant equipment – means that teachers in England have had little time to devote to lesson structures and consideration of teaching styles. Teachers in England have, of necessity, become more occupied with classroom management and less with pupil interaction and instruction. Equally, it appears that while several highly regarded research studies have provided evidence on classroom organisation, including seating arrangements, this has not influenced classroom practice. Teaching in primary classes in England is also adversely affected by frequent interruptions to lessons for administrative reasons: it is suggested here that these should be discouraged and that it should be clearly established that the activity of teaching is of paramount importance.

The teaching methods and forms of instruction commonly used by Japanese teachers are precisely those that have been shown by other research studies as best in promoting the development of slower learning children, who might, under different circumstances, be predicted as becoming 'low attainers' in the field of mathematics. While the methods predominantly used in Japanese classrooms are identified as those advantaging slower learning children, there is no evidence (either from this study or from large-scale international studies) to suggest that higher-achieving children are being held back in their development or in any other way disadvantaged by the use of such teaching methods.

8

Exemplars of contrasting pedagogy

Introduction

The previous chapter examined the differences between classroom practice in the teaching of mathematics in England and Japan, from which it is suggested that:-

(i) despite influences from outside the classroom, the decisions taken by teachers and their subsequent actions within the classroom are of crucial importance to the way in which children develop mathematical understanding;

(ii) pre-school/kindergarten experience in Japan develops skills and rituals of social/classroom behaviour among *all* children, and provides a 'levelling experience', so that teachers are able to implement a 'whole-class' approach to teaching and learning more easily. In England, an emphasis on formal learning in pre-schooling, combined with a diversity of educational/social experience within the family setting, widens the range of skills among children as they begin formal schooling. By the time children in England are aged 6 and 7 years old, there are practical difficulties in using the whole-class approach which is thought to be especially effective in the teaching of mathematics;

(iii) other characteristics of the Japanese classroom model which encourage more effective teaching of mathematics include:

• active participation of all children;
• use of contextualised problems;

- emphasis on conceptual understanding *before* procedural competence;
- emphasis on oral language;
- careful sequencing of topics within mathematics curriculum, and of steps within topics.
- expectation for all children to reach a required standard.

It is argued here that children need a secure understanding of the basic mathematical concepts relating to number, its underlying logical structure and arithmetical operations, before any understanding of more complex concepts can be attempted. We also need to understand the problems children encounter in creating conceptual structures of the logical principles that underpin later learning of more formal complex mathematics (Piaget, 1965). Only when these difficulties are understood (it is argued here) can teachers provide appropriate help for children that will serve to advance their mathematical development.

This chapter examines in greater detail the classroom practice and teaching approach observed in the introduction of two key topics in early mathematical learning: subtraction and place value. Evidence from other research studies suggesting that children experience difficulty in understanding these topics is briefly reviewed (Clements, 1980; Baroody, 1984; Fuson, 1986a).

Subtraction

This section is concerned with identifying the difficulties that pupils in England experience in answering subtraction questions, and, by contrasting the teaching approaches used in England with those in other countries, to suggest some ways in which these difficulties might in some way be reduced and consequently performance increased. The performance of children at a relatively early stage of primary schooling in England is compared with children of a similar age in Japan; in particular, the types of errors made by them in the process of subtraction, and what these errors tell us about the levels of understanding is considered. It is argued that the nature of the errors made, and, in particular, the incidence of multiple errors made by English pupils, reveals a lack of understanding of the logical structure of number which is compounded by confusion over place value. It is suggested that this lack of basic understanding among pupils in the early stages of schooling arises from flawed teaching approaches, and, given the distinctly cumulative or 'linear' nature of learning mathematics, has serious implications for later learning.

Results from earlier research on the topic of subtraction

It is generally accepted that, for pupils of all ability levels, questions involving the process of subtraction cause greater difficulty and produce more wrong answers than questions involving addition (Clements, 1980; Baroody, 1984). This is partly because understanding the *concept* of subtraction causes more difficulty among young children – due at least in part to its lack of commutativity – and also that the *process* of subtraction is more complex (Deboys and Pitt, 1979). Further, the different types of subtraction problems that may be encountered at an early stage and the range of vocabulary associated with them makes the process of identification of subtraction as the correct operation more difficult for young children. Newman (1977) in his research on the difficulties encountered by 917 children in the solving of word problems identified a 'hierarchy of error causes' which had five levels. These arose from:

- reading of the words of the problem;
- comprehending its meaning;
- transforming the problem into the appropriate mathematical 'model';
- applying the necessary process skills;
- encoding the answer.

At any stage of solving word problems, however, carelessness can produce a wrong answer and so errors due to carelessness form a separate category. The results of Newman's study – which involved interviewing children regarding reasons for errors made on a previously completed written test – suggested that, for children in the sixth grade, almost half of all errors made in the solving of word problems arose through difficulties in reading, comprehending or transforming the problem into a mathematical form. This result was supported by later research with fifth grade children (Clements, *op.cit.*). However, since an error made in reading, comprehending or transforming leads inevitably to a wrong answer, it is not possible to know whether the remaining two stages would have been completed successfully or not. For this reason, language-free, decontextualised questions may be used to compare competence in subtraction, since these eliminate both problems of reading and of comprehension. It is also important that the nature of the operation should clearly be understood to be subtraction, in order to eliminate difficulties of transforming the word problem into the correct operational process.

While the research studies by Newman and Clements are both useful in demonstrating that, in relation to the solving of word problems, many errors are non-mathematical in nature, they are not concerned to understand the reasons for making errors of a mathematical type, nor to understand the nature of the misconceptions underlying these errors. To gain some understanding of the nature of misconceptions, we need to examine carefully answers that children provide in response to subtraction questions.

Existing comparative research

Until recently, there has been little data of a comparative nature regarding the understanding and competence of pupils of a similar age in different countries with regard to subtraction questions. The publication of the findings of the 1995 TIMSS survey relating to the performance of pupils in the primary and middle years of schooling, however, provides valuable information on this topic, and Table 2.6 (in Chapter 2) has shown that the performance of English pupils on the specific, language-free, algorithmic question presented in vertical format:

$$\begin{array}{r} 6000 \\ -2369 \end{array}$$

was notably poor in comparison to Japan.

Does this perceived superior ability of Japanese children to answer algorithmic subtraction questions correctly merely reflect competence in a memorised process (which might arguably with benefit be replaced by use of a calculator), or does it indicate a better fundamental understanding of the concept of subtraction? It is not possible to provide answers to these questions from the purely statistical results available from TIMSS. From results of the objective written test to seven-year-olds in this study, however, we can examine the types of errors made on subtraction questions.

Comparison of levels of mathematical competence in the early years of schooling among pupils in Japan and England

The full results of the written test used in this study are included in

Table 8.1 *Percentages of questions involving the process of subtraction answered correctly by seven-year-old pupils: Japan and England*

Question	England %	Japan %
Contextualised: Oral		
'How many are left?' (6 – 2)	93	99
'How many more?' (7 – 3)	66	92
Language-free: written		
8 – 3	84	99
6 – 0	89	97
13 – 5	53	87
Combined operations: 3 + 6 – 2	60	85
Algorithmic without decomposition (28 –15)	48	67
Algorithmic with decomposition (52 – 29)	5	54
No. of pupils in sample	108	106

Appendix B. It is of interest here, however, to note that in *all* the questions in which the process of subtraction was involved, the percentages of seven-year old Japanese pupils answering correctly (see Table 8.1) were significantly higher than those of seven-year old English children. Most of the questions involving subtraction either were simple, contextualised word problems (these were read to the children in order to avoid confounding the results with levels of literacy skills) or presented in horizontal format with numbers less than 10. It is encouraging that 93 per cent of children in England were able to answer an oral question involving number bonds up to 10 when it was presented in a straightforward subtraction format "How many are left?" It is clear that children found greater difficulty with the format involving "How many more?", reflecting a less secure understanding of the concepts and applications of subtraction. Two of the subtraction questions given in written format were presented vertically and involved numbers up to 100. These were:

A.   28   B.   52
      –15   –29

These two-digit questions involved a similar operational process to that required in the four-digit subtraction question included in TIMSS, although only 'B' required the application of the technique of 'decomposition' (referred to as 'renaming' by Baroody, 1989, and as 'trading' by Fuson, 1986b). Both questions were presented in an 'open-ended' format. While the performance of Japanese children was superior on both questions, the results of English children on Question B were significantly poorer than their results on Question A. That only 5 per cent of English children (tested in November of Year 3) were able to answer question B correctly must be a matter of great concern, especially since English pupils have had the benefit of at least one year's additional education in comparison to Japanese pupils of the same age.

If the results are examined more closely, it is possible to identify and classify the types of errors made by the children, and thus to reach some understanding of the misconceptions held by them about the structure of numbers. From other earlier research studies (Van Lehn, 1983; Baroody, 1989), we know something of the difficulties faced by children in questions involving the process of decomposition and the nature of the errors commonly made. For example, we know that some children will often persist in subtracting the smaller digit from the larger, regardless of position – thus in 52 – 29 the 2 would be subtracted from the 9 leading to the answer '37'. We also know that children correctly attempting to apply the technique of decomposition to the units, will forget to carry that through to the tens, leading to the answer '33'. Children are also likely to (attempt to) perform the process of addition rather than subtraction: however, it is unclear whether this results in general from a carelessness in noting the operational sign, or a fundamental lack of understanding of the difference between the two processes. These three types of error predominated among the wrong answers provided by English pupils in response to questions A and B above; however, the *range* of error types was far greater, and, importantly, in many cases it was clear that wrong answers arose from *multiple* errors.

From the incorrect responses of English children to question A, 24 different types of wrong answers were seen which are categorised in Table 8.2. The nature of the operation required in response to question B was more demanding, and a total of 27 different types of wrong answer was noted. These are categorised in a similar way in Table 8.3.

It is clear from comparing the nature of the errors made on subtraction, that the majority of errors made by Japanese children derived from their misreading (or failing to note) the minus-sign in the calculation and performing an addition calculation (correctly) instead. English pupils were more likely to make errors which resulted from inadequate knowl-

Table 8.2 *Errors made on subtraction question A:* 28
−15

Type of error	Examples of wrong answers seen	No. of pupils making this error	
		England	Japan
Single errors:			
Wrong operation: addition performed (correctly)	43	18	26
Lack of knowledge of number bonds	14, 12, 03, 16	5	1
Confusion over place value	31	4	4
Multiple errors:			
Addition performed incorrectly	33, 23, 53, 41, 51	15	
Addition; confusion over place value	61,313	2	
Unfathomable answers	30, 60	2	
Not attempted/not reached		10	4
Total number of wrong answers		56	35
Total number of pupils		108	106

edge of number structure, number bonds, or procedures. The analysis of errors has been made only from the written answers and does not have the benefit of pupils' comments on the reasoning behind the wrong answers, yet it is clear that many of the wrong answers given by English pupils are the result of a fundamental lack of understanding. In order to find out why this situation exists with English pupils to a greater extent than with Japanese pupils, we need to look more closely at the way concepts are introduced in the course of teaching. Considerable practice with oral and mental subtraction problems in order to secure an understanding of both the concept and the process is regarded as vital before the introduction of any written algorithms. The errors that are typically made in vertically written subtraction questions reflect a use of a memorised algorithm which is not tied to understanding, and indicate a less secure basis of understanding (Baroody, *op.cit.*).

Teaching approaches

Many teachers would agree that subtraction is best introduced through the use of concrete materials demonstrating a 'story' or word problem

Table 8.3 *Errors made on subtraction question B:* 52
                                                    −29

Type of error	Examples of wrong answers seen	No. of pupils making this error	
		England	Japan
Single errors:			
Wrong operation: addition			
performed (correctly)	81	12	22
Smaller digit from larger	37	30	10
2 − 9 = 0	30	1	
Decomposition not carried			
through	33	1	5
Multiple errors:			
Addition; performed incorrectly	91, 71	8	
Addition; confusion over			
place value	18, 711	3	
Addition; 2 − 9 = 0	70	2	
Smaller digit from larger;			
other errors	57, 47, 77	3	
Decomposition not carried			
through; other errors	35, 133	3	2
Mixture of operations	31, 22, 66	3	
Unfathomable answers	52, 19, 39, 3, 12, 11	10	8
Not attempted/not reached		27	2
Total		103	49
Total number of pupils		108	106

situation, orally described. In Japanese textbooks and associated teaching materials, this is achieved through an example of physical movement involved in, for example, fish swimming away. The importance of establishing a sound understanding at this stage, before any formal recording is attempted is an agreed essential first stage (Carpenter and Moser, 1984). The next stage is to replace the concrete materials by a diagrammatic method illustrating the 'story' situation: in both these stages children will initially use a counting strategy to solve the problems rather than an arithmetic strategy or known number bonds and relationships.

Only at a much later stage, when the concept of subtraction is securely fixed, should more abstract 'language-free' questions be introduced: according to Baroody (1985), these may be solved either by using a modelling and counting strategy (a reconstructive process) or by retrieving known number facts (a reproductive process). At a still later stage of development in mathematical understanding and competency, children may use a combination of both types of process in the solution of problems – they may hold number facts in their memory and apply reconstructive procedures involving known processes. Children are likely to increase their efficiency in mental calculations at this stage if they can be encouraged to adopt more sophisticated strategies than the simple 'counting on' algorithm.

Detailed observation of Japanese and English lessons suggests that differences may arise in the following ways:

- from the order in which different types of subtraction problem are introduced;
- from the strategies for mental calculation which children are encouraged to use;
- from the approaches used to teaching.

These are discussed in the following sections.

Different types of subtraction problems

First, the broad typology of subtraction problems to which children are introduced generally during their first year of schooling, at age 5 or 6, depending on age of beginning statutory schooling, may be divided into three main groups:

(i) *Separating* (including problems of 'taking away', partitioning and reduction)[1]
Example: Jane has 6 sweets. She gives 2 to Tom. How many does she have left?

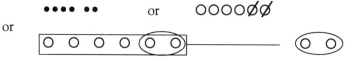

or

---

[1] This categorisation is not necessarily standard among all authors: for example Haylock (1995) adopts four categories of subtraction questions by placing questions involving a 'reduction' structure in a separate fourth category.

(ii) Comparison (including problems of difference and 'how many more?')
Example: Jane has 6 sweets. Tom has 2. How many more does Jane have than Tom?

O O O O O O

O O

(iii) Equalising (including problems of complementary addition, joining and 'how many more are needed?')
Example: Jane has 6 sweets. Tom has 8. How many more does Jane need in order to have the same number as Tom?

O O O O O O

O O O O O O O

(Further subdivisions of these three main groups may be identified and are discussed, *inter alia*, by Carpenter *et al.*, 1981, Carey, 1991 and Fuson, 1992.)

There is a strong argument for introducing children to the 'separating' group of problems first, since this category of questions clearly involves action which may be demonstrated more easily to young children using concrete materials. The 'comparison' category involves a more

Figure 8.1 *Atarashii Sansū, 1 (p. 31)*

static relationship between quantities which is less easy to demonstrate (Carpenter *et al.*, 1981), and whereas some 'equalising' problems also involve action, this may be less clear to young children. Another complicating factor arising with the category of 'equalising' problems is that the inverse relationship between the processes of addition and subtraction is not immediately perceived by children – it is only with later practice and consolidation that this becomes apparent and can be used as a problem-solving strategy.

In educational practice in Japan, an understanding of the 'taking away' action involved in the 'separating' group of problems is secured in children's minds before other types of subtraction problems are introduced. The illustration shown in Figure 8.1 is taken from the first lesson on subtraction. All examples used involve the element of physical movement: in addition to fish being caught in a net or swimming away,[2] examples refer to cakes and strawberries being eaten, birds and balloons flying away, cars being driven away, turtles swimming away and children running away. In addition to demonstrating the process, great emphasis in placed in the first introductory lesson on 'separating' and 'joining' actions: this also helps to develop an awareness of the inverse nature of the addition/ subtraction process.

In the second lesson on the 'taking away' category of subtraction questions, however, the 'visualisation' of the removal of the objects is not made explicit. The examples below taken from two worksheets illustrate this point (see Figures 8.2 and 8.3). In the first example, children see five ladybirds on a leaf; three then fly away. However, the use of the separate illustrations prevents children from using a 'counting strategy' to answer the questions. Instead the children need either to imagine three of the original five flying away, or, as the diagram beneath the illustrations suggests, use appropriate symbolic notation to construct the abstract calculation and to use their knowledge of number facts to answer it.

Another example (see Figure 8.3) shows four sheets of *origami* two of which are used to make cranes (*tsuru*), but the two sheets themselves are not removed. Again the children must construct the abstract form of the sum for themselves, and are prevented from using a 'counting strategy' as a means of solving the problem. This represents an important transitional stage between contextualised word problems and use

---

[2] The popular use of fish to demonstrate examples in mathematics reflects also the parallels often drawn between children in a class group and fish 'swimming happily in a pond altogether.'

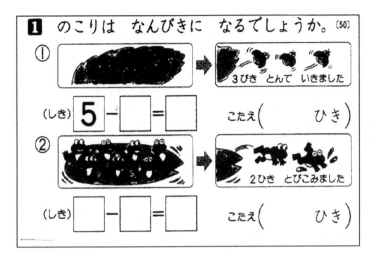

Figure 8.2 *Japanese subtraction work-sheet 1*

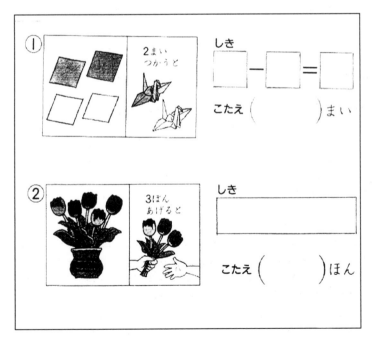

Figure 8.3 *Japanese subtraction work-sheet 2*

of concrete materials, to the use of symbolic notation and abstract thought.

Teachers' manuals provide clear, specific instruction on the extensive demonstration to be given by teachers – and pupils – of the concept of 'separating', together with the specific questions to be asked of the children, the vocabulary to be introduced and the mathematical language to be emphasised.[3] Only after extensive consolidation and practice with the idea of 'taking away' will the 'comparison' category of subtraction problems be introduced. 'Comparison' problems require an understanding of a 'one-to-one' relationship involving matching members of two sets and counting the remaining unmatched members. Problems in the third 'equalising' category which require an appreciation of the complementary addition aspect of subtraction are not introduced until a considerably later stage in mathematical development.

In Japan, the requirement of textbook approval leads to greater standardisation of material and less choice for teachers. In England, there is more diversity of content and methods within the main published schemes for the teaching of mathematics in primary schools: the comments made here refer to the most popular of those schemes (Keys *et al.*, 1996).[4] Although the most commonly used series of mathematics textbooks first introduce the topic of subtraction through the 'taking away' category of problems, there is less emphasis on modelling through the use of concrete materials and contextualised problems than at the comparable stage in Japanese textbooks.

Although, in the earliest stages of subtraction, children will model the situation with concrete objects by first representing the larger quantity (minuend) followed by taking the smaller quantity (subtrahend) from it, and then counting the remaining items: children will progress more quickly in England than in Japan to using a diagrammatic approach to modelling and then to a number line to calculate the answer. Children in England also progress more quickly than children in Japan to types of

---

[3] Examples of questions to be asked in relation to the fish in the tank (see Figure 8.1) include "What is the girl doing?" (make sure that pupils understand that fish are being caught) "How many fish are left in the tank?" "How many would be left if only one was taken out?" Teachers are also instructed to demonstrate modelling the situation by using concrete materials, and to explain step-by-step the movement of these materials.

[4] According to TIMSS (Mullis *et al.*, 1997) the most popular primary mathematics schemes in England were those published by Cambridge University Press, Heinemann Educational and Nelson.

subtraction questions involving approaches other than the single 'taking away'. Yet 'comparison' and 'equalising' problems require either an understanding of a 'one-to-one' matching, or an ability to count *on or back*. Evidence indicates that the ability to count backwards represents a higher level of cognitive development (Piaget, 1941), and the difficulties encountered by young children attempting to count back or down have been documented by Fuson (1986a) who has successfully introduced children to a method of 'counting up' from the smaller number to the larger in situations where the more cognitively demanding approach of 'counting down' would have been used. This suggests that these subtraction types are better left until understanding and competence with a 'taking away' subtraction type is secure.

Strategies for calculation

The use of a counting strategy in solving subtraction problems is given greater prominence in English (and American) teaching approaches than those found in Japan, where more emphasis is given to children progressing rapidly to 'knowing their number facts up to 10' and encouraging the use of efficient reproductive processes. While the simple subtraction question faced at the initial stage may be solved *either* by counting *or* by the retrieval of known number facts, when more difficult problems are encountered it becomes increasingly important to use procedures that are more efficient than counting. Children in Japanese classes were observed using a rapid 'fact retrieval method' within a few weeks of being introduced to subtraction – any child attempting to rely on a 'counting' strategy would have had difficulty keeping up with the rest of the class.

For both addition and subtraction problems involving numbers larger than 10, Japanese children are explicitly taught a two-stage strategy. It should also be remembered that children in Japan are introduced to numbers between 10 and 20 as a special category. For example, in addition questions children will be taught to find the answer to $8 + 5$ by considering it as $8 + 2 + 3$: in another words to break the addend into two parts, with the first part representing the amount needed to make 10, leading to $8 + 2 + 3 = 10 + 3 = 13$. This strategy is not necessarily the simplest one (for example, in the case of $6 + 6$ children may to prefer to use their number fact knowledge of 'doubles' rather than breaking it into $6 + 4 + 2$); its merit lies in its general applicability to all situations. With subtraction problems, however, two different two-stage strategies are found in Japanese textbooks – the difference between them is demonstrated most easily through an example:

(i) $14 - 6 = 14 - 4 - 2 = 10 - 2 = 8$
(ii) $14 - 6 = 10 - 6 + 4 = 4 + 4 = 8$

In the first two-stage strategy, the subtrahend is separated into two parts, so that the minuend is first taken down to 10 (or a multiple of 10). In the second strategy, the minuend is separated into two parts, namely 10 and a remainder, with the subtrahend being subtracted from 10 before the remainder is added.

Some authors (Fuson *et al.*, 1988) have suggested that the first method involving taking the minuend down to 10 is more easily used by Japanese pupils since the counting language used is 'regular'. For example, $14 - 6$ would be heard as the equivalent of 'ten-four subtract six' – thus clearly indicating that 4 needs to be subtracted from 14 to reduce it to 10, whereas in English – and most other European languages irregular 'teen' words produce 'fourteen subtract six' and many young children in the early years of schooling do not automatically know the tens patterns for these words.

While method (i) more closely corresponds to the recommended strategy for addition, it is method (ii) that Japanese children are introduced to first. A justification for method (ii) was provided by Japanese primary teachers who explained that in *practical* situations the subtrahend would first be subtracted from 10: for example, a girl paying for an item costing 6 yen when she had 14 yen in her hand would not hand over the 14 yen – instead she would get 4 yen change from the 10 yen, leaving her with $4 + 4$ yen. A further justification for introducing Japanese children first to method (ii) is that they have already developed considerable facility in subtracting unitary numbers from 10 (see Chapter 7). Method (ii) also reinforces the importance attached to the concept of 'ten' in Japan for developing understanding of numerical structure. Japanese teachers agreed, however, that the two-stage method (i) would be taught at a later stage of mathematical calculation and might well be preferred in calculations involving larger numbers.

The greater attention given by Japanese textbooks to explaining the process is demonstrated by the explanation accompanying the above two-stage method, which is broken down into four steps as follows;

1. $4 - 6$ cannot be done;
2.   14 is $10 + 4$;

3.   10 subtract 6 equals 4;
4.   4 add 4 equals 8

The different strategies for two-stage operations described, however, have two common features: firstly, they depend on knowledge and rapid retrieval of number bonds up to 10, and they emphasise the importance of 10, by either subtracting *down* to 10, or subtracting *from* 10. The effect of using either of the two-stage operations described is the same – namely, to provide all children with a general strategy for calculations which can be applied in *any* subtraction situation, and can easily be extended to apply to problems involving larger numbers.

In contrast, English schemes do not appear to suggest the use of any strategies other than counting. One scheme, for example, shows 12 – 5 as a 'string' of 12 beads with 5 crossed out, with the remaining number to be counted:

(Source: Ginn Maths 2, pp.26–7).

English textbooks tend to use illustrative diagrams that permit counting of the number of objects remaining, in contrast to the Japanese examples shown earlier where children are required to visualise the number remaining. Another scheme in use in English primary schools suggests that, after some revision of the meaning of 'difference' and 'how many more', subtraction up to 20 (e.g. 13 – 6) should be performed by means of counting back on a number line. The comment in this scheme that "The children may need to be reminded that subtraction by counting back involves moving towards the smaller numbers and that it is the number of *jumps* which they count – they should not tap the starting point" (*Nuffield Maths*, 1979), suggests that children are likely to lack fundamental understanding of, first, number, and, secondly, the subtraction process. This scheme requires children to use a counting strategy or the number line to solve 13 – 4, although "mental recall is hoped for" (*ibid.*, p. 35).

Similar approaches may be found in other English schemes: for example one popular scheme revises subtraction, first, by demonstrating 'Jason jumping back on the number line' (requiring facility and accuracy in counting backwards) and, secondly, by presenting a decontextualised number line for use in the subtraction sums involving numbers up to 20 (and crossing the tens boundary) (*Cambridge Primary Maths.*,1989). While a range of activities is included in these textbooks – for example, for 'counting back' a 'hundred square' or a number line may be used, pictures of children in rows may be used to illustrate 'finding the difference', and mental work (TU – U, not crossing the 'tens boundary') is used to encourage the observation of patterns in number work, yet the two-stage operation for use in subtraction sums crossing the 'tens' boundary does not appear to be encouraged.[5] The use of Dienes' apparatus to develop conceptual understanding of the technique of 'decomposition', which is encouraged by most of the schemes, is extremely helpful to children in the early years stages, but in order to move from the use of concrete materials to a competence with subtraction questions in a purely symbolic form, some further mental strategy is necessary, if children are to progress from being dependent on 'counting'.[6]

A valuable contribution is made by Putnam *et al.* (1990) on the use of 'derived fact' strategies in addition and subtraction. This describes ways in which children may use their existing knowledge of number combinations to develop strategies for finding hitherto unknown number combinations, without being taught a standard strategy for such calculations. It is suggested from the basis of their research that children will use a range of strategies relating to known facts. For example, 14 – 9 might be solved by using the known fact that subtracting 9 is the same as subtracting 10 and adding 1 (i.e. using knowledge of subtracting 10), whereas 14 – 6 might be solved by knowing that 14 – 7 = 7 (i.e. using 'doubles' knowledge) and then using 14 – 6 = 14 – 7 + 1. It is argued by Putnam that "these strategies are desirable and more sophisticated than simple counting procedures because they build on the structure and relationships among the basic combinations." Yet all the strategies described by Putnam, which are typical of the class of operations constituting 'derived fact strategies', apply to particular number combinations and hence are far less robust than the procedures taught in Japan, since they need to be constantly adapted to fit the particular numbers in the sum presented.

It may be argued that children in England typically face greater

---

[5] A triangular diagram illustrating a two-stage operation may be found in Deboys and Pitt (1979, p.45) which provides useful advice for teachers rather than being a mathematics scheme as such – but this two-stage operation does not involve taking the minuend down to ten.

[6] The recent publication of the Teacher Training Agency document which suggests a range of strategies including that of 'bridging' is welcomed (TTA, 1998).

difficulties with regard to subtraction problems due to the considerable range of vocabulary available in the English language associated with subtraction. It may well be that the range of subtraction vocabulary used in other languages is not as great – to illustrate this point, some comparisons may be made with the subtraction vocabulary in Japanese. For example, while the word *hiku* corresponds to *subtract*, and *toru* to 'take away', there would appear to be no specific separate Japanese equivalent words used with elementary school children for *difference* and *minus*. Further, when subtraction problems involving comparisons occur, the single Japanese word *yori* is used with young children in any comparative question, in contrast to the range of English expressions such as *greater than, more than, less than, further, longer, shorter, heavier*, and so on. It is, therefore, arguably easier for a Japanese child to identify a problem involving subtraction, by listening to the vocabulary used and it may be more difficult for English children to *comprehend* the nature of problems and to appreciate that the appropriate mathematical model involves subtraction. This, however, only serves to underline the need for clear, effective teaching.

Teaching methods

Accepting that difficulties arise with dealing with subtraction questions, firstly, due to the conceptual complexity and, secondly, to the greater procedural complexity, accentuates the need for effective teaching. The concept of subtraction is best introduced through teacher demonstration, and using a whole-class approach which maximises teacher–pupil interaction is arguably the most teacher-efficient way of achieving this. In addition to the initial demonstration using concrete materials, the concept needs to be explained and discussed, requiring further teacher-pupil interaction. This, too, is most efficiently achieved through a whole-class approach, in which all children have the opportunity to answer questions, demonstrate to the class and listen to each other. Mathematical language is more easily understood if it is frequently heard used in the appropriate context; children are seen to develop confidence in their correct use of key mathematical terms when they are provided with plenty of examples.

Reference has been made to the greater use of detailed 'teachers' manuals' in Japan which accompany the pupils' textbooks and provide a step-by-step approach to each new concept. In the case of subtraction (*hikizan*), the aim of the first lesson (as given in the Teachers' Manual for *Atarashii Sansū*, p. 76) is "to understand the meaning of subtraction in the case of 'separation' questions" and then "to construct a mathematical sentence describing subtraction as illustrated by 'separation' examples".

The instruction in the teachers' manual explains that teachers should begin the first lesson on subtraction by discussing the illustration of children removing fish from the tank (included earlier in this chapter), including asking children to check the number of red fish, the number of black fish, and the total number of fish. The same situation should then be demonstrated (the manual continues) by the illustration of the same situation using blocks or other concrete materials: "We want to find out the number of black fish: let's use the blocks so that everyone can see and understand". The manual continues by stressing that since the aim is for children to be able to illustrate the relationship between the total and the constituent parts by using the blocks, this is more easily achieved if blocks of different colours are used – for example, by using yellow and white blocks as well as red and black blocks.

From observation of this introductory lesson on the concept of subtraction, it was clear that the repeated demonstration of separation and joining of the two sets of groups constituting the whole enabled children to develop a secure understanding not only of the *concept* of subtraction but also of the *relationship* between addition and subtraction. Discussion of other examples followed, demonstrating similar situations to the removal of fish, and the way in which mathematical sentences could be used to describe symbolically the physical situations. Many children were given the opportunity to demonstrate the process of 'separation' and 'joining' to the class, appearing to revel in the extended repetition involved rather than becoming bored with the lesson. The teacher was careful to involve the slower members of the class in the demonstration – they received praise and encouragement for their participation.

The teachers' manual provided additional explanation for the benefit of the teacher on the importance of children beginning with the 'separation' process, explaining that since children found it easy to split a 'whole' into two constituent parts without using the concept of subtraction ("with numbers up to 10, they would know the 'missing part' from their knowledge of addition up to 10"), it was important for children first to develop an understanding of the relationship between the 'whole' and the parts . Only then should the children be led to understand that *hikizan* refers to the calculation to find the number of objects remaining after some objects have been removed. Examples for the children (written in

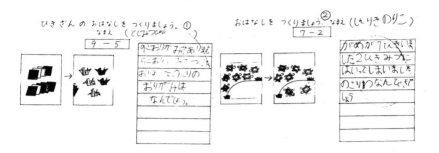

Figure 8.4 *Examples of Japanese children's word problems to describe an illustrated question*

Notes: Left-hand diagram: the children wrote "There were 9 sheets of origami. 5 sheets were folded to make cranes. How many sheets were left?"

Right-hand diagram: "There were 7 turtles. 2 of them went into the water. How many turtles are left?"

simple language that all could read) included: "There are 6 fish including 3 red ones. How many black ones are there?" "There are 8 children; 5 of them are girls. How many boys are there?" The aim of the second lesson on subtraction was to encourage children to construct their own 'subtraction stories' which might then be described by specific mathematical sentences (see Chapter 7). In order to 'make a story' from which the mathematical question '7 – 3' might be symbolically constructed, the manual suggested that in discussion the example: "There are 7 flowers and 3 of the flowers are white. How many red ones are there?" might be used as an illustration. In the ensuing discussion, children showed not only an understanding of appropriateness of the situations, but also a level of inventiveness in suggesting 'subtraction stories'. All were able to put their 'stories into pictorial form: a few experienced difficulties and were helped accordingly. Examples of the mathematical questions given are included: "There were six glasses of milk. Two were drunk. Four were left." "I have five cakes. Three were eaten. Two were left." "I have seven cars. Two are red. How many are blue?" A number of separate and distinct stages followed. Children were asked to *write* stories to describe specific contextualised visual subtraction situations. Two examples of completed worksheets are shown above (Figure 8.4) which were typical

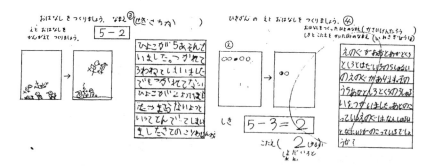

Figure 8.5 *Examples of Japanese children's own subtraction word problems (shown in pictures and words)*

Notes: Left-hand diagram: the children wrote "5 chickens were playing. 3 of them became tired and went to sleep. Meanwhile, there were 2 chickens that were not tired. They became bored and flew away. How many chickens are left?"

Right-hand diagram: "There are 5 types of paints; blue, red, black, white and flesh-coloured. 3 paints (red, white and black) were used. How many types of paint and which colours are left?"

of the standard achieved by six-year-old children of some six weeks experience of formal schooling.

The next stage was for children to be given a contextualised subtraction situation but without the visual image, which they provided before writing the story. Two examples are shown in Figure 8.5, from children who were judged to be of an average standard, which demonstrate the creativity and inventiveness of the children.

Children were also provided with extensive practice in completing the abstract calculations from a contextualised visual presentation. Each work sheet included only a small number of examples – perhaps only two or three – in order that children could feel a sense of achievement in completing a task, and also so that the teacher was constantly checking work from individual children and errors in understanding would be quickly identified. In the two examples shown in Figure 8.6, children are given "problems to persevere with" for which they must provide the abstract form of the sum illustrated in the pictures.

The final stage was to complete abstract subtraction questions with no contextualisation, language, or visual presentation. An example of one work sheet of this type is shown in Figure 8.7. Ten work sheets of this last type were completed by *all* first-grade children during the last ten

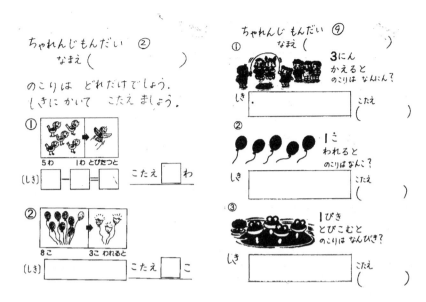

Figure 8.6 *Work sheets requiring an 'abstract' form of subtraction*
Note: The descriptions provided with each illustration respectively explain: 5 birds; 1 flies away. 8 balloons; 3 burst. 3 children are going home; how many are left? 1 balloon bursts; how many are left? 1 frog jumps in; how many are left?

Figure 8.7 *Example of Japanese work sheet with decontextualised subtraction questions*

minutes of the observed lesson. The sheets were placed around the class-room and children raced to complete them, in order, and to have their work checked by one of the two teachers present in this lesson. The few children who had one or two work sheets outstanding at the conclusion of the lesson collected them voluntarily and took them home for completion.

This detailed description of the introduction of subtraction to children in Japan illustrates that the thoroughness of the introduction to the underlying *concept* is followed by practice and demonstration with the *process*; the development of mental strategies for calculation at a later stage, together with the clarity of the teaching on the significance of place value, provide both the understanding and skills necessary for the correct solution of subtraction questions. The rigour and clarity of the teaching, supported by the instruction provided in the teachers' manuals, is a major factor in preventing the types of errors identified in responses from English children.

Once children are confident with a basic concept, applying the appropriate process becomes less problematic; however, it is clear that in the case of subtraction, a sound knowledge of number bonds and a correct understanding of place value are prerequisites for correct solutions to abstract problems. Decomposition as a technique to aid more difficult subtraction questions can only be developed once the basic knowledge is there; in many cases it was apparent that children in England were attempting to apply an incomplete knowledge of decomposition to a faulty basic understanding of the concept and the process of subtraction.

Conclusion

Apart from linguistic considerations, it appears that there are two common features associated with the teaching of subtraction to young children in Japan. First, *all* children should be provided with a sound understanding of both the concept and *then* the process. Considerable practice with oral and mental subtraction problems in order to secure an understanding of both the concept and the process is vital before the introduction of any written algorithms; errors made in vertically written subtraction questions reflect a use of a memorised algorithm not tied to understanding, and indicate a less secure basis of understanding (Baroody, 1989). Each step in the understanding of subtraction is identified and taught before progressing to the next stage.

Secondly, the importance of providing all children with a strategy for mental calculation which has general applicability to all situations is re-garded as vital: while it may be argued that children may sometimes prefer to use derived fact strategies – for example, in their use of 'doubles' or near doubles – the fundamental point is that all children should have a general strategy within their range of skills. An additional advantage of using the two-stage procedure is that children will also constantly be applying their knowledge of number combinations up to 10, thus improv-ing their retrieval speed. If problems are solved using only 'counting strategies' then existing levels of facility with number combinations will be unused and may well be forgotten. The strategies outlined have the additional merit of emphasising the importance of the number '10', and thus further secure understanding of number structure.

It is clear that many English children lack an understanding of the concept of subtraction and a sufficiently secure understanding of number structure. Greater demonstration by teachers of the concept and the process, together with full discussion and encouragement for children to create their own subtraction problems, could well help children to over-come the difficulties they experience at present. While we can accept that children differ in the speed with which they understand and apply new mathematical concepts, it is vital that all children should be pro-vided with the opportunity, repeated as often as necessary, for securing the basic understanding which is essential for further achievement in mathematics.

Place value

Introduction

In the numeration widely used today, each digit in a multi-digit number has a different value according to its position or place: for example, we know that in the number '334', one '3' represents '300' and the other '3' represents '30' by their positions in relation to one another. Acquiring an understanding of the concept of 'place value', and an ability to apply the meaning of the concept properly in subsequent calculations and prob-lems, causes difficulty among a significant proportion of weaker pupils in England – and often this difficulty is not resolved during the years of primary schooling. From classroom observation of secondary school pu-pils in England, it is not uncommon for a weaker pupil in Key Stage 3 on hearing the number 'two thousand three hundred and eighty four' to record it symbolically as '2000300804'.

Research studies concerned with the failure of US children to develop an adequate understanding of place value have argued that children need to construct multi-unit conceptual structures of numbers beyond 20 (Fuson, 1990). Initially, children's conceptual structures for number-names relate only to unitary numbers, but since number names and written symbols for multi-digit numbers involve these same numbers, it is essential that children understand how to construct these multi-digit numbers.

An understanding of the concept of place value is thought to accompany the development of an understanding of the structure of multi-digit numbers. Fuson concludes that English-speaking children may need "considerable and extended support in the classroom for constructing multi-unit meanings based on ten" because of irregularities in the number name system and the fact that in two-digit numbers the 'tens' are not explicitly named (Fuson, 1990, *op. cit.*, p. 278).

It is clear that an accurate understanding of place value is essential before any calculations with multi-digit numbers can sensibly be attempted. Errors occurring in responses of the sample of seven-year-old English children to the two-digit subtraction questions have already been discussed; many of these arose from a failure to understand the significance of the positioning of the digits – although in many cases additional misconceptions were involved in the wrong answers given.

This section considers, first, the different demands made on English and Japanese pupils in the nature of the required understanding of place value according to the differences in their respective numerative and symbolic counting systems. Are Japanese children, by virtue of the regularity of their numeration system, provided with a significant advantage in understanding of number structure? Does the relative irregularity of the English system of numeration imply that a greater emphasis on the direct teaching of this topic is required to secure an understanding? Secondly, the methods used to introduce multi-digit numbers and place value are contrasted, according to analysis of lesson materials and drawing extensively on classroom observation of teaching approaches.

It is argued that the greater use made of visual aids in the teaching of this topic in Japan, together with the consistent use of colour, emphasis on oral language and the precise meaning of the specific mathematical vocabulary associated with place value, combine to encourage the development of a sounder level of understanding of place value among second-grade pupils.

Background

The term 'place value' is a shorthand for a concept which involves understanding both the base of a numeration system and the underlying logic of the number structure. Both the English and Japanese counting systems, in common with other developed countries, use a base of ten, [7] although until relatively recently in England pupils were expected to perform calculations involving transformations to counting systems using other bases. For example, prior to decimalisation of money in 1971 and the subsequent introduction of the metric system for weights and measures into schools, [8] children would routinely perform calculations involving base 12 by trading from pence to shillings, base 14 by trading from pounds to stones, and base 16 by trading from ounces to pounds. Also, the mathematics syllabus leading to Certificate of Secondary Education examinations for several years required pupils to manipulate a number of different bases (from 2 to 9) and to perform simple calculations in them.[9] Both these activities required a facility with numerical procedures which is not currently expected of English pupils who, in the main, perform calculations only with numbers in base ten and thus need only a competence and understanding of the base ten number system.

In addition to understanding the base 10 nature of the numeration system, however, children must also understand the logic of grouping objects or units into bundles of ten and then into a hundred, and that the position of a figure within a number determines its value. For example, they must comprehend that a bundle of 14 objects can be perceived of as 1 ten and 4 ones (Baroody *et al.*, 1983; Baroody and Gannon, 1984;

---

[7] There are several examples of counting systems using bases other than 10; for example the Mayan civilisation used a base of 8 for its counting system.

[8] Although there was an initial declaration of the government's intention to switch to a metric system, this was never implemented, with the result that in the 'real world' in England outside schooling, weights and measures based on the earlier Imperial system, such as feet, inches, pounds, ounces, are still widely used. The extent to which this dual system has contributed to confusion in understanding measurement, leading to later difficulties in performing calculations in mathematical problems can only be the subject of speculation.

[9] The CSE examinations were designed for pupils who would not normally have taken GCE examinations, and were, therefore, intended to be set at a lower level of difficulty. It was a source of some puzzlement that the CSE syllabus included the relatively complex topic of 'changing bases', while many of the different syllabuses for GCE examinations did not include this. This anomaly continued until both CSE and GCE examinations were abolished and replaced by the single GCSE examinations in 1988.

Baroody, 1987a). This has not always been the case in all numeration systems; it was the introduction of a character to denote 'zero' by the Hindu-Arabic system that enabled position of a character to indicate value – for example, without '0', the difference between '45' and '405' would be lost.[10] When they see the number '725', for example, children need to understand that this represents "7 groups of one-hundred, 2 groups of ten, and 5 units or ones". This assumes, however, that a prior understanding exists of the fact that one group of ten represents 10 units, and one hundred represents 10 groups of ten. These are complex ideas to be grasped, and many children have difficulty in successfully applying this structure to large numbers. Children find particular difficulty, for example, in providing the symbolic notation for 'two hundred and five' heard aurally, which will often be transcribed as '2005'. Applying the same logic, 'two thousand three hundred and five' will appear as '20003005', which suggests that although children are familiar with the notation they lack an adequate understanding of the logical numeration structure and place value. It has been argued elsewhere that many children throughout their primary school years have a weak grasp of the ideas of place value, which can represent a major obstacle to the understanding and use of multi-digit numeration and computation (Ross, 1986; Baroody, 1989). Before considering the difficulties associated with understanding the significance of the position of a number, however, some differences between the numeration structure of Japan and England should be identified.

Counting systems

We need to consider the extent to which Japanese children benefit from using a different and *more regular counting system*. A number of research studies regarding early development of understanding of number structure have suggested that the differences between languages may be a contributory factor, and that this may also be related to later differences

---

[10] The Roman system which used only I,V,X and L to number up to 99 was economical in the number of different characters used but depended on 'counting on' and 'counting back' to indicate the value of a number and was useless for performing calculations. The Egyptian hieroglyphic system was easier to use for calculations, but depended on repetitions of the characters for hundreds, tens and units, having no concept of the position of a character indicating its value. Baroody (1989, pp. 269–73, Ch.10) argues that the Egyptian numeration system is an "ideal vehicle for bridging children's informal knowledge and formal base ten place value representation of number".

in mathematical attainment (Miura, *et al.*, 1988; Fuson and Kwon, 1991; Miura, 1993; Nunes and Bryant, 1996).

The counting system used in Japan is entirely regular, in the sense that the numbers from one to ten reappear in a logical and systematic form to provide all other numbers up to 99, with '11, 12, 13...' up to '20' being heard and written as the equivalent of 'ten-one, ten-two, ten-three...' up to 'two-ten'. The base ten system is repeated systematically, with '31' becoming 'three-ten-one', and so on. Such a regular counting system may be termed 'generative' in the sense that once the logical structure of the system is understood, it may be used to generate new numbers not previously encountered. In contrast, the counting system used in the English language, in common with most other European languages, contains irregularities in the numbers beyond ten, especially in the 'teens' and words for multiples of ten.[11] Thus the learning of number words in the correct order is more demanding for English children using an irregular, non-generative counting system in which all the number words up to twenty need to be learnt in the correct order, and also the words for multiples of ten.

In the Japanese system which uses only the words for numbers up to ten to generate all numbers up to 99, the word order demonstrates value, which may later assist understanding of place value. Other studies have suggested that there is a significant advantage for young children in using a logical and structured numbering system (Fuson, 1988; Nunes and Bryant, *op.cit.*) in which the importance of base ten is underlined by the way 'ten' is repeatedly heard in all numbers above ten. A further study of US and Korean children found better understanding of multi-digit numbers among the Korean children who also use a regular system for numeration (Fuson and Kwon, 1992); it was additionally suggested that a sound understanding of the system of multi-digit numbers influenced and affected children's choice of strategies for solving problems (Fuson, 1990). Comparative studies of five-year old American and Chinese children have shown that the latter group, using a generative number system similar to that used in Japan make fewer errors in counting and show better understanding of the importance of ten in the number structure (Miller and Stigler, 1987; Miura and Okamoto, 1989; Miura *et al.*, 1994). Geary (1994, p.244) suggests that this difference could give Asian

---

[11] A notable exception to the irregularity of European languages in relation to counting systems is Welsh, which has a regular counting system similar in construction to that of Japanese.

children "an early edge in mathematics" and might be an important contributory factor in the faster progress of Asian children in mathematical understanding in the early years of schooling. The findings of these studies, however, will be affected to some extent by cultural influences at the societal level, home background, and parents' expectations, although it is generally accepted that the extent to which social influences affect progress is less in mathematics than in attainment in other curricular subjects. A study of five-year-old children in parallel classes in Wales, taught either through the medium of Welsh or English depending on the language spoken at home, casts doubt on the importance of this factor. Children taught through the medium of Welsh, which has an entirely regular number-name system, showed only marginally greater counting skills and understanding of the structure of number than did the children in parallel classes taught in English (MacLean and Whitburn, 1996). Geary (*ibid.*) noted that Asian children also did better on non-number work and concluded that the regularity of number-name systems was "probably only a minor influence and one of a multitude of influences on mathematics development and achievement". It is suggested that while the use of a regular counting system may facilitate the acquisition of an ability to count, [12] by the time that children reach the age of six to seven, they are likely to have mastered the skills of counting regardless of the nature of the system being used.

While many studies have been concerned with the advantage of regular counting systems on the early development of counting skills, very little attention has been given to the effect of a regular counting system on the development of an understanding of place value with larger numbers. The Cockroft Report drew attention to the importance of this concept which it described as knowing that "the 2 stands for 2 units in the number 52, for 2 tens in the number 127, and for 2 hundreds in the number 263" (Cockroft, 1982, p.87). With a generative numbering system, such as exists in Japanese, the '5' in '52' has only one description or label, namely the equivalent of 'five-ten'. On the other hand, in English, with its non-generative numbering system, two distinct ways of describing the '5' in '52' may be identified: firstly, the name given to the number '50' may be used (fifty), or, secondly, it may be described as 'five

---

[12]It is generally accepted that children's understanding of the significance of counting may only safely be assumed when there is evidence that three basic criteria are understood: that counting displays the use of a one-to-one relationship; that a stable order is maintained; and that the last number counted may be used as a description of the whole.

tens'. While the second label arguably is more helpful in the way it describes the place value of the '5', the unique defining labelling of the single quantity '50' is lost. The greater difficulty experienced by children using a non-generative system in constructing named value meanings for multi-digit numbers has been established (Fuson and Briars, 1990, pp. 180–206); the authors also commented on the need to provide greater support for children in constructing such ten-structured conceptions in irregular numbering systems.[13] The greater difficulties experienced by children in developing an understanding of place value also affect their ability to understand and master the techniques of decomposition which are necessary in subtraction algorithms.

There is, however, a further difference between the number systems used in Japan and England in terms of the *symbolic* notation used. Although both countries use the Hindu-Arabic symbolic notation, Japanese children need also to master the corresponding *kanji* characters. Separate *kanji* characters exist for numbers from one to ten, with additional characters representing 'hundred' and 'thousand', and provide an alternative system for denoting all counting numbers. They are not used for calculations, which are performed in the Hindu-Arabic notation, but are sometimes used in written text.

Nunes, in her chapter on 'Ethnomathematics and Everyday Cognition' (Nunes, 1992, p. 561), comments on the similar use of characters in the Chinese written representation of multi-digit numbers and notes that: "This explicit reference to the base or a power of a base in written representation may facilitate the understanding of the meaning of written numbers, but I know of no research that has investigated this issue." The classroom observation in Japan which is discussed later in this chapter, however, addresses this issue.

It might be imagined that the need to learn yet another system for writing numbers would confuse young children further. In Japan, first-grade children in their first term meet only the Hindu-Arabic symbolic notation with *kanji* characters gradually being introduced later during their first year of schooling. When numbers over 100 are introduced during the second grade, children are already familiar with the *kanji* char-

---

[13] Children in Germany and German-speaking parts of Switzerland face a greater challenge in mastering the logic of two-digit numbers, since the 'tens and units' are reversed in the oral version, with '24' being heard as the equivalent of 'four and twenty'. Teachers comment on the difficulty they have in teaching children when writing the symbolic notation corresponding to the heard number to write the 'tens before the units' i.e. from left to right.

acters involved, but must master the rules for indicating multi-digit numbers in *kanji;* for example, that no '0' is used (302 being denoted by 三 百 二 and 320 by三 百 二 十) and that a single hundred or ten requires only the character itself and not a quantity (310 seen as三 百 十). This does not appear to cause any additional difficulty, and from direct observation is perceived as reinforcing their knowledge of place value.

It would be possible for a similar approach to be adopted in England by using to a greater extent the HTU notation (hundreds, tens and units) which is used to introduce place value, by denoting 325 (for example) by 3H 2T 3U. This idea is commonly found in German textbooks (the equivalent is 3H 2Z 3E, or 3 Hundert-2 Zehn-3 Eins) where it is used to reinforce the children's understanding of place value, and to provide consolidation when children practise breaking up multi-digit numbers into their constituent parts: however, it has not been observed to be used to any significant extent in England.

Lesson materials and teaching approaches

There are some broad similarities between the initial approaches used in Japan and England to introduce the concept of representation of numbers larger than ten and a hundred; for example, in both countries rods or strips (Dienes' rods in England) are used to represent ten single units, and squares are used to represent 10 rods or 100 single units. This idea is illustrated in textbooks and concrete materials are used in demonstrations to pupils. Children are encouraged to practise exchanging one 'ten' for 10 single units, and vice versa.

There are also some major differences, however, in the stages at which children are introduced to the concept of place-value, and also in the detail of the teaching approaches used. For example, in Japan, children will be formally introduced during the first grade to numbers larger than 10 and up to 20; this will involve discussion of the different ways in which such numbers of objects might best be arranged for ease of counting, which leads on naturally to the idea of 'grouping' in tens, and then to counting bundles of ten. First-grade Japanese children will use the concrete materials in their personal *sansū setto* to arrange a quantity of magnetic squares on their boards, and to exchange ten individual squares for a strip representing ten. The amount of practical demonstration with concrete materials was observed to be greater in Japanese lessons than in English lessons: this observation is supported by the findings of the

Michigan studies which contrasted the classroom practice in Japan, America and Taiwan. These studies found that: "even though Japanese teachers placed a lot of emphasis on verbal explanation, they used more manipulatives and real-world problem-solving scenarios than American teachers. Furthermore, the manipulatives were used in different ways in Asian classrooms. While American teachers were found to use a great variety of objects (e.g. Popsicle sticks, poker chips, bags of oranges, Dienes' blocks and Cuisenaire rods) the Japanese teachers used a very limited number of materials (for example, objects similar to Dienes' blocks) and used them repeatedly for different instructional purposes." (Robitaille and Travers, 1992, p. 706)

The formal introduction of all Japanese children to numbers greater than ten and up to twenty at a specific stage in the first-grade curriculum provided all children with the opportunity for discussion, demonstration and explanation of the way in which ten separate objects might be exchanged for one 'representing' ten. One entire lesson was devoted to whole-class consideration and discussion of the 'best' way of arranging 17 objects; by the end of the lesson children had reached the conclusion that it would be helpful to group 10 of the objects together. No such opportunity has been observed in English classrooms; classroom observation (supported by text-book analysis) suggests that discussion of the representation of numbers between 10 and 20 is glossed over and does not receive separate consideration. The use of Dienes' rods in the development and discussion of the meaning of place value has been observed to take place generally when numbers greater than 20 are first encountered and usually as a small-group activity. This may be due to the lack of sufficient quantities of concrete materials for demonstration; a typical primary classroom in England may be unlikely to have sufficient quantities of Dienes' apparatus to allow all children in a class to participate simultaneously in an activity to demonstrate 'exchanging 10 ones for 1 ten'.

The formal introduction of Japanese children to numbers greater than 100 is delayed until the second grade, by which time children are experienced and confident in both their conceptual understanding and their procedural ability in operations involving numbers of this size.[14] The first

---

[14] One lesson to second-grade children observed early in the school year – when children had not formally been introduced to numbers greater than 100 – was concerned with the topic of measurement in cm. The lesson involved demonstration of the teacher's metre ruler on the board and the counting by the class of children together of the centimetres. As the '90' boundary was crossed and '100' grew nearer, there was mounting excitement in the class as they anticipated reaching '100' for the first time!

lesson on 'numbers greater than 100' involves discussion over the possible ways of arranging such large numbers of objects that will facilitate counting of them – following the idea and approach used in the introduction of numbers up to 20. Subsequent lessons use visual demonstrations of numbers between 100 and 1000 (crossing the '1000' boundary occurs at a later stage in the curriculum, and again merits a formal introduction); with a formal discussion of the way 10 strips, each representing 10 units, may be exchanged for a single square representing 100. Colour is used to good effect both in this initial demonstration and in textbooks. In the *Sansū* scheme, for example, a large light blue square was consistently used both in board/classroom demonstration and in the textbook to represent '100', a yellow strip represented '10' and small pink squares represented 'ones'. Combinations of squares and strips were attached to the board in turn to represent a variety of different three-digit numbers and used by the teacher in whole-class demonstration and discussion of the numbers thus represented. The teacher was particularly careful to distinguish, for example, between 405 and 450. Children were called upon to demonstrate numbers individually to the whole class; other children then identified numbers depicted on the board. With each number demonstrated, its value was read aloud and the concept of place value was reinforced through the regularity of the numeration system through which children repeatedly heard that, for example, '235' represented 'two-hundred-three-ten-five'.

Children were then introduced to the *kanji* number notation to label the areas in which the 'hundreds, tens and units' were shown. The use of a further system of notation appeared to reinforce pupils' understanding and to add to it, rather than causing confusion. It should be recognised, however, that by the time children reach the second-grade in Japan, not only are they proficient in reading with the phonetic *hiragana* sound-writing system, they are also systematically being introduced to a completely different *kanji* writing system which is ideographic in structure and form.[15] It would appear that children develop an ability to move easily between the different notational systems without confusing them but apparently keeping them distinct in their minds. This ability

---

[15] Since *kanji* characters give no clues to pronunciation, children need to develop visual and aural memory skills, together with a degree of precision and accuracy in writing, in order to master this additional writing system, which is a prerequisite for literacy in everyday life. It can be argued that the development of precision and accuracy through the reading and writing of *kanji* encourages precision and accuracy in other areas of learning, in particular that of mathematics.

to hold different facts and systems simultaneously may also facilitate mental arithmetic skills, in which, from an early stage, the ability to hold one number to act as a 'counter' while at the same time carrying out another operation not only increases the choice of strategies for mental calculations but also increases the speed and accuracy with which these may be carried out.

An approach combining visual, oral and aural demonstration was observed to be used in later lessons in second-grade Japanese classes when three digit numbers were used in addition and subtraction problems. The techniques of 'exchange' and 'decomposition' were continually and repeatedly demonstrated by teachers and pupils – always for the benefit of the whole class – and all children were expected to participate in oral contributions and answering questions. In every lesson observed, following the teacher–pupil and pupil–pupil demonstration and discussion of place value and multi-digit numbers, written practice for consolidation was provided. In the first lesson, this involved the translation of a visual representation of three-digit numbers into the abstract mathematical notation (and vice versa): parallel practice in English classes was observed with individual pupils using Dienes' apparatus to represent three-digit numbers. It was clear, however, that the amount of practice provided for Japanese pupils was more extensive than that provided for English pupils at a similar stage, and also that following the completion of a particular short exercise, answers would immediately be provided by individual pupils and discussed by the teacher. This immediate discussion of answers allows for speedy correction of errors, and enables the nature of misconceptions to be clarified and corrected. Such immediate feedback is of great value in preventing misconceptions to become embedded in pupils' minds, and represents an important difference between classroom practice in Japan and England. There is an expectation in England that all written work will be collected in and laboriously marked by teachers before its return on a later (sometimes much later) occasion; this creates not only a significant delay in the correction process but also does not allow an opportunity for discussion of errors and underlying misconceptions.

In one of the later lessons on place value, which focused on the *kanji* notational system for multi-digit numeration, pupils were given substantial amounts of written practice – again following the oral discussion and demonstration – which was immediately discussed. Not all pupils were able to write correctly numbers such as 820 using *kanji* – one girl was seen to write the equivalent of 802 instead – but such errors that were observed were quickly and openly discussed. By the end of that lesson, all pupils appeared capable of recognising and understanding the meaning of three-digit numbers using both the usual Hindu-Arabic system and also the *kanji* system.

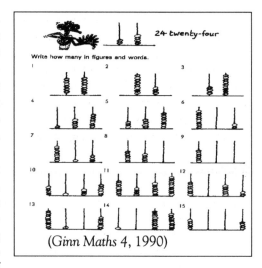

(*Ginn Maths 4*, 1990)

In contrast, a significant minority of Year 3 pupils in English classes who were observed working individually on 'place value', using Dienes' apparatus to demonstrate the value of numbers such as '28' were seen to have difficulty in understanding the use of one rod to represent 10 squares or 'units'. Fewer pupils, however, were observed to have difficulty representing three-digit numbers in a similar way by using the apparatus, which suggests that there is a conceptual hurdle that needs to be surmounted at the stage when numbers greater than 10 are first introduced. This brings us back to the starting point – namely the greater need for detailed direct teaching of place value when the numeration system does not emphasise and reiterate the 'base ten' nature of the system used. A summary of this view is provided by Geary: "for Asian children, it is likely that their language's number words make induction of the base-10 system relatively easy and certainly make direct teaching of the structure straightforward. For other children, those whose language does not facilitate the induction of the base-10 structure of multi-digit numbers, direct teaching of this structure appears to be necessary and can be successful in the second grade" (Geary, 1994, p.46).

A further point in relation to the teaching of place value in England relates to the relative unhelpfulness of the visual representations commonly used in English textbooks. Frequently, rather than depicting large squares, rods/strips and small squares to illustrate a three-digit number, a three-spike abacus with a number of discs on each spike will be illustrated. The example on the right extends the abacus idea to four-digit numbers.

This provides no clues for weaker children who lack both familiarity or experience with using an abacus and also the conceptual understanding of what is represented by each spike in moving from right to left. Using a pictorial representation of an abacus is very close to using an abstract symbolic notational system for multi-digit numbers, and does not provide the visual reinforcement that is provided in Japanese textbooks by their use of both different shapes and different colours. Equally, an 'abacus' approach to illustration does not permit any demonstration of 'exchange' or 'decomposition', both of which are essential skills for later computation involving 'crossing the tens' or 'crossing the hundreds' boundary.

Summary

Japanese children are thought to have some advantage over English children in their initial understanding of place value due to the regularity of their base-ten numeration system and the reinforcing of the importance of base-ten by the constantly heard repetition of the 'ten'. In contrast, the irregularities of the English numeration/ counting system increase the difficulties of understanding the logic of the number structure, and the counting words used give little in the way of indicating the importance of 'ten' in the structure of number. These irregularities increase the importance of rigorous, direct teaching of an understanding of place value. Unless children develop a sound understanding of the concept of place value in relation to two-digit numbers, it is unlikely that they will successfully use and apply a multi-digit system. The whole-class interactive formal introduction to Japanese children, first, to two-digit numbers in the first grade, and to three-digit numbers in the second grade (in a similar way) provided a vital opportunity for demonstration and explanation. Children's errors and misconceptions were identified, discussed and corrected. Japanese teachers, supported by the detailed teaching materials and teachers' manuals, used a range of activities to establish that all children have a secure understanding of the concept and meaning of place value before attempting computational applications to acquire procedural competence.

9

Discussion and conclusions

Discussion of main findings

Introduction

The aim of this research was to test the hypotheses and address the research questions posed regarding the acquisition of mathematical
knowledge by primary school children. The use of an international perspective enables, first, the identification of variables which are
instrumental in the achievement of pupils in a high-attainment country
such as Japan and, secondly, a comparison with the practice in relation
to those variables in England. Thirdly, as Rohlen put it: 'Rather than
borrowing certain instructional techniques, the most important lesson
may be to see more clearly, via a rich comparison, what we do and why:
to become conscious of the basic assumptions we make about learning.'
(Rohlen and Letendre, 1996, p. 3); and the use of a comparative perspective in education enables us to question some of those basic
assumptions.

Despite some criticisms regarding the validity and reliability of data
from large-scale international comparative studies, it is now generally
accepted that these studies have cumulatively provided indisputable evidence of the relatively poor performance of English pupils in the field of
mathematics. Their inferior performance is apparent already in the primary stage of schooling, when international comparisons are made of
pupils at 8 and 9 years.

The first question addressed by this study concerned the stage at which
differences in performance among pupils first become apparent. It was

244

hypothesised that, on entry to formal schooling at age six, the performance of Japanese children would not be greater than that of English children.

Results of tests administered to samples of Japanese and English children supported this hypothesis. At age six the mathematical attainment of English children was superior to that of Japanese children (mean scores were 67 per cent and 37 per cent respectively), showing, perhaps, some initial educational advantage deriving from the comparatively early start to formal schooling in England.

It was also hypothesised that between the ages of six and seven, children in Japan make faster progress in mathematical development and understanding, so that after one year of formal schooling their average mathematical competence is significantly ahead of that of children of the same age in England. This was supported by evidence from the study which showed samples of English and Japanese children aged seven scoring 82 per cent and 92 per cent respectively on the same test. Thus the *rate of progress* of Japanese children during their first year of schooling was considerably greater than the progress of the English children during Year 2 of schooling. If a constant rate of progress for the English children is assumed, this suggests that they would need a further eight months to reach the average standard achieved by Japanese children aged seven. This is consistent with the findings of international studies that suggest that by the age of nine, Japanese pupils are approximately eighteen months ahead of English pupils of a similar age.

This chapter summarises the major factors that have been identified in relation to faster progress in mathematical learning and the implications they have for educational policy. It is generally accepted that pupil achievement and the development of learning within the classroom are affected by the values and attitudes of society, the nature of the education system and models of teaching, and that children's learning reflects the combined effect of cultural influences *and* teaching processes. These external factors are summarised before factors at the classroom or instructional level are considered.

Influences from outside the classroom

From society

There are two major differences between the attitudes of Japanese and

English society that affect children's learning. The first of these relates to the perceptions of the respective contributions of innate ability and perseverance to achievement. In England, innate ability is perceived as being the major contributing factor in children's progress and attainment; effort or perseverance is regarded as of little value, especially in relation to mathematical achievement. In contrast, the ability to persevere is greatly valued in Japan, and confidence is publicly expressed in the capability of all children to reach the expected standard. The proverb, 'the slow bird must start out early', illustrates this point of view in Japan.

Secondly, in England greater importance is attached to development of the individual and the consequent need for education to provide diverse learning opportunities. In Japan, greater importance is attached to the ability to behave as a member of a group, giving support and help as appropriate in order for the group to move forward together and to maximise the chances of group success.

Pre-schooling

Cultural influences on children as they begin schooling will have been derived principally from two sources, the family and their experience of pre-school education. Differences in the latter are thought to have a significant effect on the rate of children's learning when they begin formal schooling, and are the main focus of this section.

In Japan, parents have a clear understanding of the role, functions and aims of pre-school education; these are made more explicit and specific than those in England. In addition, it has been argued here that there is relative consistency in Japan between the social and behavioural values held by the family and those to which children are exposed in pre-school education. This avoids the creation of any conflict between the views held and the cultural expectations of the two groups. Equally, it has been argued here that, among the institutions delivering pre-school education, there is a greater uniformity in Japan with regard to their learning aims and the content of the children's experience than exists in England. This is for two reasons: first, the educational aims, objectives and content of pre-school education are stated by *Monbushō* in Japan in a more specific way, and include greater level of detail, than they are by the DfEE in England. Secondly, while the functions of the two main agencies (*yōchien* and *hoikuen*) providing pre-schooling in Japan differ, their educational aims and content are the same. In contrast, pre-schooling in England is provided by a range of institutions; different objectives may be found between and within types of institution. The role, function and aims of pre-schooling in England may range from purely educational to purely child-care, although many providers of early learning attempt to achieve a mix of both.[1]

Although the within-country differences in England make it difficult to generalise about the nature of children's pre-school educational experiences, there is one major difference between England and Japan which underpins all later learning. In Japan, there is an agreed focus on *preparing* children for beginning school which includes the development of those social and behaviour skills needed for formal schooling. In England, while a professed aim of pre-schooling is also to prepare children for formal schooling, nursery schooling *may anticipate* formal learning in a way that is specifically prevented from occurring in Japan. For example, while the stated aims of the government for nursery schooling in England include social skills, teachers are also encouraged to assist with the development of formal skills of reading, writing and recording of number, which in Japan would be perceived as anticipating and trespassing on the elementary school curriculum. In England, the curriculum for nursery schooling (SCAA, 1996a, revised 1999) places greater emphasis on the development of the more formal skills of reading and writing than the kindergarten curriculum of Japan, even though nursery children in England are younger (3–4 years) than Japanese kindergarten children (aged mainly 4–6 years).

The already early age at which children begin schooling in England is becoming even earlier through the growing tendency for schools to have a single entry point to reception classes in the September following a child's *fourth* birthday. This is increasing the number of four-year-olds in reception classes; accompanied by the downward thrust of the National Curriculum from Year 1 into the reception class curriculum, this means that many four-year-olds are receiving a curriculum which gives considerable emphasis to the development of formal learning skills. The introduction of a 'foundation stage' of schooling, including the period from age three to the end of the reception year, is welcomed (QCA, 1999); this could have positive benefits if it enables greater emphasis to be placed on the development of skills which facilitate later learning but take great care not to anticipate them.

---

[1] The announcement by the Secretary of State for Education of the decision to extend the remit of OFSTED to include nurseries, playgroups and childminders (August 1999) may reduce the division between day-care and nursery education.

Also, children in pre-school education in England, as in later formal education, are encouraged in their differentiated development on an individual basis. It is accepted, even expected, that some children will progress consistently faster than others during their pre-schooling, and that by the beginning of formal schooling many children will already be able to read and write, while other children who naturally develop more slowly will have a lower starting point. At present there is no expected learning or behavioural standard for children beginning schooling; teachers are expected to build on a great range of children's existing levels of achievement and not to encourage children to repeat tasks unnecessarily. The wide variety in pre-school education combined with the lack of any expected standard in learning or behaviour makes it difficult for parents to have any clear understanding of the aims of pre-school education, or what they can reasonably expect their children to have achieved by the time they begin schooling.

In Japan, the educationists' view is that, if children are to begin formal schooling at the same age, then it is important that all begin from (as nearly as possible) a similar developmental stage, and that all participate in learning together on an equal footing. This is vital if children are to receive equal educational opportunities and the principle of uniformity of educational experience (throughout the statutory years of schooling) is to be aspired to. Differences will inevitably exist between children's early development, reflecting differences in parental and family influences, but it is seen as vital that these are not increased by pre-school learning experiences. Any existing differences in children's capabilities on entry to schooling do not receive official endorsement by the provision of differentiated learning for children on beginning schooling. For example, teaching of reading in Japan begins with the introduction of 'hiragana' characters, even though the teacher may be aware that these are already familiar to a number of children in the class. To acknowledge this would imply approval of parental efforts to develop formal reading and writing skills as early as possible. On the contrary, parents anticipating the learning of these formal skills may be seen as creating difficulties in two ways; first, they make it more difficult for teachers to begin from the beginning and to take the appropriate small, sequenced steps in formal learning; secondly, they may undermine informal learning such as memory and co-ordination by the implication that this is of less value than formal learning.

In Japan, it is accepted that for children to gain maximum benefit from the experience of formal schooling, they need a range of different types of skills. Social and behavioural skills needed include being able to behave as a member of a group and to respond accordingly; to be aware of other children's feelings and to act considerately; to be able to listen and answer questions appropriately. Other skills needed include auditory and visual memory skills, the ability to concentrate for extended periods of time, and fine and gross motor skills. The development of these skills involves a different approach to learning in pre-school education and three main differences between the methods used in pre-school education in England and Japan are identified. First, a greater use is made of routine in Japanese pre-schooling; this introduces children to the concept of group behaviour and at the same time familiarises children with many of the ritual-like routines that they will encounter in formal schooling. Secondly, 'free play' activities are used to encourage a form of child-centred discipline through which a child gradually develops responsibility both for him/herself and to the larger group. This is seen as a highly complex process; teachers persevere in developing this aspect, using their professional skills and judgement in challenging situations. An awareness of group behaviour, including an ability to consider the feelings of others, is not easy for young children to acquire, especially since prior to pre-schooling they have been the centre of attention in the family, but it is seen as vital for becoming a member of the class community in school. Thirdly, teacher-directed activities will be used in Japanese pre-schooling to develop other skills needed for formal learning. Auditory and visual memory skills will be developed through the use of music (singing, dancing and using percussion instruments). Attention span will gradually be increased as children are expected to concentrate for longer periods of time on a single activity. The ability to listen and to answer questions will be developed through story telling and group discussion. The development of fine and gross motor skills will be the deliberate focus of activities such as *origami* (paper folding), the correct use of scissors and ball control. These teacher-directed activities will often be organised on a whole-group basis, with all children involved simultaneously in the same activity, in which the teacher is then able to provide instruction and advice. This also enables a high degree of teacher-pupil interaction that improves vocabulary knowledge and oral skills.

In contrast, activities in nursery classes in England are arranged on a more informal basis; for a large part of a daily session, children will have their individual choice of activities (although the range of activities available may be controlled by the teacher). Many children will play or work individually even though they may be engaged on the same activity; levels of interaction were observed to be low among children. Also, due to the individual or small group organisation of the activities, only a small amount of teacher interaction or instruction is possible. Pupils may be encouraged to attempt formal writing without proper instruction and before they possess the level of fine motor skills needed for this.

In summary, the variable nature of English pre-schooling, the lack of specificity in aims and objectives, and the promotion of early formal skills can lead to a diversity and inconsistency of experience. Moreover, the organisational approaches observed tend to encourage differential development among children. Differences in children's development due to parental and family influences are increased by children's pre-school experiences with the result that a wide range of attainment already exists when children begin statutory schooling.

Control of educational systems and the effect on children's classroom experience

When children begin schooling, their attitudes towards learning in the classroom will already have been affected by their pre-school experience, and will continue to be affected by those of the wider society and the value placed on education. There are, however, further factors that affect children's learning that are external to the classroom and are independent of class teachers' actions. For example, the degree of central control on an education system to a great extent determines the choices open to teachers and the degree of autonomy which they enjoy in the classroom. It has been argued here that in Japan the greater degree of central control in two key areas, namely curriculum and teaching materials, is instrumental in achieving a relative uniformity of pupil experience which may be contrasted with the between and within school variation that is a feature of pupil experience in England.

In the specification of the curriculum there are two main differences between practice in Japan and England. *Monbushō* provides clear guidelines for teachers regarding the programme of work for each subject and each year of schooling. This programme of work relates to the *whole cohort* of pupils each year, and thus *Monbushō* effectively establishes minimum standards which *all* pupils are expected to achieve during a particular year of schooling. Especially in the early years of schooling in Japan, '*Minna to issho*' or 'all together' is a fundamental principle of teaching the curriculum. In contrast, the National Curriculum in England sets out areas to be covered during each Key Stage rather than specifying year-by-year requirements. The National Numeracy Strategy will have helped teachers in this respect by providing a year-by-year framework. A considerable amount of preparatory work by the individual teacher, however, is still required. Further, an implicit assumption of the National Curriculum is that children will experience differentiated rates of progress and will achieve highly different levels of attainment. Thus there is little guidance on the standards of attainment that might reasonably be expected to be achieved or exceeded by the majority of pupils – indeed, to do so would be inconsistent with the assumption of differential patterns of learning and progress. The tradition in primary schools in England during the last thirty years in which teachers are given the responsibility for maximising the *individual* development of their pupils – and it is expected that the range of attainment, especially in mathematics, will widen with years of school experience – contrasts with the responsibility of Japanese teachers for helping *all* their pupils to achieve the expected standard. The increasing diversity of attainment among English pupils steadily increases the difficulty of catering for the different learning needs of pupils in successive years.

The degree of centralised control of teaching materials also has a significant impact on teaching. The requirement of *Monbushō* approval for textbooks in Japan results in a relatively small choice of approved textbooks, with decisions on the textbook scheme being taken by an education committee rather than by teachers in the classroom. This clearly restricts the freedom of teachers to draw on a wide range of teaching materials and textbooks, as is practised by English primary teachers who provide their pupils with a diversity of lesson materials which is not found in Japan. There are, however, some important advantages of the system in which materials need approval. First, in order to obtain *Monbushō* approval, the textbooks and associated materials need to have undergone extensive trialling in schools and involved extensive consultation and participation by practising classroom teachers, and, consequently, they are of a high standard. This is not to suggest that textbooks produced by the publishing houses in England are not of a high standard; they are subject to market forces and there are clear incentives for the publications to be of high quality, but it is difficult for those in schools making decisions regarding the choice of textbook schemes to have adequate opportunity for the extensive and detailed examination of each of the various schemes available in a highly competitive market.

Secondly, Japanese textbooks are only one part of a comprehensive scheme of teaching materials including teachers' manuals, work sheets and other supporting materials (such as posters for display). The teachers' manuals play a crucial part in enabling teachers to achieve high standards of lesson delivery, quality of questioning and careful sequencing of finely graded mathematical concepts. The considerable time – measured in years not months – required to develop and trial teaching materials for a mathematics scheme is often overlooked; it may well be that the greater elapse of time in Japan between alterations to the National Curriculum facilitate the development of detailed teachers' manuals. Although some of the English mathematics teaching schemes available now include a teachers' manual and additional materials, the teachers' manuals tend to be more general in the advice and support given to teachers – perhaps because there is insufficient time for the thorough preparation of materials to fit into the National Curriculum.

At present, teachers' manuals appear to be used to a much lesser extent in England than in Japan; two main reasons for this are suggested. First, from discussion and observation it seems likely that there will be only a single copy of a teachers' manual in a school, in contrast to the situation in Japan where each teacher is routinely provided with a personal copy. Secondly, with the substantial range of pupil attainment found in English classes, teachers' manuals are simply less relevant to individualised or group work than in Japan where a greater uniformity of pupil attainment is expected and is associated with a largely whole-class teaching approach.

The requirement of official approval for mathematics teaching materials results in a greater degree of uniformity of pedagogical approach to the sequencing of topics and the methods used for introducing new concepts. Consistency of approach is achieved both between and within schools, and encourages teachers to have a clear knowledge of pupils' previous experience of mathematical learning, making it easier for learning to be developed in a systematic and consistent way. This greater uniformity is also thought to encourage pedagogical discussion at a higher level among teachers: the knowledge that they share the same broad approach to the same sequenced curriculum enables them to have informed discussions on difficulties likely to be encountered by individual pupils, and the best way to facilitate their progress.

Models of childrens' development and approaches to pedagogy

It has been argued that theory of learning in England has, for the last three decades, been dominated by a combination of Piagetian ideas and the impact of the Plowden Report, as interpreted in educationist circles. Piagetian ideas are based on the assumption that children are active learners and need to construct mathematical knowledge for themselves. A further principle which was embedded in the Plowden Report (but was perhaps, given unintended importance and emphasis in subsequent application at school and classroom level) relates to the fact that the construction of mathematical knowledge is different for individual children. The Plowden Report emphasised that the way in which such construction of mathematical knowledge takes place varies with individual children, and that teaching must respond to and reflect an awareness of such individual differences. A highly-differentiated teaching approach was the logical outcome which, as implemented in the classroom, produced a scenario in which teachers honed their management skills but neglected their pedagogical skills.

The relative lack of interest in pedagogy in England may be seen as having a further effect, namely, on the content of teacher training. In the area of mathematics, it has long been said, there is a greater need for teacher expertise in presenting the development of a new topic in a carefully sequenced step-by-step procedure; in other words, teachers need skills in translating their theoretical knowledge into a practical teaching model in the classroom. Yet training courses for intending primary teachers in England have been able to provide very little instruction on the question of how best to approach and develop specific mathematical topics. This is even more vital in an education system in which teachers do not, on the whole, have access to good quality teachers' manuals but are required to put together their own pack of teaching materials for each lesson they deliver. Perhaps due to extreme curricular and extracurricular responsibilities, there appear to be fewer opportunities for pedagogical debate among teachers. There is also very little in the way of a tradition of peer observation of teaching, which can raise perceptions of teaching issues and promote a positive atmosphere among teaching staff. Overall, it would appear that there is less in the way of pedagogical support for the teaching of mathematics by primary teachers in England, than in Japan where teachers not only have access to a more detailed curriculum, clearly specified standards of pupil attainment and good quality teachers' manuals, but also appear to have greater opportunities for exchange of ideas with colleagues and forums for pedagogical debate.

Inside the classroom

Teachers

When teachers' backgrounds are compared, differences in subject knowledge are thought to have a greater influence on quality of teaching than differences in salary structure, qualifications or age profiles. The ability of teachers in England to provide adequately for the teaching of mathematics is thought to be adversely affected by the early specialisation which characterises the educational system. Many primary teachers will have achieved only the minimum qualification in mathematics. In contrast, all elementary teachers in Japan will have continued with the study of mathematics during upper secondary schooling, a level of subject knowledge significantly beyond that required for GCSE. Differences in levels of subject knowledge between teachers in England and Japan will affect levels of self-confidence as well as competence in the teaching of mathematics.

Management and climate of the classroom

Within the classroom, it would appear that in Japan far more detailed consideration has been given to the multitude of small aspects that might affect children's learning. Beginning with those physical aspects of the classroom which are most apparent; desks, for example, will be arranged in the way that is most appropriate for the particular subject being taught, and will be rearranged several times during a day. In England, the widely used grouping of desks or tables (usually four or six) remains a permanent feature and does not appear to be adjusted to accommodate learning in a particular subject.

Storage of children's belongings in Japan reflects the need that children have for access to them; children have ready access to their books and pencils that are needed throughout the day and stored in their desks. There was a greater observed need in English classrooms for equipment to be collected or distributed from different points in the classroom. This caused delay and resulted in valuable lesson time being lost; it also caused disruption to pupils' levels of concentration.

In Japan, large magnetic blackboards – used with a wide range of magnetic objects – facilitate teacher and pupil demonstration. Flip charts used for demonstration in classes in England are regarded as unsatisfactory for several reasons: they provide a relatively small area; they are unstable;

they cannot be seen by all pupils, and pupils have difficulty in writing on them.

Pupils in Japan are provided with a personal set of good quality mathematical equipment in the first year of schooling that encourages participation and enjoyment of mathematics. In classes in England, pupils need to share the cumbersome and unattractive sets of linking cubes that are the most common form of classroom equipment. Not only does sharing equipment present problems, but the inferior quality of the equipment – and the difficulty that young children without fine motor skills experience in using them – leads to frustration.

In Japan, the activity of teaching is acknowledged as having priority in lesson time and interruptions are rare. Lesson time can thus be used efficiently. In England, lessons are frequently interrupted for non-educational reasons and valuable lesson time is lost.

The short break that follows each lesson in Japan serves a vital purpose in providing young children with an opportunity for intense physical activity, a chance to let off steam, and enables them to refocus their attention on the next lesson. It also helps in the demarcation of lesson time – this is carefully restricted to a 45-minute length. In England, many lessons were observed which lasted well over an hour with only a single break being provided during the morning session. Children were observed to have difficulty in maintaining their attention during the longer lesson time.

Taken individually, these are minor illustrations of the detailed planning and organisation that – often invisibly – underpin Japanese primary teaching. Taken together, they are vital for the creation of a positive atmosphere for learning.

Teachers' attitudes

Classroom practice reflects the broad aims of teachers, and there are two main ways in which the aims of English and Japanese teachers are perceived as differing and which have a significant effect on children's attainments. These are, first, in relation to progress of pupils and, secondly, to the emphasis given to conceptual or procedural knowledge.

With regard to progress of pupils, there is a fundamental dichotomy between the aim of maximising progress of pupils *individually*, or of the whole cohort or class of pupils. This reflects the influence of social values and attitudes, yet the impact of this on educational models and hence on teaching methods means that a cultural factor becomes, in effect, a classroom factor. Choosing between these two fundamental and apparently incompatible aims dictates much of the resulting teaching methods and classroom organisation. English teachers are under pressure from a variety of sources (for example, from parents and Ofsted inspectors) to ensure that each and every pupil achieves the maximum possible attainment level in each of the core subjects, regardless of any unevenness in achievement that may be created within the class. Japanese teachers are equally under pressure of a different type, namely, to teach in such a way that the whole class may proceed together. Both these tasks are far from easy. In Japan, despite all attempts at 'levelling up' that are made during pre-schooling, it is almost inconceivable that all children, regardless of family and maturation differences, will begin schooling at the same developmental level. Thus an in-depth understanding of each child's 'zone of proximal development' is required. This awareness of the state of each individual child's mathematical understanding, with an associated ability to anticipate and assist with conceptual difficulties likely to be encountered, has been described by Japanese teachers and educationists as the most important element for the successful teaching of mathematics. While Japanese teachers appreciate and even accept that some children will develop faster than others, they are able to use their pedagogical knowledge and expertise to help all children individually to reach the required level of understanding in order to move forward with the rest of the class. It is paradoxical that in order for the 'all together' approach to be remotely achievable, the knowledge possessed by teachers regarding the state of each individual child's capability in mathematics must be at least as great as that of English teachers who are concerned to maximise the progress of each individual.

The second way in which the aims of Japanese and English teachers are perceived as differing is in the emphasis given to conceptual understanding and procedural competence. It has been argued that these are two separate and distinct aspects of mathematics and both are essential for success in mathematics. Whereas it is often suggested that there is an emphasis on rote-learning in Japan that would lead to an expectation of a concentration of procedural competence at the expense of conceptual understanding, in fact direct observation of classroom practice indicated that Japanese teachers place great value on the need to develop sound conceptual understanding *before* attempting practice with the application of procedures. In England, although teachers appreciate the need for conceptual understanding, the complex classroom management of a large number of activities means that teachers in reality have little time to spend on this aspect, and that in practice children spend more time on written application of procedures – which is a more easily managed activity. Japanese teachers appear able to address the two distinct areas of learning separately and independently of each other; it may be that they have more time for this since they do not need to prepare a range of lesson activities.

The development of conceptual understanding can often best result from consideration and discussion of a particular carefully selected contextualised problem. This appears particularly true in the early years of schooling. Japanese teachers seem exceptionally proficient at presenting a problem which is susceptible to a number of possible methods of solution, and in encouraging pupils to develop their own independent ideas which are then discussed by the class. For example, second-grade children were encouraged to develop their own ways of measuring; this was then skilfully directed by the teacher towards a discussion of the qualities of a satisfactory system of measurement. Whole-class discussion enables children to share and compare different problem-solving strategies, to learn from one another and to develop better awareness of specific mathematical vocabulary. This is particularly helpful to weaker children. Peer evaluation of problem-solving approaches, including the identification of errors and underlying misconceptions, is encouraged in Japan. Discussion of these clarifies concepts and adds to understanding. From the teacher's point of view, discussion, probing and analysis of errors provide valuable insight into pupils' conceptual understanding; at the same time other pupils may secure their own understanding. Research evidence from other studies has shown the value to pupils of opportunities to explain their reasoning and mathematical strategies. Not only does this improve their oral skills, it requires them to be clear about their reasoning and the logical steps involved in their reasoning process. The correct use of mathematical vocabulary can be encouraged, and pupils develop self-confidence in their ability to express themselves to an audience. Less able children benefit from hearing explanations by their peers, who may give more emphasis to explaining points that they themselves found difficult; this may be of more help than further teacher explanation. Pupils also learn the importance of giving support and not being unnecessarily critical when other pupils are providing explanations.

Given the greater importance attached in England to conceptual understanding and 'thinking in a mathematical way' than to practice with procedural applications, it might be expected that English pupils would display greater levels of conceptual understanding than their Japanese counterparts. In Chapter 8, however, which focused on the learning of two specific topics within the mathematics curriculum, it was demonstrated that English pupils made errors on subtraction questions that revealed a fundamental lack of conceptual understanding. For example, on the subtraction question requiring decomposition, English pupils aged seven made a far greater number of errors than Japanese children, and a large proportion of those errors by English children revealed a poor understanding both of place value and the base-ten system of numbers. In spite of the alleged importance of conceptual understanding, it would appear that English classroom instruction has failed to secure this at an adequate level.

The development of procedural competence in mathematics, however, requires a different approach from that which is appropriate for developing conceptual understanding. Children need to be able to recall simple numerical facts and to be able to apply correct mathematical procedures without hesitation. That requires practice over time. For many years in England there has been a widespread view that the development of basic cognitive skills – such as fact retrieval and the application of numerical and other simple mathematical procedures – is unnecessary and irrelevant for success in mathematics. This view has been given greater emphasis with the extensive use of calculators throughout schooling, often by children as young as five who may have little conception of either the structure of number or the operation that is being implemented when using a calculator. Many of those with important voices in the world of mathematics education have publicly expressed the view that computational skills are now largely an irrelevance, especially given the way that the world of work has been transformed in recent years with the advent of sophisticated technology, and that increasingly what matters is an ability to think in a mathematical way. It has been argued here, however, that this view misses the purpose of developing calculating skills and procedural competence. The structure of number is the first example that children meet of a logical structure which behaves entirely consistently in the way in which rules are observed and obeyed. Understanding the fundamental structure and principle of number is a prerequisite for children's later understanding of the rules of logic and their ability to apply invariant rules to a wide range of different problem-solving situations (which need not be of a mathematical nature) (Nunes and Bryant, 1997). The development of procedural competency also aids the development of other important faculties such as memory. With practice, access to short-term memory where factual information is stored improves and retrieval of this information becomes faster.

Depriving children of adequate mental and written practice in computation is doing them no favours in the long run; they need to establish confidence and accuracy in applying simple procedures in order, at a later stage, to apply correctly the more complex procedures required in, for example the multi-stage solution of equations. The difficulty that English pupils of secondary school age have with this and other aspects of algebraic topics is well-documented; this point again demonstrates the need for mathematical understanding to be built up layer by layer on a previous well-established foundation.

In addition to developing conceptual understanding and procedural competence, Japanese teachers were observed to add a further stage to their pupils' mathematical learning. After extensive practice with a wide variety of problems (often contextualised), carefully graded to increase in difficulty, so that the use of a procedure had become embedded and automatic, teachers encouraged their pupils to turn their attention to constructing their own word-problems to fit specific mathematical situations. Teachers strongly expressed the view that only when children could successfully create their own word problems, was it certain that children had both a sufficiently deep conceptual understanding *and* could apply the correct procedure. While all the teachers observed in Japan introduced this stage, often in the concluding lesson on a particular topic, none of the teachers observed in English schools used this technique, and it is not certain that it exists to any great extent in the repertoire of teaching methods in England.

Differences in classroom practice: teaching methods and approaches

The lessons observed in Japan were characterised by clear learning objectives, common lesson structure and often included a summary of the main learning points at the conclusion. While much of the detail of the lessons – the structure, the questions to be asked of the pupils, the possible points of misunderstanding, the mathematical vocabulary to be emphasised – is provided by the teachers' manuals and not by the teachers themselves, this enables teachers to concentrate on other aspects essential for successful learning, namely, identifying clearly the level of understanding of individual children, targeting them with appropriate questions and ensuring that no one is left behind. Involving all children in a class in answering questions, providing explanations and board demonstration requires a high level of skill and depends on the supportive, co-operative and essentially non-competitive atmosphere of the class being well established. The strong oral content of each lesson – typically occupying about 60 per cent of observed lesson time – further helps to develop the whole-class feeling of unity; extensive periods of lesson time on written work can lead to a splintering of the class and uneven progress among pupils. The *quality* of the oral content reflects the professional skills of teachers in, for example, using a variety of different levels of questions; achieving this quality of whole-class interactive discussion is seen as one of the most challenging tasks for teachers.

Pupil motivation/participation

The relationship which elementary school teachers in Japan appeared to have with their class of pupils was observed to be different from that of English teachers. From observation, it would seem that Japanese teachers are able to create an atmosphere in which they and all their pupils share common aims and are looking forward in the same direction. Japanese teachers and their pupils appear to be set on sharing the way forward together; the role of teachers may be seen as helping all their pupils along the way together. Time spent dealing with behaviour problems is perceived by both parties as a pointless and unnecessary distraction from the business of learning. Pupils play a large part in achieving expected standards of discipline – partly through the *tōban* rota system for class organisation, and partly through the co-operative, supportive class spirit. Both of these aspects are built upon foundations laid in pre-schooling, and again point to the importance of consistent, highly specific pre-school education. Pupils seem secure in the knowledge that guidance will be provided by their teachers, and are reassured by this, leading to a self-confidence that is evidenced by their willingness to take part in whole-class demonstration, only a few weeks after beginning school. Their self-confidence is not undermined, as is often seen in England, by teachers who, with the best of intentions and wishing to provide evidence of effective differentiation within the classroom, set work of a less demanding nature for pupils who are perceived to be less able. In Japan, a uniformity of educational experience for all pupils within a given class, which includes fair distribution of teacher time and attention among all pupils, is seen as important in enabling pupils to share a common goal with their teacher.

In contrast, English teachers are occupied to a greater extent by looking in towards their pupils' behaviour, which distracts them from looking forward to the main learning objective. The earlier age of beginning schooling, coupled with the diversity of pre-schooling experience, combine to produce a range of social and behavioural skills among children in formal schooling; a great deal of teacher time and attention is required for the resolution of resulting behavioural problems. Children are less likely to have had experience of whole-group participation during their pre-school experience, and may lack knowledge of how to participate. They may also not have in place the skills of listening and responding that enable them to contribute successfully to group discussion.

Expectations for pupils

In Japan, there is a clear expectation that all pupils in a class will attain the expected standard, which is clearly specified by the curriculum requirements. Parents understand these requirements and support their children and the teachers in achieving them. The same high standards of attainment, precision, accuracy, and in presentation of written work are expected by teachers of all their pupils; this is seen as a reasonable expectation since all pupils have begun from a more equal point and have had the same experience of step-by-step teaching. While it cannot be assumed that there is a greater level of homogeneity among children's inherent ability than in England, the different approach to teaching means that Japanese teachers are required to accommodate the variation within their whole-class teaching approach. To achieve this, they will use a range of different approaches to convey a single mathematical concept that can then be mastered by all children, which will be followed by a considerable quantity of consolidation and practice examples in order to establish procedural competence. Japanese teachers may also spend time outside the class with children who need additional assistance; this helps to raise class standards. Children are aware of, and readily accept, their obligations as a member of the class to complete all the work set by the teacher; implicit in this is acceptance that only by effort can mastery be gained and that a degree of persistence is required to achieve this.

In contrast, the classroom culture in primary schools in England has, for the last thirty years, emphasised the importance of maximising individual development, while failing to provide any standard or yardstick against which acceptable progress could be measured. More recently, the government has established that Levels 2 and 4 in the National Curriculum represent the standards which children are 'expected' to achieve by the end of Key Stages 1 and 2 respectively. However, these levels are described in only broad terms in the National Curriculum, making it difficult for parents to have a clear picture of what an acceptable standard of achievement represents. Additionaly, there is growing concern that the year-on-year improvement nationally in the percentage of children attaining these levels reflects teachers' ability to 'teach to tests' rather than any real improvement in standards.

In England, methods for teaching mathematics currently being developed for use with *low-attaining pupils* include highly structured lessons with a clear learning objective, a high oral content, a whole-class interactive approach, and plenty of consolidation and practice. It would appear that these have much in common with the methods used with great success with pupils of all abilities in Japan and, rather than allowing only those children with learning difficulties to benefit from them, it would be to the advantage of children of all levels of ability in England to be taught in such a way.

Conclusions

It is not suggested that all Japanese teachers are equally effective, but they are assisted in the delivery of a competent lesson by, first, a more detailed curriculum and, secondly, detailed teachers' manuals that can be translated with ease into logically sequenced classroom instruction. Time and effort thus saved can be used to focus on individual pupils' needs.

At the classroom level, in England the educational policy of differentiation has had a huge impact on classroom practice and children's learning experience. Teachers have needed, in effect, to become classroom managers, and have had little opportunity to use their pedagogical knowledge in order to develop conceptual understanding of pupils. The principles and practice observed in Japanese classrooms were not exceptional; many aspects of the methods used in Japan are those which previous research studies have shown to be the most effective, especially with children for whom learning mathematics is not easy. Japanese teachers emphasised a problem-solving approach through which conceptual understanding was developed prior to practice in procedural competence. The thoroughness of Japanese teaching was evident in the way in which pupils were taught each step in a new concept, carefully and without haste, using a variety of methods to demonstrate mastery of a concept. Teachers checked at each stage to ensure that every pupil had constructed an adequate and correct understanding. Procedural knowledge was introduced as a separate learning objective, and the application of both the concept and the procedure was practised in a series of carefully graded examples. The final stage in embedding understanding was for pupils to construct their own examples and often to demonstrate these to other pupils.

Pupils demonstrated a self-confidence which was aided by the attitude of their teachers, and supported by the co-operative atmosphere carefully fostered by the teacher. Pupils were also confident that they would not be expected to solve a problem for which they did not have the necessary understanding, knowledge or capability; that is, they would be provided with the appropriate tools for a particular task. In contrast, teachers in England are encouraged to provide pupils with questions of a 'challenging' nature which can serve to undermine the self-confidence of pupils who are less secure in their mathematical knowledge.

Recent changes

Recognition of the fact that in England schooling standards of mathematical attainment are lower than might reasonably be expected has led to a plethora of government directives and initiatives during the last two years in order to address this situation. At the pre-school level, a review of early learning goals has led to the establishment of a 'foundation stage' of schooling (up to the end of the reception class year), although the learning goals remain broadly unchanged. At the systemic level, while the publication of a new National Curriculum (to take effect from the year 2000) has provided greater detail of topics to be covered than the previous 1995 curriculum, the curriculum content is still described in terms of each Key Stage of schooling (rather than for each year of schooling) and lacks a degree of specificity comparable with that of the Japanese 'Course of Study'.

Perhaps a more significant step forward is represented by the introduction of the National Numeracy Strategy into primary schools in September 1999, which provided teachers with a year-by-year detailed framework of the topics to be covered within the mathematics curriculum. The National Numeracy Strategy has also been instrumental in establishing a common structure to mathematics lessons in primary schools, and its inclusion of an element of whole-class teaching is welcomed. The complexity and difficulty of achieving effective whole-class interactive teaching should not, however, be underestimated; this requires extensive and rigorous training for all teachers. It has been taken for granted for many years that teachers will carry out all government directives and initiatives on request, even where these involve considerable additional burdens. Incorporating an element of whole-class interactive teaching in their range of teaching approaches involves a major shift for many teachers from the individualised or group instruction that has been the English model for thirty years, and represents an approach for which they may well not have had any training or, indeed, have had any experience when they were pupils. Teachers deserve to be given adequate support and training to develop an understanding of the associated pedagogy and teaching techniques involved (such as questioning of pupils); it is not clear that this is being provided at an adequate level. Additionally, the National Numeracy Strategy does not provide detailed lesson materials and teachers still need to construct their lessons from a variety of resources and to provide a range of pupil activities for different levels of attainment.

Finally, it is difficult to predict the effect of the new requirement (in the year 2000) for all teacher trainees to demonstrate an appropriate standard in numeracy in order to be eligible for Qualified Teacher Status. The aim of improving the mathematical competence and subject knowledge of those entering the profession as primary teachers is laudable. Until such time that the mathematical knowledge of the average English school leaver is comparable to his/her Japanese counterpart, however, it is important to provide an adequate level of directed help in mathematics as appropriate for those wishing to enter the teaching profession. Intending teachers who possess all the diverse attributes necessary for becoming a successful primary teacher except that of an adequate subject knowledge in mathematics should not be discouraged from entering teaching by the daunting prospect of a numeracy test; it may well be that those students who had difficulties themselves in achieving mathematical competence have the potential to become the best teachers of basic mathematical concepts – since they appreciate misconceptions and errors. It is important to break the cycle of ineffective mathematics teaching in England by improving the subject knowledge of intending teachers, developing their self-confidence and self-esteem with regard to mathematics, and ensuring that they understand the detailed sequencing of topics and steps that is necessary for the development of mathematical understanding.

It is difficult for any government to reconcile the need for short-term gains (within an elected term) with the fact that real improvements in education take time (measured in years) and can only be effected after careful consideration and planning. In spite of the recent government initiatives, fundamental issues regarding primary mathematics education still need to be addressed and recommendations resulting from this study are summarised below.

Recommendations

The main recommendations for changes to English practice which are likely to improve mathematical attainment are identified under the following broad areas of influence:

At the pre-school level:
- it should be clearly understood that all educational provision before Year 1 is regarded as pre-schooling;
- the aims, objectives and content should be given greater specificity;
- it should be clearly understood that in terms of educational aims these relate to the development of informal learning and not the formal skills of reading, writing and recording of number;
- greater emphasis should be placed on the learning of social behaviour and preparation for school;
- additional help should be provided for those children perceived as lacking identified educational and behavioural skills in order that all children can begin schooling on equal terms.

At the systemic level:
- the National Curriculum requirements should be specified in more detail and for each year of schooling;
- every child should have a textbook;
- every teacher should have a good quality teachers' manual (with specific notes on the mathematics to be taught, on methods to be used, on answers to be expected, on how to deal with slower and faster learning children) written specially to accompany the text book. Such manuals require considerable development time, and thus adequate time must be allowed between the promulgation of a new curriculum and its implementation in schools;
- the quality of text books should be improved to reflect current research knowledge about how topics are most efficiently taught.

At the classroom level:
- improve teachers' subject knowledge and competence through additional in-service training in the short-term (on pedagogical issues rather than in response to government directives) and changes to initial teacher training in the longer term;
- place greater emphasis on the need for all children to reach the level specified in National Curriculum requirements, and thus remove the need for differentiated teaching;
- improve teachers' awareness of the mathematical pedagogy that can be used to develop conceptual understanding of *all* pupils on an individual level, and especially for those pupils for whom this is not easy;
- increase the level of oral interaction and pupil participation in lessons;
- encourage teachers to discuss approaches to problem-solving with their pupils and to encourage pupils to construct their own problem questions to fit particular situations;
- ensure that teachers distinguish between teaching approaches which are effective for the development of conceptual understanding and those that improve procedural competence;
- develop quality of questioning and teacher-pupil interaction.

One response of governments to the disappointing standards of mathematics among pupils in England has been to set targets in order to raise the proportion of pupils attaining an 'expected' level. For a real improvement in attainment standards, however, target setting is not enough. This detailed examination and comparison of contrasting ways of acquiring mathematical skills has indicated essential changes necessary for real improvement. It may appear that this study has given undue focus to the development of children's cognitive learning and improving their achievement in mathematics, and that there may be wider, more important goals for education. But children are required to meet the demands of school achievement and, by comparing their performance with that of others, they become aware of their relative success or failure. Improving the chances of those low-attaining pupils of achieving success in the early years and thus adding to their chances of success in the later years of schooling and beyond must be an important goal.

Appendix A

National comparisons: England and Japan

Table A.1 *Summary statistics for pupils in primary/elementary schooling: England and Japan*

	England Maintained primary schools 1997[a]	Japan Local public elementary schools 1997[b]
No. of pupils ('000s)	4271	7740
No. of schools ('000s)	18	24
Average school size	220	320
No. of full-time teachers ('000s)	182[c]	416
Pupil:teacher ratio	23.4	18.6
Average class size	27.5	27.8
No. of hours per week Year 2/1st grade	22.0	18.75 (25.0)[d]
No. of hours in mathematics per school year Year 2/1st grade	137[e]	102 (136)
Year 3/2nd grade	137[e]	131 (175)

Sources: DfEE (1998) Statistics of Education in England, 1997; (London, DfEE), Tables 6, 7, 15, 17; Monbushō (1998) Statistics of Education (Tokyo, Monbushō). NIER (1999), An international comparative study of school curricula' (NIER; Tokyo).

Notes: [a]Primary schools consist mainly of infant schools for children aged 5–7, junior schools for those aged 7–11 and all through primary schools for children aged 5–11. Some 'first' schools, however, cater for children aged 5–8. Many primary schools provide nursery classes for children under 5. A nursery class is one which includes amongst its staff a qualified nursery assistant. [b]In Japan, there are three categories of school: private, local public, national. The 'local public' category corresponds most closely to the maintained sector of schools in England. [c]Or full-time equivalent. [d]One school 'hour' is defined as a class period or 45 minutes, giving a total of 18 hours 45 minutes teaching time each week for a total of 25 'hours'. [e]Recommended.

Table A.2 *Summary statistics for pupils in nursery/kindergarten: England and Japan*

		England Nursery classes/units	Japan Kindergarten	
			Local public	All
No. of pupils ('000s)	Full-time	9	360	1790
	Part-time	14	360	1790
No. of schools ('000s)		0.5	6.1	14.7
Average school size (per half-day session)		93	59	122
No. of full-time teachers ('000s)		1.6	25.0	103.8
Pupil:teacher ratio		18.9	14.4	17.2

Sources: DfEE (1998) Statistics of Education in England, 1997; (London, DfEE), Tables 6, 7, 15, 17; Monbushō (1998) Statistics of Education (Tokyo, Monbushō).

Note: ᵃMore than 98% of pupils of elementary school age are educated in 'local public' schools. The comparable figure for children in 'local public' kindergarten is only 20%, however, and so figures relate to all types of kindergarten (including private and national) are also provided here.

Appendix B

Results of written tests

Table B.1 *Percentages of correct answers by pupils: England and Japan*

		6-year-olds				7-year-olds			
		Mean	SD	SE	n	Mean	SD	SE	n
England									
School	A	62	18.0	3.7	24	86	8.7	1.6	28
	B	75	15.0	2.9	27	78	13.9	2.7	26
	C	71	13.8	2.4	32	83	11.7	2.1	30
	D	60	21.3	4.3	24	79	16.7	3.4	24
All Schools		67	19.9	1.9	107	82	13.3	1.3	108
Japan									
School	E	33	4.8	0.9	28	91	8.6	1.7	27
	F	37	10.5	1.9	30	90	8.2	1.3	39
	G	40	11.5	1.9	36	94	8.9	1.4	40
All Schools		37	9.9	1.0	94	92	8.5	0.8	106

Table B.2 *Seven-year-old pupils answering individual question correctly: England and Japan*

Question	England		Japan	
	No of pupils	As % of all pupils	No of pupils	As % of all pupils
1. How many dots are there?	106	98	106	100
2. What is the number that comes after 6?	104	96	104	98
3. What is the number that comes before 9?	102	94	96	91
4. How many flowers are there altogether?	106	98	100	94
5. 5 ducks are on a pond. 2 more arrive. How many ducks are there altogether?	99	92	103	97
6. 5 add 1	103	95	101	95
7. There are 5 birds and 4 sets of birdcages. Which set of birdcages has one birdcage for each bird? Put a ring round that set.	102	94	102	96
8. Which tree has more apples?	107	99	106	100
9. Which basket has fewer eggs?	98	91	106	100
10. How many dots are there?	103	95	104	98
11. There are 6 cars parked in a street. 2 drive away. How many are left?	100	93	105	99
12. Jane has 7 books and Ann has 3. How many more books does Jane have?	71	66	97	92
13. 5 add 4	104	96	106	100
14. 10 add 6	99	92	104	98
15. 8 subtract 3	91	84	105	99
Average for questions 1–15	100	92	103	97

Questions 16-26 were language-free and were presented in written form as shown	England		Japan	
	No of pupils	As % of all pupils	No of pupils	As % of all pupils
16. 73, 74,□, 76, 77, 78, □, □, 81, 82	94	87	106	100
17. 100, 200, 300,□, 500, 600,				
□, 800	102	94	103	97
18. 6 – 0	86	80	103	97
19. 15 + 3	95	88	95	90
20. 18 + 4	82	76	90	85
21. 13 – 5	57	53	92	87
22. 3 + 6 – 2	65	60	90	85
23. 37				
+21	79	73	96	91
24. 46				
+15	52	48	86	81
25. 28				
– 15	52	48	71	67
26. 52				
–29	5	5	57	54
Average for questions 16–26	76	70	90	85
Average for all questions 1–26	85	80	97	92
No. of pupils	108	100	106	100

Note: Questions 1–15 were read to the children

Appendix C

Results of lesson observation

Table C.1 *Number of mathematics lessons observed*

	1995	1996	Total
England			
School A	9	8	17
School B	7	8	15
School C	10	9	19
School D	11	12	23
Total	37	41	78
Japan			
School E	14	10	24
School F	12	12	24
School G	16	10	26
Total	42	32	74

Table C.2 *Pupils' attendance rates: England and Japan*

	Pupils attending as % of those on roll		
	1995	1996	Total
England	93	92	92
Japan	97	98	98

These rates are consistent with the results from the TIMSS survey which found that, on a typical day, 5 per cent of English primary school pupils were absent compared with 2 per cent in Japan (Martin *et al.*, 1999, table 6.1).

Table C.3 *Pupils observed to be 'off task' during lessons*

per cent

England	1996
School A	18
School B	21
School C	22
School D	28
All lessons	21
Japan	
School E	6.2
School F	6.8
School G	2.9
All lessons	5.1

Table C.4 *Pupils' activity during observed lessons: 1996[a]*

	% of lesson time	
	England	Japan
Development section		
Listening	7	7
Answering questions	3	25
Class discussion	3 } 13%	13 } 49%
Pupil explanation and board demonstration	0	4
Collaborative group work	0	3
Consolidation and practice		
Working individually on non-differentiated activity	0	42
Working individually on differentiated activity	65	0
No activity recorded	22	7
Total	100	100

Note: [a]Time-sampling of pupils' activity and non-activity was recorded in greater detail during the 1996 fieldwork than in 1995.

Appendix D

Oral responses of children

In addition to the written mathematical tests administered to all children in the classes observed, oral questioning and informal interaction with individual children took place when opportunities arose, during the mid-morning and lunch breaks. Children questioned informally were not selected systematically but care was taken to include children of all levels of attainment.

Six-year-old children
In Japan, children were, firstly, shown pictures of different numbers of objects (for example, 6 tulips and 8 daisies; 4 red balloons and 5 blue balloons) and were asked to say how many objects there were altogether. About 80 per cent of children were able to answer immediately; the remainder either visibly counted or paused long enough to permit a counting process to take place.

The second stage was to pose simple language-free addition sums involving number bonds up to 10 (for example, 6 + 2, 4 + 5, 2 + 7, etc). This produced an immediate and accurate response. All children appeared to have instant recall of these number bonds; there was no evidence of fingers being used for counting.

In England, similar questions were initially put to individual children, but the responses were so negative that the exercise was abandoned in order to avoid the risk of causing stress to the children. A few appeared able to count objects correctly, but none was able to answer correctly the questions involving addition. Some began to use their fingers for counting (some of these wrongly) but all appeared dependent on a counting aid.

Seven-year-old children
In Japan, children were given more difficult language-free addition questions involving numbers up to 20 and crossing the tens boundary (for example, 9 + 4, 6 + 11, 6 + 9). These were answered correctly and immediately in 83% of cases. In 5% of cases correct answers were given after hesitation (and possibly using a counting or alternative strategy); 5% of answers were incorrect and in 7% of cases no answer was offered.

In England, similar questions were initially put to individual children. It quickly became clear, however, that without a counting aid (fingers were insufficient for these questions), children had no method for finding an answer. The exercise was abandoned in order to avoid stress.

274

Appendix E

Glossary of Japanese terms

amae	emotional dependence
'Atarashii Sansū'	'New Arithmetic'
awasete	add; put together
bakufu	military government; the administration headed by the shogun
bento	packed lunch box
burakumin or dowa	'Japanese untouchables'; descendants of the outcast class of the feudal period – by tradition, tanners, butchers and undertakers
chigai	difference
chūgakkō	lower secondary or junior high school
daigaku	college or university
doryoku	effort
dōtoku	moral education
dohyō	circle used in sumō-game
empitsu	pencil
fueruto	add; increase, gain
gakkō	school
gaman	persistence, determination
gambaru	to persevere
gambatte kudasai!	Please persevere!
Gochisōsama	expression of thanks for a meal
han	small group of children within a particular class
hansei	self-reflection
hato	dove
hensachi	measure (deviation value) used to assess scores in competitive entrance examinations for high school and university
hikizan	subtraction

hiku	to subtract
hiragana	phonetic alphabet used by children
hoikuen	day care centre
honne	real feelings, opposite of tatemae
ichinensei	pupil in first grade of elementary school
ii ko	good child
ijime	bullying
ikimasu	to go
Itadakimasu	'Bon appetit'
Jibun no koto o jibun de suru	self-reliance
jikanwari	school timetable for lessons
juku	private preparation evening schools
kaerimasu	to return home
kami-zumō	traditional children's game involving paper sumo wrestlers
kanji	ideographic Chinese characters
kejime	ability to distinguish situations in which each type of behaviour (honne and tatemae) is appropriate
ken	prefecture; one of 47 regional districts of Japan
kamishibai	traditional picture cards used for story telling
koinobori	large flying fish
kokugo	(Japanese) language
kotae	answer
kōtōgakkō	upper secondary or high school
kumi	school class
kyōiku	education
kyōiku mama	literally, 'education mother' but used pejoratively to refer to the obsessively supportive attitude of some Japanese mothers towards the education of their children and their determination for their children's academic success.
manga	cartoon books
Meiji jidai	reign of Emperor Meiji; 1868 to 1912
minna	everyone
minnade	add; all together
Monbushō	Ministry of Education, Science & Culture
Nan desu ka?	What is it? What are they?
nendo	modelling clay
Nikkyōso	Japanese Teachers' Union
ninensei	pupil in second grade of elementary school
nokoriwa	to remain
ongaku	music
origami	the art of paper folding
pianika	musical instrument used in first-grade of elementary school – a cross between a keyboard instrument and a recorder

randoseru	school rucksack
ringo	apple
rōmaji	Roman alphabet
rōnin	students who have failed the university entrance examination and are resitting the following year: literally "masterless samurai"
sakana no hikizan	subtraction with fish
samurai	warrior class of the Tokugawa period
sansū	elementary school mathematics or arithmetic
sansū setto	set of mathematics equipment provided for each first grade pupil
seikatsu	life sciences
sensei	teacher; a term of respect
shijuku	private academies of the Tokugawa period
shiki	question, problem
shōgakkō	elementary school
shōgun	'barbarian-subduing great general'; title held by members of the Tokugawa family 1603–1868
shūdan seikatsu	ideal of group living
soroban	Japanese equivalent of the abacus
sunao	compliant, guileless
tabemasu	to eat
taiiku	physical education
tatemae	apparent behaviour
teragoya	parish schools for commoners in the Tokugawa period
tōban	class rota system for responsibility
tobimasu	to jump
tomodachi	friend
Tokugawa jidai	From 1603 to 1868 the descendants of the Tokugawa family held the office of shogun
toru	to take away
tsuru	cranes (birds)
wakaraseru	getting (the child) to understand
Yamatano-orochi	traditional story about a snake of this name
yōchien	kindergarten or nursery school
yobikō	juku specialising in preparing students for university entrance examinations
yori	more than, greater than, longer than
yutaka na kokoro	confident, sensitive heart
zenbude	add; all together
zukō	handwork

Appendix F

Physical arrangement
in classrooms

Physical arrangement in Japanese classrooms: 1st grade classes

Classrooms in all three schools were similar in lay-out and size

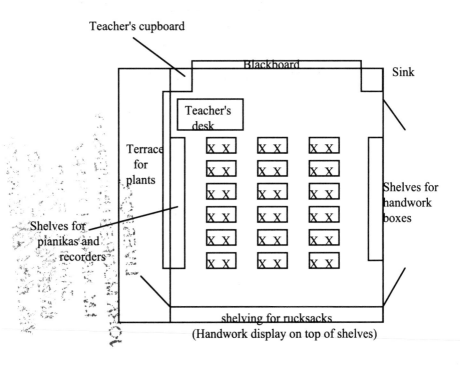

Physical arrangement in English classrooms: Year 2 classes

Example given below: minor differences existed between the schools.

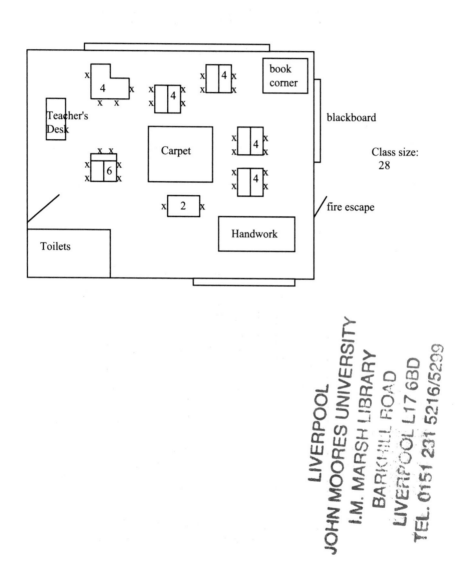

Appendix G

Examples of timetables for Japanese classes

For first-grade children

	Mon	Tues	Wed	Thurs	Fri	Sat
8.50–9.35	Music	Japanese	Handwork	Moral education	Music	Japanese
9.40–10.25	Japanese	PE	Handwork	Life sciences	Japanese	Japanese
10.45–11.30	Life sciences	Japanese	PE	Japanese	PE	Life sciences
11.35–12.20	Maths	Maths	Japanese	Maths	Maths	Special activities
			LUNCH TIME			
1.40–2.25	–	Japanese	–	–	–	–

In order not to forget anything, get everything ready the day before.
In the morning check again.

280

For second-grade children

じかんわりひょう　2年1くみ

	月	火	水	木	金	土
1	こくご	音がく	こくご	こくご	音がく	こくご
2	たいいく	さんすう	ずこう	生かつ	ずこう	どうとく
3	さんすう	こくご	としょ	さんすう	こくご	さんすう
4	生かつ	生かつ	たいいく	たいいく(中)	さんすう (タイム)	学きゅう
5		こくご		かきかた	(松原)	

◇わすれものを しないように、まえの日にようい して、あさ もう一ど たしかめましょう。

 名まえ(　　　　　　　　　)

	Mon	Tues	Wed	Thurs	Fri	Sat
8.50–9.35	Japanese	Music	Japanese	Japanese	Music	Japanese
9.40–10.25	PE	Maths	Handwork	Life sciences	Handwork	Moral education
10.45–11.30	Maths	Japanese	Library	Maths	Japanese	Maths
11.35–12.20	Life sciences	Life sciences	PE	PE	Maths	Special discussion activities
		LUNCH TIME				
1.40–2.25	–	Japanese	–	Hand-writing	Special school programme	–

In order not to forget anything, get everything ready the day before.
In the morning check again.
Name (　　　　　　　　　)

Bibliography

Alexander, R. (1992), *Policy and Practice in Primary Education* (London: Routledge).

—(1995), *Versions of Primary Education* (TJ Press: Padstow).

—, Rose, J. and Woodhead, C. (1992), *Curriculum Organisation and Classroom Practice in Primary Schools* (London: Department of Education and Science).

Altbach, P.G. and Kelly, G.P. (1978), *Education and Colonialism* (New York: Longmans).

—(eds.) (1986) *New Approaches to Comparative Education* (University of Chicago Press: Chicago)

Anderson, C.A. (1977), 'Comparative education over a quarter of a century: maturity and challenges', *Comparative Education Review*, 21, 3, pp. 405–16.

Anghileri, J. (Ed.) (1995), *Children's Mathematical Thinking in the Primary Years: Perspectives in Children's Learning* (London: Cassell).

Atarashi Sansū series (1995), (Tokyo: Shoseki Kabushiki Kaisha).

Aubrey, C. (1994b) An Investigation of Children's Knowledge of Mathematics at School Entry, *British Educational Research Journal*, 20, 1, 94, pp. 105–20

Ausubel, P. (1968), *Educational Psychology: A Cognitive View* (New York: Holt, Rhinehart & Winston).

Axelrod, H., Hall, R.V. and Tams, A. (1979), 'Comparison of two common classroom seating arrangements', *Academic Therapy*, 15, pp. 29–36.

Azuma, H. (1986), 'Why study child development in Japan?' *in* Stevenson, H. *et al.*, *Child Development in Japan* (New York; Freeman).

—Kashigawa, K. and Hess, R.D. (1981, 1986), *Maternal Attitudes, Behaviour and Children's Cognitive Development: A Cross-National Survey Between Japan and the US* (Tokyo: Unwartz of Tokyo Press).

Ball, Sir C. (1994), *The Importance of Early Learning* (London: RSA).

Barnes, J. (1985), 'Teaching experience and instructions' *in* Husen, T. and Postlethwaite, T.N. (Eds), *The International Encyclopaedia of Education, 9*, pp. 5124–8 (Oxford: Pergamon Press).

Baroody, A.J. (1984), 'Children's difficulties in subtraction: some causes and questions', *Journal for Research in Mathematics Education*, 15, 3, pp. 203–13.

—(1985), 'Mastery of basic number combinations', *Journal for Research in Mathematics Education*, 16, 2, pp. 83–98.

—(1987a), *Children's Mathematical Thinking* (Teachers' College: New York).

—(1987b), 'The development of counting strategies for single-digit addition', *Journal for Research in Mathematics Education*, 18, pp. 1411–557.

—(1989), *A Guide to Teaching Mathematics in the Primary Grades* (Mass.: Allyn & Bacon).

—(1990), 'How and when should place value concepts and skills be taught?' *Journal for Research in Mathematics Education*, 21, 4, pp. 281–6.

and Gannon, K.E. (1984), 'The development of the commutativity principle and economical addition strategies', *Cognition and Instruction*, 1, pp. 321–39.

Baroody, A.J., Ginsburgh, H.P. and Waxman, B. (1983), 'Children's use of mathematical structure', *Journal for Research in Mathematics Education*, 14, pp. 156–68.

Beaton, A.E., Martin, M.O., Mullis, I.V.S., Gonzalez, E.J., Smith, T. A. and Kelly, D.L. (1996), *Mathematics Achievement in the Middle School Years: IEA's Third International Mathematics and Science Study* (TIMSS International Study Center, Boston College, MA).

Beauchamp, E. (1978), *Learning to be Japanese* (Connecticut: Haunden).

—(1991), *Windows on Japanese Education* (New York: Greenwood Press).

Becker, J.P., Silver, E.A., Kantowski, M.G., Travers, K.J. and Wilson, J.W. (1990), 'Some observations of mathematics teaching in Japanese elementary and junior high schools', *Arithmetic Teacher*, 38, 2, pp. 12–21.

Befu, H. (1971), *Japan, An Anthropological Introduction* (San Francisco: Chandler Publishing Co.).

—(1986), 'The social and cultural background of child development in Japan and the United States' *in* Stevenson, H. *et al., Child Development and Education in Japan* (Freeman: Stanford, California).

Ben-Ari, E. (1997), *Japanese Childcare: An Interpretive Study of Culture and Organization* (London: Kegan Paul International).

Benjamin, G.R. (1997), *Japanese Lessons* (New York: New York University Press).

Bennett, N. (1988), 'The effective primary school teacher: the search for a theory of pedagogy', *Teaching and Teacher Education*, 4, 1, pp. 19–30.

—and Carre, C. (1991), *Learning to Teach* (London: Routledge).

Bennett, N., Desforges, C., Cockburn, A. and Williamson, B. (1984), *The Quality of Pupil Learning Experience* (London: Lawrence Erlbaum Ass.).

Bennett, N. and Dunne, E. (1989), *Implementing Co-operative Group Work in Classrooms* (Exeter: University of Exeter, School of Education).

Bereday, G. (1964), *Comparative Method in Education* (New York: Holt, Rinehart and Winston).

—(1967), 'Reflections on comparative methodology in education; 1964–1966', *Comparative Education*, 3, 3, pp. 169–88.

Berliner, D.C. (1987), 'Simple views of effective teaching and a simple theory of classroom instruction' *in* Berliner, D.C. and Rosenshine, B.V. (Eds), *Talks to Teachers*, (New York: Random House), pp. 93–110.

—(1992), 'The nature of expertise in teaching' *in* Oser, F.K. *et al.* (Eds), *Effective and Responsible Teaching – The New Synthesis* (San Francisco, CA: Jossey-Bass), pp. 227–48.

Berrueta-Clement, J.R. (1984), *Changed Lives: The Effects of the Perry Pre-Schooling Program on Youths through Age 19* (Ypsilani: High Scope Press, Monograph of the High Scope Education Foundation no. 8).

Bierhoff, H. (1996), *Laying the Foundations of Numeracy* (National Institute of Economic and Social Research: Discussion Paper No. 90).

Blackstone, T. (1971), *A Fair Start* (London: Allen Lane Penguin).

Blinco, P. (1991), 'Teaching of mathematics in Japanese schools' *in* Beauchamp, E., *Windows on Japanese Education* (New York: Greenwood Press).

—(1993), 'Persistence and education: a formula for Japan's economic success', *Comparative Education*, 29, 2, pp. 171–84.

Bloom, B.S. (1966), 'Twenty five years of educational research', *American Educational Research Journal*, 3, pp. 206–19.

—(1971), 'Mastery learning' *in* Block, J.H.B. (Ed.), *Mastery Learning Theory and Practice* (New York: Holt, Rhinehart & Winston).

Boden, M. (1977), *Artificial Intelligence and Natural Man* (Brighton: Harvester Press Ltd).

Boocock, S. (1991), 'The Japanese pre-school system' *in* Beauchamp, E., *Windows on Japanese Education* (New York: Greenwood Press).

Bracey, Y.G. (1992), 'The second Bracey Report on the condition of public education', *Phi Delta Kappan*, 74, pp. 104–17.

Brophy, J.E. and Good, T.L.C. (1986), 'Teacher behaviour and student achievement' *in* Wittrock, M.C. (Ed.), *Handbook of Research on Teaching* (3rd ed.) (New York: Macmillan).

Brown, J.S. and Burton, R.R. (1978), 'Diagnostic models for procedural bugs in basic mathematical skills', *Cognitive Science*, 2, pp. 155–92.

Brown, J.S. and Van Lehn K. (1982), 'Towards a generation theory of 'bugs'' *in* Romberg, T. *et al.* (Eds), *Addition and Subtraction Developmental Perspectives*, (Hillsdale, NJ: Lawrence Erlbaum Associates).

Brownell, W.A. (1935), 'Psychological considerations in the learning and the teaching of arithmetic' *in* Reeve, W.D. (Ed.), *The Teaching of Arithmetic: The 10th Yearbook of the National Council of Teachers of Mathematics* (pp. 1-31) (New York: Teachers College Press).

Bruner, J.S. (1960), *The Process of Education* (Cambridge, Mass: Harvard University Press).

—(1966), *Towards a Theory of Instruction* (New York: Norton).

—(1985), 'Vygotsky, a historical and conceptual perspective' *in* Wertsch, J.V. (Ed.), *Culture, Communication and Cognition* (Cambridge: Cambridge University Press).

Bull, R. and Johnston, R.S. (1996), 'Children's arithmetical difficulties: contributions from processing speed, item identification and short-term memory, Paper given at British Psychological Society Conference.

Bynner, J. and Steedman, J. (1995), *Difficulties with Basic Skills* (London: Basic Skills Agency).

Carey, D. (1991), 'Number sentences; linking addition and subtraction word problems and symbols', *Journal for Research in Mathematics Education*, 22, 4, pp. 266–80.

Carpenter, T.P., Hiebert, J. and Moser, J.M. (1981), 'Problem structure and first grade children's initial solution processes for simple addition and subtraction', *Journal for Research in Mathematics Education*, 12, pp. 27–39.

Carpenter, T.P. and Moser, J.M. (1984), 'The acquisition of addition and subtraction concepts in grades 1–3', *Journal for Research in Mathematics Education*, 15, pp. 179–202.

Case, R. (1983), *Intellectual Development: A Systematic Re-interpretation* (New York: Academic Press).

Charles, C.M. (1980), *Individualizing Instruction* (St. Louis: Mosby).

Clements, M.A. (1980), *Analysing Children's Errors in Written Mathematical Tasks*, Educational Studies in Mathematics, II, 1 (Dordrecht and Boston, D. Reidel Publishing).

—(1982), 'Careless errors made by sixth-grade children on written mathematical tasks', *Journal for Research in Mathematics Education*, 13, 2, pp. 136–44.

Cockroft, W.H. (1982), *Mathematics Counts: Report of the Committee of Inquiry into the Teaching of Mathematics in Schools* (London: HMSO).

Cole, M. (Ed.) (1978), *Mind and Society: The Development of Higher Psychological Processes: L S Vygotsky* (Cambridge, Mass: Harvard University Press).

Coleman, J.S. (1979), *Equality of Educational Opportunity* (Washington: US Office of Education).

Comber, L.C. and Keeves, J.P. (1973), *Science Education in Nineteen Countries: An Empirical Study* (New York: Wiley).

Cresswell, M. and Gubb, J. (1987), The *Second International Mathematics Study in England and Wales* (NFER – Nelson).

Croll, P. and Hastings, N. (Eds) (1996), *Effective Primary Teaching* (London: Fulton).

Croll, P. and Moses, D. (1988), 'Teaching methods and time on task in junior classrooms', *Educational Research*, 30, pp. 90–97.

Crump, T. (1992), *The Japanese Numbers Game* (London: Routledge).

Cummings, W.K. (1980), *Education and Equality in Japan* (Princeton: Princeton University Press).

—(1989), 'The American perception of Japanese education', *Comparative Education*, 25, pp. 293–302.

—(1995), 'The Asian human resource approach in global perspective', *Oxford Review of Education*, 21, 1, pp. 67–81.

—, Amano, I. and Kitamura, K. (Eds) (1979), *Changes in Japanese University* (New York: Praeger).

Davie, R. Butler, N.R. and Goldstein, H. (1972), *From Birth to Seven* (National Child Development Study: Longmans).

Dearden, R.S. (1976), *Problems in Primary Education* (Birmingham: University of Birmingham Press).

Dearing, R. (1994), *The National Curriculum and its Assessment: Final Report* (London: SCAA).

Deboys, M. and Pitt, E. (1979), *Lines of Development in Primary Maths* (Blackstaff Press: Belfast).

Department for Education (DFE) (1994a), *School Teachers' Pay and Conditions Document 1994* (London: HMSO)

—(1994b), *The Code of Practice on the Identification and Assessment of Special*

Educational Needs (London: HMSO).

—(1995), *Statistical Bulletin,* May (London: HMSO).

Department for Education and Employment (DFEE) (1996), *The Next Steps* (London: DfEE).

—(1997a), *Excellence for all Children: Meeting Special Educational Needs* (London: The Stationery Office).

—(1997b), *Teaching: High Status, High Standards* (Circular No. 10.97) (London: DfEE).

—(1998a), *Numeracy Matters: The Preliminary Report of the Numeracy Task Force* (London: DfEE).

—(1998b), *Form 7* (London: DFEE).

—(1998c), *Key Stage 2 Results* (London: DfEE).

—(1998d), *Statistics of Education: Teachers* (London: The Stationery Office).

—(1998e), *Homework: Guidelines for Primary Schools* (London: DFEE).

—(1999), *The National Curriculum for England* (London: DFEE).

Department of Education and Science (DES) (1989), *Standards in Education 1987–8* (London: DES).

Dillon, R.F. and Schmeck, R. (Eds) (1985), *Individual Differences in Cognition* (New York: Academic Press).

Dore, R. (1965), *Education in Tokugawa Japan* (London: Routledge & Kegan Paul).

—(1987), *Taking Japan Seriously* (Stanford: Stanford University Press).

—(1997), (Second Edition) *The Diploma Disease* (London: Allen and Unwin).

Duffin, J. (1994), *Calculators in the Classroom: Reports of the National Evaluation of the CAN Component of the PrIME Project 1986–9, and of the CAN Continuation Project 1990–1992* (Hull: University of Hull Numeracy Centre).

Fogelman, K., Essen, J., and Tibbenham, A. (1978), 'Ability grouping in secondary schools and attainment', *Educational Studies,* 4, 3, pp. 201–12.

Foxman, D. Ruddock, G., McCallum, I. and Schagen, I. (1991), *APU Mathematics Monitoring* (Phase 2) (NFER).

Fraser, B.J., Walberg, H.J., Welch, W.W. and Hattie, J.A. (1987), 'The need for educational productivity research,' *International Journal of Educational Studies,* 11, pp. 147–252.

Fraser, S.E. (1964), *Jullien's Plan for Comparative Education 1816–1817* (New York: Teacher's College, Colombia University).

Fuson, K.C. (1986a), 'Teaching children to subtract by counting up', *Journal for Research in Mathematics Education,* 17, 3, pp. 172–89.

—(1986b), 'Roles of representation and verbalisation in the teaching of multi-digit addition and subtraction', *European Journal of Psychology and Education,* 1, pp. 35–36.

—(1988), *Children's Counting and Concepts of Number* (New York: Springer Verlag).

—(1990), 'A forum for researchers: issues in place value and multi-digit addition and subtraction learning and teaching', *Journal for Research in Mathematics Education,* 21, 4, pp. 273–80.

—(1992), 'Research on whole number addition and subtraction' *in* Grouws, D.A. (Ed.), *Handbook of Research on Mathematics Teaching and Learning* (New York:

National Council of Teachers of Mathematics).

—, Stigler, J. and Bartsch, K. (1988), 'Grade placement of addition and subtraction topics in Japan, China, the USSR, Taiwan and the US', *Journal for Research in Mathematics Education*, 19, pp. 449–56.

— and Briars, D.J. (1990), 'Using a base-ten blocks learning/teaching approach for first-and-second-grade place-value and multi-digit addition and subtraction', *Journal for Research in Mathematics Education*, 21, 3, pp. 180–206.

—, Carroll, W.M. and Landis, J. (1996), 'Levels in conceptualisation and solving addition and subtraction compare word problems', *Cognition and Instruction*, 14 3, pp. 345–71.

— and Kwon, Y. (1991), 'Chinese-based regular and European irregular systems of number words: the disadvantages for English-speaking children' *in* Durkin and Shire, *Language of Mathematical Education* (Milton Keynes: Open University Press).

— and Kwon, Y. (1992), 'Korean children's single digit addition and subtraction: numbers structured by 10', *Journal for Research in Mathematics Education*, 33, 2, pp. 148–65.

—, Smith, S.T. and Cicero, A.M.L. (1997), 'Supporting first-graders ten-structures thinking in urban classrooms', *Journal for Research in Mathematics Education*, 28, 6, pp. 738–66.

Gagné, R.M. (1965), *The Conditions of Learning* (New York: Hole, Rinehart and Winston).

Galton, M. (1983), *Changing Schools –Changing Curriculum* (London: Fulton).

—(1998), *Reliving the Oracle Experience: Back to Basics or Back to Structure?* (Warwick: University of Warwick, Centre for Research in Elementary and Primary Education).

—, Fogelman, K., Hargreaves, L. and Cavendish, S. (1991), *The Rural Schools Curriculum Emnhancement National Evaluation (SCENE) Project: Final Report* (London: Department of Education and Science).

— and Simon, B. (Ed.) (1980), *Progress and Performance in the Primary Classroom* (London: Routledge & Kegan Paul).

—, Simon, B. and Croll, P. (1980), *Inside the Primary Classroom* (London: Routledge and Kegan Paul).

Geary, D.C. (1994), *Children's Mathematical Development* (Washington DC: American Psychological Association).

Gellman, R. and Gallistel, C.R. (1978), *The Child's Understanding of Number* (Cambridge, MA: Harvard University Press).

Genishi, C. (1982), 'Observational research methods for early childhood education *in* Spodek, B. (Ed.), *Handbook on Research on Early Childhood Education* (Free Press: New York).

Ginsburg, H.P. (1977), *Children's Arithmetic: The Learning Process* (New York: Academic Press).

—(1983), *The Development of Mathematical Thinking* (Academic Inc.; London).

Gipps, C. (1992), *What We Know about Effective Primary Teaching* (London: University of London, Institute of Education).

Goldstein, H. (1993), *Interpreting International Comparisons of Student Achieve-*

ment (UNESCO).

Grossman, P.L., Wilson, S.M. and Shulman, L.S. (1989), 'Teachers of substance: subject matter knowledge for teaching' *in* Reynolds, M.C. (Ed.), *Knowledge Base for the Beginning Teacher* (Oxford: Pergamon Press).

Hanna, G. (1993), 'The validity of international performance comparisons' *in* Niss, M. (Ed.), *Investigations into Assessment in Mathematics Education* (Amsterdam: Kluwer).

Hans, N. (1949), *Comparative Education: A Study of Educational Factors and Traditions* (London: Routledge and Kegan Paul).

Harnisch, D.L. (1986), 'Cross-national differences in mathematics attitudes and achievement among seventeen year olds', *International Journal of Educational Development*, 6, 4, pp. 233–44.

—(1994), 'Supplemental education in Japan: Juku schooling and its implication', *Journal of Curriculum Studies*, 26, pp. 323–34.

Harris, S. and Henkhuzens, Z. (1998), *Mathematics in Primary Schools* (Slough Bucks: NFER).

Harris, S., Keys, W. and Renandez, C. (1996), *Third International Mathematics and Science Study: Second National Report Part I* (Slough: NFER).

Haylock, D. (1986), 'Mathematical low attainers' check list', *British Journal of Educational Development*, 56, pp. 205–6.

—(1991). *Teaching Mathematics to Low Attainers 8 – 12* (London: Paul Chapman Publishing).

—(1995), *Mathematics Explained for Primary Teachers* (London: Paul Chapman Publishing Ltd).

Helmke, A. and Schrader, F.W. (1988), 'Successful student practice during seatwork: efficient management and active supervision not enough', *Journal of Educational Research*, 82, pp. 70–75.

Hendry, J. (1985), 'Peer pressure and kindergartens in Japan', *Social and Economic Research on Modern Japan*, 57 (Berlin, Ute Schiller).

—(1986a), *Becoming Japanese* (Manchester: Manchester University Press).

—(1986b), 'Kindergarten and the transition from home to school education', *Comparative Education*, 29, 2, pp. 53–8.

—(1993), *Wrapping Culture* (Oxford: Oxford University Press).

Her Majesty's Inspectorate (HMI) (1989a), *Increasing Pre-school Provision* (London: HMSO).

—(1989b), *The Teaching and Learning of Mathematics* (DES: London).

—(1991), *Aspects of Upper Secondary and Higher Education in Japan* (DES: HMSO).

Hess, R.D., Kashiwagi, K., Azuma, H., Price, G.G. and Dickson, W.P. (1980), 'Maternal expectations for the mastery of development tasks in Japan and the US', *International Journal of Psychology*, 15, pp. 259–71.

Hiebert, J. (1986), *Conceptual and Procedural Knowledge: The Case of Mathematics* (Hillsdale NJ: Erlbaum Associates).

Hirahala, H. (1995), *A Comparative Study of Mathematics Education for Students Aged 16-18 in the UK and Japan* (Kagawa, Japan: Bikousha Press Co. Ltd).

Hohl, W. (Ed.)(1994–6). *Mathematik 1–3* (Zurich, Lehrmittelverlag des Kantons Zurich)

Hollenbeck, A.B. (1978), 'Problems of reliability in observational research', *in* Sackett, G.P. (Ed.), *Observing Behaviour, Vol. 2* (Baltimore, MD; University Park Press).

Holmes, B. (1965), *A Comparative Approach to Education* (London: Routledge).

—(Ed.) (1985), *Equality and Freedom in Education: A Comparative Study* (London; Allen and Unwin).

Horio, T. (1990), 'Conflicting approaches to the reform of Japanese society: economic liberalism versus educational liberalism' *in* Moon, B , (Ed.), *New Curriculum, National Curriculum* (Milton Keynes: Open University).

Howarth, G. (1993), *Britain's Educational Reform* (London: Routledge).

Howson, A. G. (1984), 'Seventy-five years of the International Commission in Mathematical Instruction', *Educational Studies in Mathematics,* 15, pp. 75–93.

—(1991), *National Curricula in Mathematics* (Leicester: Mathematical Association).

Huelskamp, R.M. (1993), 'Perspectives on education in America', *Phi Delta Kappan,* 74, pp. 718–21.

Hughes, M. (Ed.) (1996), *Teaching and Learning in Changing Times* (Oxford: Blackwell).

Husén, T. (1967), *International Study of Achievement in Mathematics: A Comparison of Twelve Countries* (New York: Wiley).

Ishida, H. (1993), *Social Mobility in Contemporary Japan* (Basingstoke: Macmillan).

Jackson, J. (Ed.) (1970), *Professors and Professionalisation* (London: Cambridge University Press).

Jansen, M.B. (Ed.) (1989), *The Cambridge History of Japan: Vol. 5 The Nineteenth Century* (Cambridge: Cambridge University Press).

Joffe, L. (1981), 'Mathematical difficulties and dyslexia', *British Mathematical Association Conference,* Reading, September 1997.

Johnson, T. (1972), *Professors and Power* (London: Macmillan).

Joshi, M.S. and MacLean, M. (1997), 'Maternal expectations of child development in India, Japan and England', *Journal of Cross-cultural Psychology,* 28, 2, pp.219–34.

Joshi, M.S., MacLean, M. and Carter, W. (1997), 'Children's journeys to school – new data and further comments', *World Transport, Policy and Practice,* pp. 17–22.

Kanako, M. (1988), *The Role of the Government in Asian Higher Education Systems* (RIHE).

Kandel, I.L. (1933), *Comparative Education* (London: Harrap).

—(1955), *The New Era in Education: A Comparative Study* (Boston: Houghton Mifflin).

—(1959), 'The methodology of comparative education', *The New International Review of Education,* 5, 3, pp. 270–78.

Katz, L.G. and Mohanty, C.T. (1985), 'Early childhood education' *in* Husén, T. and Postlethwaite, T. (Eds), *International Encyclopaedia of Education, Vol.3* (Oxford: Pergamon Press).

Kazamias, A.M. (1972), 'Comparative pedagogy: an assignment for the '70s', *Comparative Education Review,* 16, 3, pp. 406–11.

Kerry, T. and Mayes, A.S. (Eds) (1995), *Issues in Mentoring* (London Routledge: Open University Press).

Keys, W., Harris, S. and Fernandez, C. (1996), *Third International Mathematics and Science Study: Second National Report Part II and Appendices* (Slough: NFER).

King, E.J. (1986), 'Japanese education in comparative perspective', *Comparative Education*, 29, 2, pp. 73–82.

Kitamura, K. (1986), 'The decline and reform of education in Japan: a comparative perspective', *in* Cummings, W.K. *et al.*, *Educational Policies in Crisis* (New York: Praeger).

Lapointe, A.E., Mead, N.A. and Phillips, G.W. (1989), *A World of Difference: An International Assessment of Mathematics and Science* (Princeton, NJ: Princeton University Press).

Lee, S.-Y., Graham, T. and Stevenson, H.W. (1996), 'Teacher and teaching: elementary schools in Japan and the United States' *in* Rohlen, T.P. and Letendre, G.K. (Eds), *Teaching and Learning in Japan* (Cambridge: Cambridge University Press).

Leestma, R.R, and Walberg, H.J. (Eds) (1992), *Japanese Educational Productivity* (Centre for Japanese Studies; University of Michigan).

Leinhardt, G. and Greeno, J.G. (1986), 'The cognitive skill of teaching', *Journal of Educational Psychology*, 78, pp. 75–95.

Lewis, C.C. (1995), *Educating Hearts and Minds* (Cambridge University Press).

Lewis, H.D. (1985), *The French Education System* (London: Croom Helm).

Light, P. and Butterworth, G. (1992), *Context and Cognition: Ways of Learning and Knowing* (New York, London: Harvester Wheatsheaf).

Lincicome, M. (1993), 'Focus on the internationalisation of Japanese education', *Comparative Education Review*, May, pp. 123–51.

Livesey, T.J. (1888), *Moffatt's 'How to Prepare Notes of Lessons'* (London: Moffatt and Page).

Lovegrove, N.C. and Wiltshire, M.J. (1997), 'IT in UK schools: its time for a strategy', *McKinsey Quarterly*, 2, pp. 220–30.

Lynn, R. (1988), *Educational Achievement in Japan: Lessons for the West* (New York: M E Sharpe).

MacLean, M. and Whitburn, J. (1996), 'Number name systems and children's early number knowledge: a comparison of Welsh and English speaking children', paper given to the International Society for Behavioural Development, Quebec, August 1996; British Psychological Society, Oxford, September 1996.

Marks, J. (1996b), *Standards of English and Maths in Primary Schools for 1995* (London: Social Market Foundation).

—(1998), *An Anatomy of Failure: Standards in English Schools for 1997* (London: Social Market Foundation).

Marshall, B.K. (1994), *Learning to be Modern: Japanese Political Discourse on Education* (Boulder, Colorado: Westview Press).

Martin, M.O., Mullis, I.V.S., Gonzalez, E.J., Smith, T.A. and Kelly, D.L. (1999), *Third International Mathematics and Science Study*, Boston College, www.timss.org.

McIntyre, D. and Hagger, H. (Eds) (1996), *Mentors in Schools* (London: David Fulton Publications Ltd).

McLean, M. (1995), *Educational Traditions Compared* (London: David Fulton Pub.).

—and Lauglo, J. (1985), *The Control of Education: International Perspectives on the Centralization -Decentralization Debate* (London: Heinemann).

McNamara, D.R. and Waugh, D.G. (1993), 'Classroom organisation: a discussion of the grouping strategies in the light of the 'Three Wise Mens' report', *School Organisation*, 13, 1, pp. 41–50.

Meadow, S. (1993), *The Child as Thinker: The Development and Acquisition of Cognition in Childhood* (London: Routledge).

Medley, D.M. (1979), 'The effectiveness of teachers', *in* Peterson, P. and Walberg, H., *Research on Teaching* (Berkeley, California: McCutchan).

Mehar, H. (1979), *Learning Lessons: Social Organization in the Classroom* (Cambridge, Mass.: Harvard University Press).

Miller, M.F. and Stigler, J.W. (1987), 'Counting in Chinese: cultural variation in a basic cognitive skill', *Cognitive Development*, 2, pp. 279–305.

Miura, I.T. (1993), 'First grades; cognitive representations of number and understanding of place value: cross national comparisons, France, Japan, Korea, Sweden and the United States', *Journal of Educational Psychology*, 85, 1, pp. 24–30.

—, Kim, C.C., Chang, C.-M., and Okamoto, Y. (1988), 'Effects of language characteristics on children's cognitive representation of number: cross-national comparisons', *Child Development*, 59, pp. 1445–50.

— and Okamoto, Y. (1989), 'Comparison of American and Japanese first grade's cognitive representations of number and understanding of place value', *Journal of Educational Psychology*, 81, 1, pp. 109–14.

—, Okamoto, Y., Kim, C.c., Chang, C.-M., Steere, M. and Fayol, M. (1994), 'Comparisons of children's cognitive representation of number: China, France, Japan, Korea, Sweden and the United States', *International Journal of Behavioural Development*, 17, pp. 401–11.

Monbushō (1989), *A Course of Study for Elementary Schools* (Tokyo: Monbushō).

—(1991), *Report from the Council for Promotion of Kindergarten Education* (Tokyo: Monbushō).

—(1994), *Education in Japan* (Tokyo: Monbushō).

—(1995a), *Statistical Abstract* (Tokyo: Monbushō).

—(1995b), *About Japan Series: Education in Japan* (Tokyo: Monbushō).

—(1997), *Education in Japan* (Tokyo: Monbushō).

—(1998), *Education in Japan* (Tokyo: Monbushō).

Mortimore, P., Sammons, P., Stoll, L., Lewis, D. and Ecob, R. (1986), *The Junior School Project: Main Report* (London: ILEA Research).

—(1988), *School Matters: The Junior Years* (Wells: Open Books).

Mullis, I.V.A., Martin, M.O., Beaton, A.E., Gonzalez, E.J., Kelly, D.L. and Smith, T.A. (1997), *Mathematics Achievement – the Primary School Years* (Chestnut Hill, MA: TIMSS Study Center).

Murray, J. (1939), 'The relative difficulty of the base number factors' *in* Scottish Council for Research in Education, *Studies in Arithmetic* (London: University of London Press).

Nagasaki, E. (1998), *Japanese Teachers' and Guardians' Attitudes Towards Mathematics Education* (Tokyo: National Institute for Educational Research in Japan).

—and Becker, J.P. (1993), 'Classroom assessment in Japanese mathematics education', *in Assessment in the Japanese Classroom* (NCTM Yearbook).

National Council on Educational Reform (1987) *Reports on Educational Reform*

(Tokyo: NCER).

National Foundation for Educational Research (1995), *Starting School* (Slough: NFER).

National Institute for Educational Research (1991), *Distinguishing Features of Japanese Education* (Tokyo: NIER).

Newman, M.A. (1977), 'An analysis of sixth grade pupils' errors on written mathematical tasks', *Research in Mathematics Education in Australia* (Melbourne: Monash University).

Noah, H.J. and Eckstein, M.A. (1969), *Toward a Science of Comparative Education* (London: Macmillan).

Noss, R. (1998), 'Missing the point on numeracy', *Times Educational Supplement*; 6 March.

Nunes, T. (1992), 'Ethnomathematics and everyday cognition', *in* Grouws, D.A., *Handbook of Research on Mathematics Teaching and Learning* (New York: Macmillan).

—and Bryant, P. (1996), *Children Doing Mathematics* (Cambridge, Mass.:Blackwell).

—and Bryant, P. (1997), *Learning and Teaching Mathematics: An International Perspective* (Hove: Psychology Press Ltd).

Office for Standards in Education (Ofsted) (1993), *Mathematics* (London: HMSO).

—(1995a), *Primary Mathematics* (London: Ofsted).

—(1995b), *Class Size and the quality of education* (London: Ofsted).

—(1996a), *Primary Subject Guidance* (London: Ofsted).

—(1996b), *The Annual Report of Her Majesty's Chief Inspector of Schools: Standards and Quality in Education 1994/5* (London: The Stationery Office).

Ohta, T. (1986), 'Problems and perspectives in Japanese education', *Comparative Education*, 29, 2, pp. 27–30.

Organisation Mondiale pour l'Education Préscolaire (OMEP) (1992), *Education and Care of Young Children in Japan* (Tokyo: Japan National Committee of OMEP).

Osborn, A.F. and Milbank, J.E. (1987), *The Effects of Early Education* (Oxford: Clarendon Press).

Ozakir, S. (1978), *The Japanese: A Cultural Portrait* (Tokyo, Japan: Charles E Turtle Co. Ltd).

Palzkill, L., Rinkins, H.-D. and Honisch, K. (Eds) (1994), *Denken und Rechnen* (Braunschwieg:Westermann).

Pascaul-Leone (1970), 'A mathematical model for the transition rule in Piaget's developmental stages', *Acta Psychologica*, 32, pp. 301–45.

Passin, H. (1982), *Society and Education in Japan* (New York: Columbia University Teachers' College).

Peak, L. (1991), *Learning to Go to School in Japan* (Berkeley: University of California).

Perry, M., Vanderstoep, S.W. and Yns, L. (1993), 'Asking questions in first-grade mathematics classes: potential influences on mathematical thought', *Journal of Educational Psychology*, 85, pp. 31–40.

Phillips, D. (Ed.) (1992), *Oxford Studies in Comparative Education: Lessons of Cross National Comparison in Education* (Triangle Books: Wallingford).

Piaget, J. (1941), *The Child's Concept of Number* (Routledge and Kegan Paul).

—(1965), *The Child's Conception of the World* (New Jersey: Littlefield, Adams).

—(1969), *Science of Education and Psychology of the Child*, trans. Coltman, D. (London: Longman Group Ltd).

Pickett, L.H. and Boren, D. (1924), *Early Childhood Education* (London: Harrap).

Plowden Report (1967), *Children and Their Primary Schools: A Report of the Central Advisory Council for Education* (London: HMSO).

Prais, S.J. (1987), 'Educating for productivity: comparisons of Japanese and English schooling and vocational preparation', *National Institute Economic Review*, February, pp. 40–56.

—(1993), 'Economic Performance and Education: The Nature of Britain's Deficiencies', National Institute of Economic and Social Research, Discussion Paper no. 52.

—(1995), *Productivity, Education and Training* (Cambridge University Press).

—(1996), 'Class size and learning', *Oxford Review of Education*, 22, pp. 399–414.

—(1997), 'How did English schools and pupils *really* perform in the 1995 international comparisons in mathematics?' *National Institute Economic Review*, July, pp. 53–68.

Pringle, M.K. and Naidoo, S. (1975), *Early Child Care in Britain* (London: Gordon and Breach).

Psacharopoulos, G. (1972), 'Rates of return to investment in education around the world', *Comparative Education Review*, 16, 1, pp. 54–67.

—(1990), 'Colloquy on comparative theory', *Comparative Education Review*, 34, 3, pp. 369–80.

Putnam, R.T., Lampert, M. and Peterson, P.L. (1990), 'Alternative perspectives on knowing mathematics in elementary schools' *in* Cazden, C. (Ed.), *Review of Research in Education*, 16, (Washington DC: American Educational Research Association).

Qualifications and Curriculum Authority (QCA) (1999), *Early Learning Goals*, London: DFEE and QCA.

Redfeld, D.L. and Rousseau, E.W. (1981), 'A meta-analysis of experimental research on teacher questioning behaviour', *Review of Educational Research*, 51, pp. 237–45.

Reform Council (1987) see National Council on Educational Reform.

Resnick, L.B. (1983), 'A developmental theory of number understanding' *in* Ginsburg, H.P., *The Development of Mathematical Thinking* (London: Academic Inc.).

Reynolds, D. and Farrell, S. (1996), *Worlds Apart?* (London: Ofsted).

Richman, L.C. (1983), 'Language-learning disability: issues, research and future directions' *in* Wolraich, M. and Routh, D.K. (Eds), *Advances in Developmental and Behavioural Paediatrics*, Vol.4 (Greenwich, CT: Jai Press).

Rieber, R.W. and Carton, A.S. (1987), *Collected Works of L J Vygotsky* (New York: Plenum Press),

Robbins, L. (1963), *Report on Higher Education* (London: HMSO).

Robinson, W.P., Tayler, C.S. and Piolat, M. (1992), 'Redoublement in relation to self-perception and self-evaluation: France', *Research in Education*, 47, pp. 64–75.

Robitaille, D. and Garden, R.A. (1989), *The IEA Study of Mathematics II: Contexts and Outcomes of School Mathematics* (London: Pergamon Press).

Robitaille, D. and Travers, K.J. (1992), 'International studies of achievement in mathematics' *in* Grouws. D.A. (Ed.), *Handbook of Research on Mathematics Teaching and Learning* (New York: National Council of Teachers of Mathematics).

Rohlen, T.P. (1983), *Japan's High Schools* (Berkeley, CA: Center for Japanese Studies, University of California).

—and Letendre, G.K. (Eds), (1996), *Teaching and Learning in Japan* (Cambridge University Press: Cambridge).

Romberg, T.A. and Carpenter, T.P. (1984), 'What children do' *in* Rombert, T.A. and Stewart, D.M. (Eds), *School Mathematics: Options for the 1990s Proceedings of the Conference* (Madison; Wisconsin: National Council for Teachers in Mathematics).

—(1986), 'Research on teaching and learning maths: two disciplines of scientific enquiry' *in* Wittrock, M.C. (Ed.), *Handbook on Research and Teaching* (New York: Macmillan).

Rosenshine, B. (1979), 'Content, time and direct instruction' *in* Peterson, P. and Walberg, H.J., *Research on Teaching* (Berkeley, CA: McCutchen).

—(1987), 'Direct instruction' *in* Dunkin, M. (Ed.), *Teaching and Teacher Education* (Oxford: Pergamon).

Ross, S. (1986), 'The development of children's place value through numeration concepts in grades two through five', American Educational Research Association paper.

Rothery, A. (1980), 'Children reading maths', Working Paper of the Language and Reading in Maths Group: Worcester College of Higher Education.

Rousseau, J.J. (1762), *Emile, or, Education* (1911, London: JB Dent).

Royal Society, The, and the Institute of Mathematics and its Applications (1988), *How To Provide For The Teaching Of Mathematics In Secondary Schools* (London: The Royal Society).

Ruthven, K. (1998), 'The use of mental, written and calculator strategies of numerical computation by upper primary pupils within a 'calculator-aware' number curriculum', *British Educational Research Journal*, 24, 1, pp. 21–42.

—, Rousham, L. and Chaplin, D. (1997), 'The long-term influence of a 'calculator-aware' number curriculum on pupils' mathematical attainments and attitudes in the primary phase', *Research Papers in Education*, 12, 3, pp. 249–82.

Rutter, M., Maughan, B., Mortimore, P. and Ouston, J. (1979), *Fifteen Thousand Hours* (London: Open Books).

Sadler, M. (1902), *Aims in Education* (Extracted from Present Day Papers, March).

Sammons, P., Hillman, J. and Mortimore, P. (1994), *Assessing School Effectiveness* (London: University of London Institute of Education).

—(1995), *Key Characteristics of Effective Schools; A Review of School Effectiveness Research* (London: Ofsted).

Sato, N. (1996), 'Honoring the individual' *in* Rohlen, P. and Letendre, G.K. (Eds), *Teaching and Learning in Japan* (Cambridge: Cambridge University Press).

Schools Curriculum and Assessment Authority (SCAA) (1995), *Planning the Curriculum at Key Stages 1 and 2* (London: SCAA).

—(1996a), *Desirable Outcomes for Children's Learning* (London; DfEE).

—(1996c), *A Guide to the National Curriculum* (London: SCAA).

Schmittau, J. (1993), 'Connecting mathematical knowledge: a dialectical perspective', *Journal of Mathematical Behaviour*, 12, March, pp. 179–202.

Schoenfeld, A.H. (1983), *Problem Solving in the Mathematics Curriculum: A Report* (Washington DC: Mathematical Association of America).

—(1984), *Mathematical Thinking and Problem Solving* (Hillsdale, NJ: Lawrence Erlbaum Associates).

Schoppa, L. (1991), *Education Reform in Japan* (London: Routledge).

Schriewer, J. and Holmes, B. (1988), *Theories and Methods in Comparative Education* (Frankfurt am Main: Lang).

Schweinhart, L.J., Weikart, D.P. and Larner, M.B. (1986), 'Consequences of three pre-school curriculum models through age 15', *Early Childhood Quarterly*, 1, pp. 15–46.

Shields, J.J. (Ed.)(1990), *Japanese Schooling: Patterns of Socialization, Equality and Political Control* (Pennsylvania State University Press).

—(1991), 'Education reform in Japan: balancing academic achievement with parental choice', mimeo.

Shimahara, N.K. and Sakai, A. (1995), *Learning to Teach in Two Cultures: Japan and the United States* (New York: Garland Publications)

Silver, E.A. (Ed.) (1985), *Teaching and Learning Mathematical Problem Solving* (Hillsdale, NJ: Lawrence Erlbaum Associates).

Simmons, C. (1990), *Growing Up and Going to School in Japan* (Milton Keynes: Open University Press).

Simon, A. and Boyer, E.G. (1970), *Mirrors for Behaviour III; An Anthology of Observation Instruments* (Wyncore, Penn.: Communications Materials Center).

Simon, B. (1981), 'Why no pedagogy in England?' *in* Simon, B. and Taylor, W. (Eds), *Education in the Eighties, The Central Issues* (London: Batsford).

—(1993), 'Some problems of pedagogy, revisited', lecture delivered to the 8th Annual Congress of the Educational Research Network of Northern Ireland.

Simon, M.A. (1995), 'Reconstructing mathematical language from a constructivist perspective', *Journal of research in Mathematics Education*, 26, 2, pp. 114–5.

Singleton, J. (1990), '*Gambaru*: a Japanese cultural theory of learning' *in* Shields, J.J. (Ed.), *Japanese Schooling: Patterns of Socialization, Equality and Political Control* (Pennsylvania State University Press).

Slavin, R.E. (1987), 'Ability grouping and student achievement in elementary school', *Review of Educational Research*, 57, 3, pp. 293–336.

—(1990), 'Achievement effect of ability grouping in secondary schools', *Review of Educational Research*, 60, 3, pp. 471–99.

Song, M.J. and Ginsberg, H.P. (1987), 'The development of informal and formal mathematical thinking in Korean and US children', *Child Development*, 58, pp. 1286–96.

Stedman, L.C. (1994), 'Incomplete explanations: the case of US performance in the international assessment of education', *Educational Research*, 23, 1, pp. 24–32.

Steffe, L.P., Glaserfeld, E. von, Richards, J. and Cobb, P. (1983), *Children's Counting Types* (New York: Praeger).

Steffe, L.P. and Gale, J. (Eds) (1995), *Constructivism in Education* (Hillsdale, NJ: Erlbaum Associates).

Stephens, M. (1991), *Education and the Future of Japan* (Sandgate: Sandgate, Kent).

Stevenson, H., Azuma, H. and Hakuta, K. (1986), *Child Development in Japan* (New York: Freeman).

Stevenson, H.W. and Bartsch, H. (1992), An Analysis of Japanese and American Textbooks in Mathematics *in* Leestnam R. and Walberg, H.J. (Eds), *Japanese Educational Productivity* (University of Michigan, Ann Arbor).

Stevenson, H.W. Lummis, M., Lee, S.-Y., and Stigler, J.W., (1990), *Making The Grade In Mathematics: Elementary School Mathematics in the United States, Taiwan and Japan* (Reston, VA: National Council of Teachers of Mathematics).

Stevenson, H.W. and Stigler, J.W. (1992), *The Learning Gap* (Summit Books: New York).

Stigler, J.W. (1988b), 'The use of verbal explanation in Japanese and American classrooms', *The Arithmetic Teacher*, 36, 2, pp. 27–9.

—and Baranes, R. (1988),'Culture and mathematics learning', *in* Rosskopf, E.Z. (Ed.), *Review of Research in Education* (Washington DC: American Educational Research Association).

—, Fernandez, C. and Yoshida, M. (1996), 'Cultures of mathematics instruction in Japanese and American elementary classrooms' *in* Rohlen, T.P. and Letendre, G.K. (Eds), *Teaching and Learning in Japan* (Cambridge: Cambridge University Press).

—, Lee, S.-Y., Lucker, W. and Stevenson, H.W. (1982), 'Curriculum achievement in mathematics: a study of elementary school children in Japan, Taiwan and the United States', *Journal of Educational Psychology*, 74, 3, pp. 315–22.

—, Lee, S.-Y. and Stevenson, H.W. (1987), 'Mathematics classrooms in Japan, Taiwan and the United States', *Child Development*, 58, 5, pp. 1272–85.

— and Perry, M. (1990), 'Mathematics learning in Japanese, Chinese and American classrooms', *in* Stigler, J.W. *et al.*, *Cultural Psychology* (Cambridge University Press; Cambridge).

Stolurow, L.M. (1965), 'Model the master teacher or master the teaching model?' *in* Krumbholtz, J.E. (Ed.), *Learning and Educational Process* (Chicago: Rand McNally).

Stones, E. (1979), *Psychopedagogy: Psychological Theory and the Practice of Teaching* (London: Methuen).

Sugiyama, Y. (1987), 'Comparison of word problems in textbooks between Japan and the US', *in* Becker, J.P. and Miura, T. (Eds), *Proceedings of the US-Japan Seminar on Problem Solving* (Carbondale, IL: Southern Illinois University).

Teacher Training Agency (TTA) (1998), *Initial Teacher Training National Curriculum for Primary Mathematics* (Annex D of DfEE Circular 4/98) (London: Teacher Training Agency).

Thorndike, E.L. (1924), *The Psychology of Arithmetic* (New York: Macmillan).

Thorpe, and Schmuller (1954), *Contemporary Theories of Learning* (New York: Wiley).

Tizard, B., Blatchford, P., Burke, J., Farquhar, C. and Plewis, I. (1988), *Young Children at School in the Inner City* (London: Lawrence Erlbaum).

Tobin, J.J. (1992), 'Japanese pre-schools and the pedagogy of selfhood' *in*

Rosenberger, N. (Ed.), *Japanese Sense of Self* (Cambridge: Cambridge University Press).

—, Wu, D.Y.H. and Davidson, D.H. (1989), *Pre-school in three cultures* (New Haven: Yale University Press).

Travers, K. and Westbury, I. (1989), *The IEA Study of Mathematics I: Analysis of Mathematics Curricula* (Oxford: Pergamon Press).

Tsuchimochi, G.H. (1991), *Education Reform in Post-War Japan* (Tokyo: University of Tokyo Press).

Turner, R. (1971), 'Sponsored and contest mobility in the school system' *in* Hopper, S. (Ed.), *Readings in the Theory of Educational Systems* (London: Hutchinson).

US Department of Education (1987), *Japanese Education Today* (Washington DC: US Government Printing Office).

Van Lehn, K. (1983), 'On the representation of procedures in repair theory' *in* Ginsburg, H.P. (Ed.), *The Development of Mathematical Thinking* (New York: Academic Press).

—(1990), *Mind Bugs: The Origins of Procedural Misconception* (Cambridge, Mass: MIT Press).

Vygotsky, L.S. (1934), 'Learning and mental development at school age', translated in Simon, B. (Ed.) (1963), *Educational Psychology in the USSR,* (London: Routledge and Kegan Paul).

—(1962), *Thought and Language* (Cambridge, Mass.: M.I.T).

—(1966), 'Play and its role', *Soviet Psychology,* 12, 6, pp. 62–76.

—(1981), 'The genesis of higher mental functions' *in* Wertsch, J.V. (Ed.), *The Concept of Activity in Soviet Psychology* (Armonk, NY: Sharpe).

—(1987), *The Collected Work of L S Vygotsky, Vol. 1* (New York: Plenum Press).

Waxman, H.C. and Walberg, H.W. (1982), 'The relation of teaching and learning: a review of reviews of process-product research', *Contemporary Education Review,* 1, pp. 103–20.

Weinert, F.E. and De Corte, E. (1996), 'Translating research into practice' *in* De Corte, E. and Weinert, F.E. (Eds), *International Encyclopaedia of Developmental and Instructional Psychology* (Oxford: Elsevier Press).

Weinert, F.E., Helmke, A. and Schrader, F.W. (1992), 'Research on the model teacher and the teaching model' *in* Oser, F.K. *et al., Effective and Responsible Teaching – The New Synthesis* (San Francisco, CA: Jossey Bass).

Weinert, F.E. and Lingelbach, H. (1995), 'Teaching expertise: theoretical conceptualization, empirical findings and some consequences for teacher training', *in* Hoz, R. and Silberstein, M. (Eds), *Partnerships of Schools and Institutions of Higher Education in Teacher Development* (Beer-Shera, Israel: University of Neger Press).

Weinert, F.E., Schrader, F.W. and Helmke, A. (1989), 'Quality of instruction and achievement outcomes', *International Journal of Education Research,* 13, pp. 895–914.

—(1990), 'Educational expertise: closing the gap between educational research and classroom practice', *School Psychology International,* 11, pp. 163–80.

Wertsch, J.V. (1985), *Vygotsky and the Social Formation of Mind* (Cambridge, Mass.: Harvard University Press).

Wheldall, K. and Glynn, T. (1989), *Effective Classroom Teaching* (New York: Basil

Blackwell).

Wheldall, K. Morris, M., Vaughan, P. and Ng, Y. (1981), 'Rows versus tables: an example of behavioural ecology in two classes of 11 year old children,' *Educational Psychology*, 1, 2, pp. 27–44.

Wheldall, K. and Olds, D. (1987), 'Of sex and seating: the effect of mixed and same sex seating arrangements in junior classrooms', *New Zealand Journal of Educational Research*, 22, pp. 71–85.

Whitburn, J. (1995a), 'Keeping the register', *Compare*, 25, 1, pp. 49–57.

—(1995b), 'The teaching of mathematics in Japan: an English perspective', *Oxford Review of Education*, 21, 3, pp. 347–60.

—(1996), 'Contrasting approaches to the acquisition of mathematical skills : Japan and England', *Oxford Review of Education*, 22, 4, pp. 415–34.

White, M. (1987), *The Japanese Educational Challenge: A Commitment to Children* (New York: Free Press).

—(1993,) *The Material Child: Coming of Age in Japan and America* (New York: Free Press).

—and Levine, R. (1986), 'What is an *Ii Ko?*' *in* Stevenson, H., Azuma, H. and Hakuta, K. (Eds), *Child's Development in Education in Japan* (New York: Freeman).

Whitebread, D. (1996), *Teaching and Learning in the Early Years* (London: Routledge).

Wittrock, M.C. (1977), *Learning and Instruction* (Berkeley: McCutchan for the American Education Research Association).

Woodhead, C. (1995), *Teaching Quality: The Issues and the Evidence in Teaching Quality: The Primary Debate* (London: Ofsted).

—(1996), *The Annual Report of Her Majesty's Chief Inspector of Schools* (London: Ofsted).

Zigler, E. (1987), 'Formal schooling for four year-olds? No', *American Psychologist*, 42, 3, pp. 254–60.